THE EXPERIENCE OF DEMOCRACY AND BUREAUCRACY IN SOUTH KOREA

PUBLIC POLICY AND GOVERNANCE

Edited by Professor Evan Berman, Victoria University of Wellington, New Zealand.

This series brings together the best in international research on policy and governance issues. Authored and edited by experts in the field, these books present new and insightful research on a range of policy and governance issues across the globe. Topics covered include but are not limited to: policy analysis frameworks; healthcare policy; environmental/resource policy; local government policy; development policy; regional studies/policy; urban policy/planning; social policy.

Titles include:

THE EXPERIENCE OF DEMOCRACY AND BUREAUCRACY IN SOUTH KOREA

EDITED BY

TOBIN IM

Graduate School of Public Administration, Seoul National University, South Korea

emerald
PUBLISHING

United Kingdom – North America – Japan
India – Malaysia – China

Emerald Publishing Limited
Howard House, Wagon Lane, Bingley BD16 1WA, UK

First edition 2017

Reprints and permission service
Contact: permissions@emeraldinsight.com

British Library Cataloguing in Publication Data
A catalogue record for this book is available from the British Library

ISBN: 978-1-78714-472-9 (Print)
ISBN: 978-1-78714-471-2 (Online)
ISBN: 978-1-78714-939-7 (Epub)
ISBN: 978-1-83867-926-2 (Paperback)

CONTENTS

LIST OF ABBREVIATIONS

ACE	Administration and cost of elections
ARPI	Audit request for public interests
A-WEB	Association of World Election Bodies
BAI	Board of Audit and Inspection of Korea
BRIAS	Bid rigging indicator analysis system
CAR	Citizen audit request
CO₂	Carbon dioxide
CSO	Civil society organizations
DAC	(OECD) Development Assistance Committee
DFID	(UK) Department for International Development
EMB	Electoral management bodies
EPB	Economic Planning Board
FKI	Federation of Korean Industries
GDP	Gross domestic product
ICT	Information Communication Technology
IDEA	International Institute for Democracy and Electoral Assistance
IFES	International Foundation for Electoral Systems
INTOSAI	International Organization of Supreme Audit Institutions
IOC	International Olympic Committee
ISFs	International Sports Federations
ISP	Information strategic plan
KOCEID	Korean Civic Education Institute for Democracy
KOICA	Korea International Cooperation Agency
KONEPS	Korea ON-line E-Procurement System

KRW	Korean won
MAS	Multiple award schedules
MGA	Ministry of Government Administration
MIA	Ministry of Interior Administration
MOU	Memorandum of understanding
NAIS	National Audit Activity Information System
NEC	National Election Commission
NGO	Non-governmental organization
NIMBY	Not in my back yard
NOC	National Olympic Committees
NPM	New public management
NPO	Non-profit organization
OAS	Organization of American States
OCOG	Organizing Committees for the Olympic Games
OECD	Organization for Economic Cooperation and Development
PM10	Per cubic meter 10 or particles less than 10 microns in diameter
PPP	Purchasing power parity
PPPs	Private-public partnerships
PPS	Public Procurement Service
PWC	Price Waterhouse Coopers
RFID	Radio frequency identification
RIA	Regulatory impact analysis
RRC	Regulatory Reform Commission
RRTFT	Regulatory Reform Task Force Team
SAI	Supreme Audit Institution
SME	Small and medium-sized enterprise
TO&E	Table of organization and equipment
TOE	Table of organization and equipment
UNDESA	United Nations Department of Economic and Social Affairs

UNDP	United Nations Development Programme
US	United States
USAID	United States Agency for International Development
WTA	Willingness to accept
WTO	World Trade Organization

LIST OF CONTRIBUTORS

Jesse W. Campbell	Assistant Professor, Department of Public Administration Incheon National University, South Korea
Wonhyuk Cho	Senior Lecturer of Public Management and Director of International Students Programme School of Government, Victoria University of Wellington, New Zealand
Hyemin (Hemin) Choi	PhD candidate, Graduate School of Public Administration, Seoul National University, Korea
Seon-Gyu Go	Professor, Korean Civic Education Institute for Democracy, Korea
Tobin Im	Professor, Graduate School of Public Administration Seoul National University, South Korea
Jisu Jeong	Associate Research Fellow Korea Institute for Defense Analysis (KIDA)
Nanyoung Kim	Senior Research Fellow, Audit and Inspection Research Institute, Board of Audit and Inspection of Korea
Hyukwoo Lee	Professor, Department of Public Administration, Paichai University, Korea
Kwang-Hoon Lee	Assistant Professor, Department of Public Administration, Kangwon National University, South Korea
Shi-Chul Lee	Professor, Kyungpook National University, Korea

NOTES ON CONTRIBUTORS

Jesse W. Campbell is an assistant professor in the Department of Public Administration at Incheon National University in South Korea. His research focuses on correlates of effectiveness in the public sector. An additional stream of research examines issues with unique relevance to the East Asian/Korean administrative context.

Wonhyuk Cho is a senior lecturer of public management and director of International Students Programme for the School of Government at the Victoria University of Wellington, New Zealand. His research interests lie in the areas of HRM, bureaucracy, organizational behavior, law enforcement organization, e-government, and performance measurement.

Hyemin (Hemin) Choi is completing her PhD in the Graduate School of Public Administration at Seoul National University. Her current research interests focus on organizational environment, competitiveness strategy, bureaucracy, urban development, and democratization.

Seon-Gyu Go is a professor of Korean Civic Education Institute for Democracy. His research focuses on election, electoral system, participation, and influential people. His current research interests are SNS election campaign and Japanese politics. He received his PhD in information science at Tohoku University, Japan.

Tobin Im is a professor at Seoul National University's Graduate School of Public Administration and director of Center for Government Competitiveness. Professor Im completed a doctoral degree in Sociology from L'Institute d'Etudes Politiques de Paris, and has been president of Korean Association for Public Administration. His outstanding researches were awarded by Korean Association for Policy Sciences(1997), Korean Association for Public Administration(2007), American Review of Public Administration(2016), and Seoul National University(2017). His research and teaching areas of interest include organizational theory, public management, and comparative administration. In an effort to create an Asian model of public administration, his current research deals with how to apply the 'time' and space concept to various realms of public affairs.

Jisu Jeong is an associate research fellow in the Korea Institute for Defence Analysis (KIDA). His research focuses on organization structure, public management, government regulation, defense policy, and comparative study. He earned a PhD from Seoul National University.

Nanyoung Kim is a senior research fellow in the Audit and Inspection Research Institute affiliated with the Board of Audit and Inspection of Korea. Her research focuses on public sector governance, performance management, policy evaluation, and public audit.

Hyukwoo Lee is a professor of Department of Public Administration at Paichai University, South Korea. He is serving as a member of the presidential committee (cost analysis subcommittee) and is also a chairman of general affairs at Korea Society for Regulatory Studies. His research focuses on government regulation, public administrative reform, and government development strategies.

Kwang-Hoon Lee is an assistant professor in the Department of Public Administration at Kangwon National University, South Korea. He received his PhD in Swiss Graduate School of Public Administration at University of Lausanne, Switzerland. His research interests include public management, organization theory, sport administration, international organizations, and comparative public policies.

Shi-Chul Lee is a professor at Kyungpook National University, South Korea. He served as dean of Strategy & Finance and Graduate School of Public Administration at KNU, director general of Transport Bureau at Daejeon Metropolitan City and as editor in chief of *Journal of Local Government Studies*. His research interests include green urbanism, urban health, and other general issues in cities.

PREFACE

The idea for this book first came to mind in 2015 when I was serving as president for the Korean Association for Public Administration (KAPA). At that time, members of KAPA raised a fundamental question about the essence of "good" public administration. Our interest was to reevaluate the true meaning of "good" when it comes to public administration and find ways for "good public administration" to vitalize both the already developed and the developing countries' social and economic circumstances.

South Korea is known for its rapid economic growth, with many even calling it a "miracle." As a professor of Seoul National University in South Korea, I have had opportunities to meet scholars from other countries. Interestingly, many of them from developing countries shared a similar curiosity of how South Korea made it. I could see that their interest was to find a way for their countries to grow economically, which South Korea experienced so rapidly from the 1960s to the 1990s. From then, I have been trying to capture the uniqueness of South Korean public policy and have thought of ways to introduce Korea's case so that the Korean experience can benefit other developing countries.

This book is part of the effort to search for "good public administration." Professor Evan Berman from the University of Victoria, Wellington, New Zealand was a great inspiration for me to edit this book. He and I once had a discussion at a beautiful café in downtown Wellington, and there he encouraged me to think more about the fundamental questions that need to be asked in the field of politics and public administration. This book is partly the fruit of this discussion. I would also like to thank all the authors of each of the chapters of this book for sharing their academic and practice experiences to support the idea behind this book. Their contribution and constructive criticisms made this book possible. I am most grateful to my editor, Rachel Wald, at Emerald Publishing for her support despite our different time zones.

Lastly, I would like to recognize my research assistants, the majority of whom work with the support of KAPA and the National Research Foundation of Korea (NRF-2014S1A3A2044898) at the Center for Government Competitiveness in Seoul National University. Hyemin Choi,

Dani Kim, Hyung-Geun Kwon, Hyunkyung Lim, and Wonbin Son worked particularly hard on reading pieces of drafts and manuscripts of this book and supported the editing process.

Tobin Im, Seoul National University

INTRODUCTION: BUREAUCRACY AND KOREAN DEVELOPMENT

QUESTION ADDRESSED IN THIS BOOK

In the 1960s, South Korea was one of the poorest countries in the world. Moreover, in the aftermath of 30 years of colonial occupation and a devastating civil war that left the country divided, the country's economic outlook was not favorable. Given this precarious starting position, Korea's subsequent economic transformation is rightly seen as remarkable. A good deal of research suggests that government was a key factor in Korea's rapid economic growth. Specifically, an effective and robust bureaucracy could implement economic policy decisively despite unstable and underdeveloped social, political, and economic conditions. This bureaucracy-driven model has come to be called Korea's developmental state (Chibber, 1999). In this model, the state coordinates investment in strategic sectors while focusing on exports and sheltering nascent industrial concerns from domestic competition. In the Korean case, this approach lead to a rapid buildup of industrial capacity and propelled the economy through several stages of economic development beginning with light manufacturing, progressing to heavy industry and construction, and finally into the high-tech era of today.

The effectiveness of this model derived in part from the highly authoritarian nature of government organization. Monopolizing the policy-making power, the executive could force industry toward the objectives that it deemed essential. Civil society was weak and there was little space for political activity outside of the narrow constraints imposed by the government (Kim & Campbell, 2014). Additionally, the state was also to resist co-option of its institutions for private gain at the expense of its development goals. Of course, there were significant levels of corruption in the relationship between government and industry (a state of affairs, which stubbornly endures even today), however, the abuse of office for private gain was not permitted to overwhelm or to take precedence over economic development. Especially in strategic ministries, recruitment and promotion were strictly merit based, and while education levels and high-quality human resources were scarce in the country. Generally, government could attract the brightest by offering them stable and decently paid positions and the opportunity to make a significant contribution to the nation.

These characteristics of the developmental state are well known. The puzzle this book aims to address, however, is not the role of bureaucracy in economic development, but in political democratization. At least in its central organs, the Korean developmental state was highly efficient, meritocratic, and fully monopolized coercive force. These resources were skillfully leveraged to shape the direction of private sector actors toward strategic initiatives. However, these very same resources should have allowed the bureaucracy to retain its power indefinitely. Instead, step by step, the resources of the bureaucracy, which during the developmental period were in the service solely of the authoritarian leadership, were exercised toward democratization. What were the conditions that made this transformation possible? Despite the voluminous literature on the developmental state in South Korea, this question has received almost no attention.

Korean economic development and particularly the role of the national bureaucracy have been studied extensively with the goal of deriving practical implications for contemporary developing countries. This volume of essays sheds light on the factors, processes, and structures that have allowed the Korean bureaucracy to play an active role in the country's equally impressive democratic development.

This book explores the ways in which bureaucracy may not only be compatible with democracy but also, more ambitiously, the conditions under which it can enhance it. To illustrate this theoretical perspective, various ways in which South Korea's bureaucracy has influenced the country's democratic transition from the late 1980s until the present day are described. This introduction gives a general overview of the Korean context as it relates to the topic and summarizes the key contributions of the book.

KOREAN BUREAUCRACY IN POLITICAL CHAOS

The modern history of South Korea formally begins in 1948, which marks the beginning of the country as a Republic. This period is related to major revisions of the Constitution and the term of the presidency. Korea is currently under the Sixth Republic period. The First Republic was a presidential system and the Second Republic was parliamentary system. The Third

Republic was a two-term four-year presidency. However, the Fourth Republic was "president for life" situation with a direct election system. The Fifth Republic was single seven-year presidency. The Sixth Republic was a single five-year term presidential system. Except the Sixth Republic, other previous Republic periods of bureaucracy were strongly influenced by the presidential leadership due to the centralized decision-making system and a high level of authority. Therefore, the presidential leadership and its administrative philosophy are critical to understand the characteristics of the evolution of the Korean bureaucracy. Table 1 provides an overview of this evolution, highlighting important changes relevant to democratization.

Era of Nation Building: President Syngman Rhee Government

Anti-Communism: A Transition to Authoritarianism

Following the independence from Japanese colonialism and the devastating Korean War of 1950–1953, Korean society under President Syngman Rhee was caught up in diverse philosophical polemics that ranged from communism to liberalism. In the aftermath of the official day of liberalization, that is, August 15, 1945, the Korean peninsula was soon put under the influence of a concurrent flow of utopian philosophies which in fact often highlighted the stark reality of the war-ridden nation: diverging political factions included nationalists, socialists, pro-American factions (under the guidance of President Rhee himself), pro-Japanese factions, and many others (Kwon, 1998: 173).

The fact that post-independence Korea had witnessed a sudden outflow of political ideologies that can be proved by the sheer number of newborn political parties upon Independence Day. In March 1946, Korea had total of 134 political parties and social factions, and the number increased to 350 in 1947. Among the newborn parties, however, there were a significant number of pseudo-parties as well, which basically were interest-driven cliques centered on a few charismatic individuals (Kim, 2006: 69). In sum, the political climate during this period can be understood more as a sudden outpour of parochial opportunistic ideologies rather than a birth of political factions with a firm basis in philosophical perspectives.

Dr. Rhee (President Rhee received a doctoral degree in political science from Princeton during his stay in the United States) was not very different from his counterparts, as he was more of an action-driven politician than a philosopher (Jeong, 2003: 179). Although President Rhee had a unique combination of international and scholarly upbringing as he spent many years

Table 1. Overview of Korean Political History.

	Nation Building	Economic Development	Transition Period	After Democratization
Presidential leadership	Rhee, Syngman (I) (Yoon, Bosun)	Park, Chung-Hee (II)	(Choi, Kyuha) Chun, Doo-Hwan (III) Roh, Tae-Woo (IV)	Kim, Young-Sam (V) Kim, Dae Joong Rho, Moo Hyun Lee, Myung Bak Park, Geun Hye Moon, Jae In
Time	1948–1961	1961–1979	1979–1980–1987–1993	1993–1998–2003–2008–2013–2017
Republic period	The First Republic (The Second Republic)	The Third Republic	The Fourth Republic The Fifth Republic	The Sixth Republic
Term of presidency	Presidential system (parliamentary system)	Two term (4 year)	Indirect election Single 7-year term	Single 5-year term
	Authoritarian			Democracy
Bureaucracy	Centralized, Strong, and Elite Formal and legalism Spoil system Inefficiency	Technocratic Merit system Efficiency and goal oriented	Process of Decentralization Efficiency Military management style, Strong anti-corruption policies	NPM Transparency, responsiveness Representative bureaucracy
Local government			National mantra (2003-2008) The first five-year comprehensive plan for devolution (2004) Sejong new administrative city Local and regional council elections (1991) Local autonomous system adopted (1995)	
Police	Political force	Myth building National Police Affairs Office established (1974)	Democratic control over the police Police Act enacted (1991)	Performance reform in policing

Election	National Election Commission established under the Constitution (1983)		
	Single Member District System (1988)		
	Parliamentary Electoral Reform (1988)		
	Financed electoral management and The Presidential Election Law Reform (1994)		
Regulation		Regulatory Reform Committee (1997)	
		Digital Petition—*Shinmungo* (2003)	
		Regulatory Reform Task Force Team (2004)	
Personnel Management	Career civil service system		
	The ceiling approval procedure (1977)		
	Individual approval system	The standard ceiling system	The total ceiling management	The fixed budget
Mega event	Ministry of Sports Established (1982)		
		Seoul Olympic (1988)	
National Audit		National Audit Activity Information System (1994)	
		E-Audit System	
Public procurement	Public Procurement Service Agency established (1961)		
	National Basic Information System project		
		Framework Act on Informatization Promotion (1995)	
		Master Plan for Informatization Promotion(1996)	
		Cyber Korea 21 (1999)	
		Korean online E-Procurement system (2002)	

in the United States, his administration often gets labeled as one-person authoritarianism (Han, 1981: 29), which then highlights an apparent absence of governing philosophy throughout his regime.

However, the fact that President Rhee's governing philosophy lacked contents does not mean that his administration lacked all substance. In fact, President Rhee himself had a firm belief in anti-communism (Jeong, 2003: 179). President Rhee's firm insistence on anti-communism was a decisive factor in cancelling-out even the slightest possibility of political cooperation across the ideological spectrum (Lee, 1989: 327–328). President Rhee's anti-communism policies served as a practical raison d'etre of Korea's First Republic, which gained even stronger momentum as anti-communism fervor swept the southern half of the Peninsula following the 4.3 Rebellion and Yeosu-Suncheon Rebellion of 1948, and finally, the outbreak of the Korean War in 1950 (Jeong, 2003: 181). It was due to such circumstances that Korea's liberal democracy during its First Republic phase could not overcome its limitation as it was effectively used as a disguise for granting legitimacy to President Rhee's iron-clad rule over the populace.

From an economic perspective, President Rhee had a strong proclivity toward free-market capitalism, which can be traced back to his past 40 years of residency in the United States (Yoo & Lee, 1997). In the aftermath of the establishment of the government of the Republic of Korea, public officials soon engaged in active discussions and dialogs on different choices among a centralized planning economy, free-market capitalism, the ratio of state-owned enterprises to private firms, and so forth (Kim, 2006: 91). Although Korea was experiencing severe economic hardship, President Rhee's economic philosophy, which showed high similarity to that of the United States insisted on minimizing the intervention of government over the market. However, President Rhee's economic drives lacked specific directions and deliverables, whereas the overall Korean economy did not have enough public infrastructure or social background for important policy, which in fact led to confusion and poverty.

From a social perspective, Korea under President Rhee was under an abysmal situation. Following the three decades of Japanese colonial rule and an all-out-war on the Peninsula, Korea was experienced extreme social fragmentation. Concerning such dire circumstances, one of President Rhee's policies was to emphasize education. From the very onset of the First Republic, the Rhee Administration secured people's right to education on the Constitution of 1948, and stipulated a six-year mandatory education on the Education Act of 1949. President Rhee's education drive was an all-out effort against the limits of schools, classrooms, textbooks, and teachers (Kim, 2006: 94). Numbers of institutes for higher-education grew to 62 in 1960, a remarkable increase from 31 in 1948, while the total number of pupils grew to 97,819 from 24,000 (Handerson, 1968: 170). Considering the dire socioeconomic circumstance that the Rhee Administration inherited, the President's education policy was indeed remarkable. Yet, its success cannot be misunderstood as the same level of philosophical inquires and discussions of contemporary Korea, as the nation during the 1950–1960s was under heavy stress of economic despair and underdevelopment.

Corruption and Chaos in Public Administration
During the First Republic, President Rhee was indeed an authoritarian leader, yet his administration lacked a stable political base and administrative background. This was due to the lack of philosophical contemplation on inquires such as "what is the role of public administrations" and "what constitutes an ideal form of bureaucracy." In short, President Rhee's tenure can be characterized as an utter absence of both political and administrative philosophy other than anti-communism.

During that time, Korea's nemesis in Pyongyang (the capital city in North Korea) was a tangible, constant threat to the national security of the South, while leftist political factions within Korea strived for the downfall of the First Republic. Facing such threats out- and inside of the nation, however, President Rhee's administration did not have enough capacity in national defense and policing (Lee, 1988: 303–305). This was due to the fact almost all of Korea's public functions (e.g., administration, education, transportation, etc.) came to a complete halt as the Japanese colonial government was dissolved in 1945. Korean society was under compressed demands and aspirations for a better future, and given that such desires were kept heavily oppressed under Japanese colonialism, intra-Peninsula disputes and divisions, and devastating poverty and chaos, Korea's lack of background capacity for administrative tasks were a serious impediment for the betterment of the populace (Kim, 1006: 87).

During the First Republic, most of the cabinet posts were filled by foreign-educated officials who had their backgrounds in the independence movement. From a dichotomous perspective of efficiency versus democracy, President Rhee's cabinet can be labeled as the latter, as its appointments had an emphasis on representative bureaucracy. Yet, President Rhee's cabinet can also be perceived more as politics-driven appointments than as an achievement of democracy, as representatives from numerous pro-Rhee factions, such as National Youth League, United Labor Union, and Nationalist Party for Women, were invited to participate as ministers.

Under President Rhee, it does not seem that the bureaucracy itself had conspicuous roots of governing philosophies. In fact, President Rhee had a quasi-permanent, unofficial personal network throughout his close circles and top political appointees across the bureaucracy, police, youth leagues, and party machines of the governing Liberal Party (Kim, 1991: 114). President Rhee often shuffled his cabinet-posts, through which those who were perceived as not loyal to the President or people with potential to become his future contenders were fired from their positions (Kim, 1991). President Rhee, personally, was a believer in liberal democracy, yet his governing tendency revealed a heavy presence of authoritarianism.

Through installing official governmental branches in place, the First Republic had initiated its public administration structure; yet most of the officials, from minister-level to policy practitioners, were novices in public administration, and most of public employees could not perform their tasks effectively (Kim, 2006: 87–88). As government officials lacked know-how and expertise in managing daily administrative tasks, they also could not conduct administrative reforms effectively, and most of their daily tasks and agendas were no more than a mere amalgamation of traditional administrative culture and habitual performances from the remnants of Japanese colonialism (Oh, 2007: 3). Facing the national agenda of prosecuting pro-Japanese collaborators, however, the Rhee Administration did not sort out public employees of the past Japanese colonial government. The rationale for such decision was an urgent need of trained professionals in the public sector, which led to a de facto clemency toward the collaborators (Kim, 1990: 234–235; Park, 1987: 47). This can be diagnosed as a problem originating from the absence of administrative philosophy within the newborn government.

Incompetent politics-dependent bureaucracy tends to reveal characteristics of its pre-modern traits. In this sense, public bureaucracy during the First Republic claimed active roles in financing resources for facilitating the upper echelon's authoritarian tactics, repressive mechanisms against opposing parties and civil society, and disseminating propaganda messages in managing the government's legitimacy over the populace (Kim, 1998: 234–235). In addition, certain branches within the bureaucracy, such as the Ministry of Internal Affairs and regional self-governance institutions, took on the role of executing illegitimate elections throughout the nation, thereby effectively bolstering President Rhee's grip on power and the authoritarian political tactics of the ruling regime (Kim, 1991: 106).

During the latter days of the First Republic, Korea's bureaucracy was dominated by numerous political appointees from the hardliners of the governing Liberal Party. Such politicization of the bureaucracy soon precipitated a close interaction between the administrative branch and the Liberal Party's nationwide networks, thereby effectively controlling both the civil society and political arena of South Korea (Kim, 1990: 237; Kim, 1991: 106). In order to maintain iron-fisted suppression over the populace, the government of the First Republic soon transformed itself into a combination of centralized bureaucracy and the repressive police agencies (Kang, 1988: 7).

In sum, President Rhee's tenure was a time of corruption and inefficiency among the nation's professional bureaucrats who lacked long-term time-perspective and capacity in policy making. In addition, most of President Rhee's public employees were both the inputs and products of a spoils system, thereby exacerbating the vicious cycle of their parasitic behavior on politics.

Era of Economic Development: President Park Chung-hee

Utilitarianism Focused on Economic Development

President Park, the strongman who governed Korea for more than a decade, was a firm believer in centralized economic planning for the betterment of the nation' material prowess. His governing philosophy was specifically centered on a nationalist sentiment through which Korea's urgent needs for modernization and industrialization were emphasized. In this sense, he thought that Korea, as a Third-World nation, was in a particular historical stage when compared to Western states. Rather than following Western-oriented democratic institutions and governance, President Park put higher priority in generating sustainable growth momentum, even when such an approach entailed rigid top-down authoritarianism.

Witnessing the increase of popular dissent and opposition against the regime's autocratic behaviors, President Park insisted on the principle of "democratic nationalism" that stressed democracy can only be achieved once the survival and welfare of the Korean people was granted. Clearly, President Park did not have a firm foothold in democratic ideals or values, as he ended up amending the constitution to uphold even more repressive elements and uncontrolled power for his regime.

Like President Rhee, Park was also a steadfast anti-communist. President Park perceived the period between the downfall of the First Republic and the success of his coup as an era of social chaos and turmoil. He strongly opposed ongoing discourses on national reunification as a mere tactic of North Korean sympathizers.

In contrast to his lack of political philosophy on democratic governance, President Park had a deep perspective in assessing Korea's contemporary status as an underdeveloped nation. His strong bias toward economic modernization came from his childhood, as his family had to endure severe economic hardship and poverty. This, combined with his perception of the chaos of post-war Korea, led to Park's continuing call for economic modernization. In this sense, his view on governance can be categorized as a strong emphasis on utilitarianism. Most of the agendas were focused on the question of how to rapidly transform the nation toward the path of material abundance, a goal for which the values of democratic governance were sacrificed.

Claiming the presidency, President Park initiated numerous economic initiatives through so-called "Five-Years Plans" on economic development. His economic policies were different from those of his predecessor, President Rhee, as Park emphasized centralized planning and control over free-market principles with minimalist approach from the government. Of course, Korea under President Park remained as a repressed society with restrictions and limitations on individual freedom in place. National mobilization through political rallies, continuing repression against the opponents, and centralized planning on socioeconomic policies were defining characteristics of President Park's presidency.

Emphasis on Efficacy and Effectiveness: Career Civil Service System
In terms of governing and managing the widespread administration apparatus, President Park was a strong believer in efficiency and efficacy. Considering Korea's underdeveloped status, he held a firm belief that a liberalist approach with minimalist intervention from the government was fundamentally unfit to Korean society of the 1960–1970s. His governing behaviors were more centered at initiating top-down guidance which did not necessarily entail agreement from below. Most of the time, he expected consent from the below, and suppressed any dissenting voices. During the Park era, government-led public administration gained a firm foothold upon the Korean society, thereby turning the bureaucracy into the machine of authoritarian governance from above.

As President Park emphasized efficiency and efficacy, and a culture of a modern bureaucracy in the Weberian sense appeared within the government. During the 1960s, most of Korea's public employees had fewer experience and lower general capacity than military officers. In order to overcome widespread skill mismatch of the public sector, President Part brought in numerous military officers into the governing apparatus. Concurrently with the entrance of military officers into the public sector, President Park sought to reform the public personnel management of the government, as he sought to bring in the principles of meritocracy. Unconventional massive administrative reforms initiated during this era and the fundamental structure of Public Servants System and Administrative System still continues to this day. Career civil service system was institutionalized in Park's era.

Era of Transition: President Chun Doo-Hwan

Extension of Utilitarianism

The Presidency of Chun Doo-Hwan was an illegitimate government as he claimed power through a military coup that was consolidated by a massacre in the city of Gwangju. Compared to the period under President Park, Chun's presidency saw a continuing outpour of dissent and a longing for democracy. People's anti-regime sentiment was simply too strong for President Chun to continue his predecessor's governing philosophy based on utilitarianism. President Chun himself defined power as "source of strength that makes the impossible possible." Clearly, President Chun believed in a clear-cut dichotomy between "us" versus "them" when faced with political resistance and opposition from the below. He even insisted that 70% of pro-democratic activists were comprised of North Korean sympathizers. He continued with his animosity toward the National Assembly by pointing out that the opposing parties did not show full consent to the ruling majority of his governing party.

Most of President Chun's national agendas were focused on economic development, as he held firm understanding that sustaining Korea's high growth rate is the only way that his regime could gain legitimacy. Such a heavy emphasis on economic indicators can be understood as a continuation of President Park's insistence on centralized economic planning. In this sense, bureaucracy under President Chun's Fifth Republic was an effective vehicle in both policy formulation as well as implementation. Yet, President Chun's economic drive has its biggest difference from that of President Park in that the Fifth Republic sought to establish a strong market economy. This was a major deviation from President Park's centralized bureaucracy-led economic modernization (e.g., Economic Planning Board). President Chun, a former military general, did not have deep understanding of the national economy, and he sought to delegate most of his authority on the professionalized bureaucracy on economic matters. President Chun accepted most of comments and advises from his inner circle on how to formulate appropriate economic policies throughout the 1980s.

President Chun's iron grip over the Korean society showed a gradual downward curve throughout his seven-year tenure. In the beginning, President Chun and his cabinet showed highly inflexible attitude toward the populace, when most of "legitimate" voice against the regime was kept suppressed. Yet, as his administration gained momentum as Korea's economic growth continued, President Chun increasingly showed some degree of leniency toward the citizens. In this sense, he can be understood as an "instrumental liberalist," as his first and primary concern was stability of his authoritarian control over the populace. For instance, in 1982, the curfew, which was effectively in-place since the Korean War of 1950 was abolished. In 1983, police officers stopped its surveillance along university campuses.

Professionalism in Bureaucracy

President Chun emphasized professionalism in the bureaucracy. Through granting professional autonomy to the bureaucratic apparatus, President Chun could effectively achieve a number of economic goals such as the stabilization of the price index, balanced development, increased productivity, and financial liberalization. Again, the lack of political, democratic legitimacy led President Chun to open his cabinet posts to subject matter experts, and President Chun himself accepted most of policy proposals from his professionalized bureaucracy. At the same time, in order to root out corruption within the bureaucracy, he introduced various policies such as "The Registration of Property of Public Officials" and initiated the simplification of administrative procedure and the zero-base budgeting system.

Regarding noneconomic areas, the Fifth Republic entailed significant degrees of authoritarianism and corruption, as the intervention from a group of politicized military officers, *Hanahoe*[1], engendered a sort of patron–client relationship throughout society. With its military wing being heavily politicized, the Fifth Republic could not uphold moral values on governance. This, combined with the lack of procedural democracy throughout the seven years was one of the major weaknesses of President Chun. Although the upper echelons of the bureaucracy showed competency and effectiveness in formulating appropriate policy prescriptions, the middle-tier managers and street-level bureaucrats remained passively entangled with rampant corruption.

Era of Delayed Democracy: The Roh Tae-Woo Administration

Democratic Experimentation?
Korea's fervor toward democratization started to gain momentum during the latter years of the Park Chung-Hee Administration. As the nation endured

seven additional years of authoritarian dictatorship under President Chun Doo-Hwan, popular dissent and frustration reached the culmination point and a massive demonstration for freedom. Facing such large-scale dissent from below, the ruling party and the administrative branch of Korea could not continue to ignore the people's longing for democracy. In this sense, the 6.29 Declaration, which proclaimed the restoration of democratic election of Korea's presidency, was a significant milestone that turned the historic tide away from the past oppression.

The 6.29 Declaration (June 29, 1987) was a comprehensive democratization proposal by presidential candidate Roh Tae-woo that was officially titled the "Special Declaration for Grand National Harmony and Progress Towards a Great Nation." This is the historical declaration in the history of Korean democratization. The Declaration comprised eight points, in which Roh promised to:

1. amend the constitution to provide for the direct election of the president;
2. revise the presidential election law to ensure free candidature and genuinely competitive elections;
3. grant amnesty to political prisoners, including *Kim Dae-jung*;
4. protect human dignity and extend the rule of habeas corpus;
5. abolish the Basic Press Law and restore the freedom of the press;
6. strengthen local and educational autonomy;
7. move the political climate toward dialogue and compromise; and
8. achieve substantial social reform.

However, there is no evidence that reforms aimed at implementing democratization were results of President Roh's inner beliefs or governing philosophy. Rather, it is more accurate to view the Administration's pro-democratic policy as a strategic response to the will of the populace.

Although President Roh's Sixth Republic was a democratically elected administration, it is rather difficult to categorize his government as having a firm with consistent philosophical branch in promoting reforms throughout the society. In this sense, most of historians and political scientists agree that his tenure was rather a time of stagnated reforms toward democratic consolidation.

Also from an economic perspective, President Roh lacked clear direction on policy making. His five years inside Korea's presidential palace was beset with new challenges both from internal and external affairs, specifically surrounding Korea's restoration of democracy. Facing such newfangled challenges, President Roh failed to provide a clear-cut strategy or mission toward the nation's future economic direction.

On the other hand, from a sociocultural perspective, the Sixth Republic showed some limited progress. Upon inauguration, President Roh proclaimed that he would pursue two major agendas, democratic reforms and people's unity, and asked for people's support and cooperation. Yet, it is more accurate to view the aforementioned policy agendas as a mere rhetoric, especially when the persistent problems of inter-provincial inequality and unjust income distribution were considered. Corruption, like his predecessors, became President Roh's biggest concern, as Roh could not control his inner circle from committing massive-scale corruption throughout his presidency. The moral hazard of the Sixth Republic meant that the President and his cabinet could not keep up their promise on implementing societal reforms against the remnants of the past years of military dictatorship. This, again, clearly shows that President Roh lacked a consistent set of governing principles for handling a diverse range of issues from democratic reforms to economic redistribution.

Bureaucracy as a Bystander? Failed Initiatives and Agendas on Reforms
The Sixth Republic's management over its bureaucratic apparatus also revealed ineptitude in providing effective public administration. As President Roh decided to extend the tenure of six government ministers from the Fifth Republic, thereby effectively ignoring the civil society's call for democratic values in governance, much damage was done to his reputation as the first democratically elected president. In addition, President Roh invited four university professors, all of whom did not have any prior experience in public administration, to his cabinet, deteriorating the overall efficiency and effectiveness of the bureaucracy. From the above, with inexperienced novices in leadership positions of government institutions, the Roh Administration revealed significant limitation in its governing capacity.

One of the defining characteristics of President Roh and his cabinet is a persistent overlap of policies and personnel appointments from the previous administration. Although the President actively promoted policies of administrative reform and anti-corruption drives, his guidance and directives could not get through his bureaucratic bodies.

Looking into the personal factors of the administration, one of the noticeable characteristics is an absence of reform-minded faction around the President. Lacking support from his inner circle, President Roh could not meet the citizens' widespread expectation toward democratic reforms. While the Sixth Republic strived toward multiple reform-oriented agendas, most of the government's initiatives were restricted within the administrative branch. In this sense, the Sixth Republic and its bureaucratic machine was an isolated island, deviating from the will of the populace. President Roh's reform agendas (e.g., marketization, democratic consolidation, a complete implementation of regional decentralization, etc.) were far from complete, failing to transform the short-span attention of the constituents toward long-term dedication and support. Meanwhile, lacking tangible fruits of reform, most of the Sixth Republic's initiatives and agendas ended up in the enlargement of size and scope of governmental institutions and agencies.

Institutionalization of Democracy: President Kim Young-Sam

Cessation of Authoritarian Legacies: Political Democratization
Although President Kim's electoral victory can be characterized as a result of strategic alliance with the governing party of President Roh, the very fact that Kim, a lifelong democratic activist, decided to merge his party with its governing counterpart highlighted that the termination of the rule of presidents with military backgrounds was the most urgent task facing Korean society. Looking into the election of 1992, it appears that Mr. Kim gained more popular support from the conservative electorates of the nation, which traditionally favored Korea's past authoritarian regime. Although his victory was based on a political merger with the governing party of the Sixth Republic, President Kim attempted to conduct decisive reforms aimed at terminating the remnants of past authoritarianism throughout Korean society.

One of the biggest accomplishments of President Kim was ending the enduring legacy of the military's intervention in politics. Upon inauguration, the President soon dissolved *Hanahoe*, an unofficial elite clique within the military, thereby effectively eliminating the military's patron–client relationship with its civilian counterpart in the government. President Kim's philosophy was concentrated on reforming the nation through cutting off ties from its authoritarian past: he held a firm belief that only through such radical turnover from the past could his administration gain credit and support from the populace. In this sense, President Kim had a deep understanding of political theories around the politicized military as the origin of evil on the third-world's drive toward democracy.

Fighting corruption was one of his main agendas as well. He viewed corruption as by far the largest obstacle against Korea's achievement of long-lasting economic prosperity. For instance, the enforcement of the Decree of the Act on Real Name Financial Transaction and Confidentiality was much more focused on eradicating corruption from the nation's financial sector.

In this sense, rather than a mere amalgamation of economic interests and pragmatic solution seeking, his reform-minded policies in the economic sector were indeed targeting the higher goal of overall reforms in the society. President Kim's reform drives were not without objection: his insistence on reforming the financial sector was often a target of criticism within the inner circle, as the President's cabinet frequently advised against such a rapid implementation of the measure.

Under President Kim, Korea succeeded in entering the coveted circle of the "First World" as it was officially invited to the Organization of Economic Cooperation of Developed Nations (OECD). This was a milestone in turning the tide of Korea's overall economic policies, as the nation could not continue its former status as a "developing nation." This meant that Korea's manufacturing firms and its conglomerates could not expect the same degree of tax breaks and tariff protection from the government. Facing the so-called "Wave of Globalization" however, most of the firms in Korea were not fully ready to engage in full-scale competition with foreign corporations. In this sense, economic liberalization and full-scale opening of Korea's financial market were perceived as threats to the homegrown firms in South Korea. For instance, as the government decided to open its financial markets, a sudden, large volume of foreign capital entered the system, while export-led manufacturing firms suffered trade imbalance. In 1996, Korea's net trade imbalance was reaching the alarming rate of 23.7 billion USD, a two-fold increase from the year before. Foreign loans also skyrocketed, leading the nation to the verge of a massive financial crisis.

Although President Kim strived for Korea's new international status as a fully democratized nation with developed economic prowess, he did not set clear-cut priorities between growth and redistribution, nor had any palpable coordination mechanism within his government. Lacking tangible content and sustainable support from within, President Kim's "globalization" reform drive soon faltered. This is due to the fact that the Administration was aiming two different targets with the same arrow one for reforms in improving the quality of life (e.g., education, social welfare, labor and reforms) and the other for globalization (e.g., increased national competitiveness, deregulation, and economic liberalization).

New Public Management in Korea
As mentioned above, President Kim's governing philosophy can be succinctly summarized as cessation of Korea's authoritarian past. From a bureaucratic perspective, the Kim Administration's defining moment occurred when the President ordered initiatives and guidelines based on enhancing transparency

and efficiency of government apparatus, thereby effectively implanting the mechanisms of New Public Management.

First, President Kim's drive toward transparency was a detailed effort, which was soon formulated in the actual policies of financial market reforms and revealing the data on the personal properties of high-level government officials. The very fact that President Kim's reform policies were pragmatic measures aimed at tangible results was a deviation from his predecessor, as Korea's past governments were reluctant in implementing their rhetoric toward enhancing transparency. This is ever more significant as President Kim's emphasis on transparency had a deep, profound connection with the zeitgeist of consolidating the newborn democracy on Korean soil. President Kim started off his policy by opening the list and amount of his personal property to the people, and soon his inner circle followed suit. This is a remarkable achievement as such measures were not legally binding at first. Korea's media and press also joined in by publishing articles and reports on hidden corruption scandals throughout the society.

Second, it was under President Kim's five-year tenure as the school of New Public Management began its expansion throughout Korea's bureaucratic apparatus. NPM can be roughly understood as bringing in management techniques of the private sector to public institutions. "Efficient but small government" was the motto of the NPM school, and President Kim had a firm understanding of the contemporary intellectual flow of public administration that had a great amount of emphasis on the globalization and professionalization of bureaucracy with information-centered organizational structures. In 1993, the first year of the Kim Presidency, the government eliminated two government branches and laid off 139 public employees. In 1994, total of 115 official positions were eliminated from the payroll, with an additional downsizing of 1002 personnel. Facing the wave of NPM-oriented reforms, the military was not an exception either, as the Ministry of National Defense, Joint Chiefs of Staff, and Military Headquarters endured significant downsizing.

From an NPM perspective, reforms concerning internal government regulations were also initiated. Regarding administrative regulations and civil complaint matters, a government ombudsman was established. The President initiated policies aimed at reducing unnecessary red tape throughout the public sector, while putting efforts (e.g., consumer protection, traffic accident management procedures, and modifying administrative penalties) on improving the actual quality of life of the populace.

Next, privatization of Korea's state-owned enterprises soon followed. Within the inner circle of the top-echelon, President Kim and his advisers held a belief that private corporations are better suited to attain efficiency and effectiveness than public entities. Their preference of private firms over public institutions was soon developed into a policy through which government officials and public employees received one-point lectures and seminars from middle-upper level managers of Korea's conglomerates. Most of the lectures and class materials were focused on advertising the success and initiatives of private firms, which obviously did not provide much help to the "students" from the government offices. This reveals that President Kim and his inner circle did not have a concrete understanding on the difference between public and private entities and the discrete environment on which each sector performs its given role. Although Kim's government was consistently active in promoting reforms throughout both the public and private areas of the nation, their blueprint and philosophy on national agendas contained a significant degree of contradiction.

Looking into President Kim's leadership on policy decision making, one can notice a significant distance from what a leader would do under the New Public Management school. President Kim repeatedly emphasized that he, and only himself, is the very first legitimate president of the Republic of Korea. His inner circle harbored moral righteousness and a sense of superiority. From the beginning of the Administration, President Kim and his advisers acted as if they were the sole representatives of justice, and that only they can bring substantial reforms to the Korean society. Their assertive attitudes engendered numerous practical problems as the President's inner circle was a small minority when compared to the overall bureaucrats in the government system. President Kim's leadership was sometimes overly assertive while insisting on his predecessor's top-down approach in delivering guidance and initiatives. More often than not, he did not follow written procedures when deciding significant policy agendas, some of which even lacked rudimentary-level discussion with his advisers before getting announced. This shows that President Kim, specifically concerning his leadership style, was not a real disciple of the New Public Management school.

From the very beginning, Kim strived to appoint "new faces" to key cabinet positions, as he believed that shuffling out government officials from the previous era was essential to achieve democratic consolidation throughout the nation. Yet, what this meant is that most of the newly appointed ministers did not have much experience with how to manage the vast bodies of Korea's administrative machine. Considering Kim's past as a devoted democracy activist, most of his inner circle did not have systemic experience in governance. In this sense, it was far difficult for the Office of the President to effectively dominate the newborn administration. As the Blue House was filled with inexperienced politicians who had devoted most of their career in fighting against the past autocratic regimes, Kim's inner circle became increasingly closed door, and ironically, started to resemble its authoritarian predecessors. In this sense, President Kim's personnel administration over his key government posts was perceived as nothing more than a kitchen cabinet, which lacked systemic reviewing procedures and democratic deliberation over the appointment. Based on his closed, clandestine nature of personnel management style, President Kim often suffered from mockeries and criticisms from his opponents who frequently referred the Blue House as "reform-minded authoritarianism" and "nonmilitary autocracy."

STRUCTURE OF THIS BOOK: DEMOCRACY AND BUREAUCRACY

The articles in this volume address the relationship between Korea's bureaucracy and the country's democratization. In a key essay in the volume, Im takes a high-level view, analyzing the relationship between bureaucracy and democracy from several different perspectives. The analysis is guided by the question that gave rise to the volume: what are the conditions necessary such that a national bureaucracy may support democratization? Following an analysis of the relationship between democracy and bureaucracy in general, Im argues that, for instance, the bureaucracy must be of a sufficient size to protect itself from the arbitrary use of political power. In addition to size, the sophistication of operations, which Im denotes by the term "red tape," may be used to prevent intervention from undemocratic political powers. The neutral competence of bureaucrats is also instrumental in shielding them from unreasonable external influence. Importantly, Im points out that ill-timed or conceived elections can often exasperate problems instead of solving them.

The remaining chapters in the volume take an issue-based approach to the question of bureaucracy and democracy in the Korean context.

Choi and Jung present an analysis of Korea's technocratic way of limiting the growth of government organizations by the political executive. Dating from 1945, a hard cap on the number of total civil servants was instituted based on an empirical analysis of the number of staff needed. The authors argue that this "ceiling strategy" effectively limits intervention into the bureaucracy by undemocratic political powers seeking to needlessly expand the bureaucracy for their own self-interest. In this sense, the strategy allows the bureaucracy to work in a stable environment and to take a long-term perspective while avoiding undemocratic political influence.

In another interesting article, Cho focuses on the reformation of the national police bureaucracy in South Korea. Tracing the roots of the national police to the Japanese colonial period, an institutional approach is used to analyze the process of change over a long period of time. The institutional approach is well established in studies of police bureaucracy. From 1987, democratic control over the police was established, and following the Asian Financial Crisis of 1997, increased pressure for efficiency was placed on the bureaucracy. Cho points out that, while today a greater emphasis is placed on community policing to facilitate legitimacy, it remains to be seen how well this strategy can remedy the deeply rooted, negative perceptions of the police.

Campbell looks at the public procurement process in Korea as well as the implementation of the country's e-procurement system. Due to the scope of procurement in the public sector, public procurement policy has the potential to positively shape the behavior of market actors as well as facilitate the entrance of groups with democratically relevant characteristics to the procurement market. The essay describes how the KONEPS e-procurement system has significantly reduced corruption in the procurement process in South Korea. Second, the essay looks at how the government has developed an active procurement policy for sustainable procurement. The essay concludes with the discussion of the possibilities for developing countries to follow Korea's path.

Lee explores the development of local bureaucracy and how it has contributed to democratization in the country. Korea is a highly centralized country where most administrative functions are carried out by the central government in Seoul. Increasingly, however, local governments have been giving greater autonomy in their operations. Examining the topic from both a political and administrative perspective, Lee points out that, while there are many challenges at the local level, there have also been several distinct opportunities to contribute to democracy. Local bureaucracies are in some ways much closer to the citizens that they serve and career bureaucrats at the local level can try to resist the inefficient use of public resources by temporarily elected officials. However, much like the national bureaucracy, there is, of course, the danger that local government will accumulate too much authority and the author points out that it remains to be seen the extent to which local bureaucracy will continue to support democratization in the future.

Lee makes an interesting argument about how sport can be a significant soft power resource for countries. Focusing on the Olympics, the author examines how the bureaucracy contributed to the success of Korea's hosting of the 1988 Seoul Olympics and he explains how the event impacted the political modernization of the country as well as the attitudes of bureaucrats. Soft power variables, such as democratic participation, have a potential influence on a successful bid for the Olympics. Interestingly, preparing for the Olympics also potentially stimulated democracy as bureaucrats needed to engage directly with citizens, which in turn increased this spirit of public participation in the country.

Go explores the role of Korean electoral management bodies in fostering democracy in South Korea. The author points out that the successful implementation of elections is not necessarily a straightforward and simple matter but rather requires a significant level of technical expertise and a highly trained bureaucracy. Especially in developing countries, where democracy often has a highly formal character, the opportunities for self-interested actors to hijack the electoral process are many. In the case of Korea, a steady increase in the authority and investigative powers of the National Election Commission has contributed greatly to the legitimacy of the country's democracy.

Lee introduces some key features of the regulatory management system in South Korea as well as the challenges that need to be overcome. In particular, the bureaucracy has worked hard to chip away at past regulations that produce rents for various private interest groups but provide little to society at large. Regulatory quality is tied closely to democracy as maintaining a fair and even playing field for entrepreneurs is a key freedom. Introducing checks and balances into the regulatory system can be an important way to facilitate this goal.

Kim explores the roles the supreme audit institution of Korea explained how the Board of Audit and Inspection of Korea have played during the democratization of South Korea over the last two decades to manage the check-and-balance system among different political powers.

The discourse of "Korean bureaucracy" has been narrowly discussed within the context of political power. Therefore, scholars tend to easily conceptualize bureaucracy through a dichotomous approach: centralized or decentralized. Rather than analyzing the result, this book tries to understand processes of internal control within the bureaucracy. The core argument is that bureaucracy can keep in check undemocratic political influences. The accumulation of these institutional efforts of bureaucracy was hidden because scholars have not been interested in this process. Therefore, revealing the efforts of the bureaucracy before and after 1987 can help us understand the role of bureaucracy and its contribution to democratization.

NOTE

1. Hanahoe ("all for one organization") indicates an unofficial group of army officers that was formed in 1963 by former presidents Chun Doo Hwan and Roh Tae-woo, both graduates of the Korea Military Academy.

REFERENCES

Chibber, V. (1999). Building a developmental state: The Korean case reconsidered. *Politics & Society, 27*(3), 309–346.

Han, S. (1981). *The heritage of the First Republic 1950*. Seoul: Hangil Publishing.

Henderson, G. (1968). *Korea, the Politics of the Vortex*. Harvard, MA: Harvard University Press.

Im, T. (2008). Philosophy of Korean presidential leadership: How has administrative philosophy changed in Korea?: A historical approach to governing philosophies appearing over the last 60 years. *Korean Journal of Public Administration, 46*(1), 211

Im, T. (2014). *Public administration from 'time' perspective*. Seoul: Parkyoungsa Publishing.

Jung, Y. (2003). *Political leadership and Korean democracy*. Seoul: Nanam Publishing.

Kang, M. (1988). Korea's national role and national organization. *Korean Political Science Review, 22*(2), 7–31.

Kim, C. (2006). *President and national management: From President Lee to Kim administration*. Seoul: Seoul National University Press.

Kim, D. H., & Campbell, J. W. (2014). Development, diversification, and legitimacy: Emergence of the committee-based administrative model in South Korea. *Public Organization Review, 15*(4), 551–564.

Oh, S. (2007). The footsteps of Korea's administrative reform and future career paths. Korean Association for Public Administration (KAPA) Winder Conference Proceeding, p. 14.

Park, J. (1989). *Korean industrialization policy and national role 1948–1972*. Korea: Korea University Press.

Yoo, S. M., & Lee, S. S. (1945). Evolution of industrial organization and policy response in Korea: 1945–1995. *The Korean Economy, 1995*, 426–467.

CHAPTER 1

REVISITING BUREAUCRATIC DYSFUNCTION: THE ROLE OF BUREAUCRACY IN DEMOCRATIZATION*

Tobin Im

ABSTRACT

While many studies have focused on the link between economics and democracy in exploring the strategies adopted by developing countries, they have tended to overlook the role of bureaucracy in democratization. This study seeks the missing link between bureaucracy and democratization. What are the conditions necessary for bureaucracy to facilitate the democratization process of a country? This chapter begins by briefly reviewing the bureaucracy literature from Max Weber and Karl Marx and then argues that despite its shortcomings, bureaucracy in its Weberian form can facilitate the political democratization of a developmental state. This study concludes that although bureaucracy is often regarded as dysfunctional, it can be instrumental in the democratization process in the context of the

*This chapter was previously published as Revisiting Bureaucratic Dysfunction: The Role of Bureaucracy in Democratization, in *The Korean Journal of Policy Studies*, Vol. 32, No. 1 (2017), pp. 127–147.

The Experience of Democracy and Bureaucracy in South Korea
Public Policy and Governance, 1–21
doi:10.1108/S2053-769720170000028001

developmental state. This article concludes that there are six conditions for the function for democratization: big enough to protect themselves from the arbitrary use of political authority, qualification and competency, "take administration out of politics" and political neutrality, red tape, consensus about the good government, and having an eye on the long-term, broader interests of the country and the government.

Keywords: Bureaucratic dysfunction; democracy; economic development; Weberian bureaucracy

THE MISSING LINK BETWEEN BUREAUCRACY AND DEMOCRATIZATION

Many scholars raise the question of what the government's role is in a country's economic development, but only a few have researched the relationship between bureaucracy and democratization. This reflects "economy first" which is the typical development strategy that many developing countries adopt, placing an emphasis on economic growth and rarely asking about democracy. Relatively, the relationship between bureaucracy and economic development in developing countries has been studied by Western economists, sociologists, and political scientists. North (1989) emphasizes the importance of institutions, such as an efficient judicial system, which can matter in the development of economies. Evans and Rauch (1999) argue in a similar way that an effective and rule-following bureaucracy significantly enhances prospects for economic growth using a sample of 35 developing countries for the 1970–1990 period. Haggard (2004) finds that institutions have played a central role in the political economic accounts of East Asia's growth, from the developmental state to the microinstitutions of industrial policy. Corruption and its effect on economic growth has also been widely addressed (Mauro, 1995; Shleifer & Vishny, 1993). Furthermore, recently a consensus has emerged to the effect that not only quantitatively factors like economic growth but also qualitative elements such as quality of life are important characteristics of successful development in developing countries (Sen, 1999).

It is understandable that many developing countries mobilize and dedicate their available resources to economic growth, since almost the entire population lives in poverty. Therefore, how to rapidly develop the economy of country is the main concern for many political leaders of developing countries as well as many global institutions such as the Asia Development Bank and World Bank. Scholars have explored the role that bureaucracy plays in facilitating economic development (Chibber, 2002). The "four tigers" – Singapore,

South Korea, Taiwan, and Hong Kong – are well-known cases that help clarify the theoretical concept of bureaucracy in a full economic developmental model. Ironically, however, politics is minimized or ignored in their case research. For example, in a study of Japan's development, Johnson (1982) stresses that bureaucracy, more precisely, the Ministry of International Trade and Industry, was the driving force behind Japan's economic development. Muramatsu and Krauss (1987), however, criticize Johnson for ignoring the role of politicians in forming the proeconomic growth consensus. Many scholars seem to generally believe that the more democratized a country is, the happier its citizens will be. South Korea is not an exception in this regard. This phenomenon is possibly shown in most of the Asian states' context due to the "economy first"[1] strategies.

There is mounting evidence that government bureaucracy is strongly connected to good government performance, which suggests that in less developed countries, where democracy is usually not well established, creating a well-functioning bureaucracy can be a prior goal (Cho, Im, Porumbescu, Lee, & Park, 2013). A strong performance on the part of the government is assumed to contribute to better economic performance in a country. This hypothesis is even more plausible when it comes to developmental states such as Singapore, for example.

Economy and politics are like two sides of the same coin because politics is related to the distribution of wealth. Therefore, if we expand the definition of politics as power and allocation of resources, more connections between the two emerge. First, decentralization can be considered part of the political democratization process to the extent that an authoritarian regime ends up sharing power with local governments. In addition, different kinds of decentralization bring different effects. Fiscal decentralization contributes to economic growth, while political decentralization does not have a significant relationship with economic growth (Im, 2010: Rodríguez-Pose & Ezcurra, 2011). Second, in a broad context, the allocation process can be part of political democratization. If the allocation process is unpredictable or unstable, political democratization can be beset by corruption. Although political modernization can diminish corruption, corruption is still widely considered to be synonymous with bureaucracy, not democracy. Many researchers, however, emphasize studies that point to the negative effects of decentralization and single out bureaucrats as the main hindrance to economic growth or democratization.

For example, Hanna Bäck and Axel Hadenius (2008) question how democratization affects state administrative capacity by using the time series method. Their conclusion is that there is a curvilinear (J-shaped) relationship between the two factors. In other words, the effect of democratization on state capacity is negative at low values of democracy, nonexistent at median values, and strongly positive at high democracy levels. However, if we examine the reverse relationship with this statistical method, using the definition of bureaucracy rather than an ambiguous concept of state capacity as a variable, the question becomes whether the bureaucracy affects democratization.

In that sense, this study examines a different version of this question, exploring whether and under what conditions bureaucracy can be an independent variable in the production of democracy. Acknowledging the current status of research on this topic, this study argues that there is a relationship between bureaucrats and the democratization of a country. How can a bureaucracy lead to democratization in a country? What are the conditions necessary for bureaucracy to facilitate the democratization process of a country? These are examples of the kind of questions that this study takes up.

CLARIFICATION OF CONCEPTS: BUREAUCRACY AND DEMOCRACY

Before diving into the argument, it is necessary to look into the meanings of the key concepts, since they are used in various senses.

Bureaucracy and Bureaucratization

"Bureaucracy" is a term that has been used in many different senses particularly in Europe (Albrow, 1978). Among them, we highlight the sense of it as "rule by officials." From the bureaucratic-polity perspective, rule by officials is viewed as a political system that is dominated by officials. Laski defines bureaucracy as "a system of government the control of which is so completely in the hands of officials that their power jeopardizes the liberties of ordinary citizens" (1930, pp. 70–74). Herman Finer views bureaucracy as "government by officials" (Albrow, 1970, p. 92), and Lasswell and Kaplan also define bureaucracy as "the form of rule in which the elite is composed of officials" (1950, p. 209). From the bureaucrats-in-power perspective, officials are understood as the ruling class. Sharp refers to bureaucracy as "the exercise of power by professional administration" (1927, p. 394), which in turn leads Brecht (1954) to question the definition of bureaucracy as "government by officials" and embrace instead the idea of it as "office-holders who exercise power."

According to Max Weber, whose theory of bureaucracy is well known, the modern form of bureaucracy can arise only when legal authority is institutionalized. Authority, categorized into three types – charismatic, traditional, and legal – in the Weberian sense of the term, has a special connotation to the effect that subordinates in a hierarchy "accept" it. Thus the primitive bureaucracies that stem from charismatic authority or traditional authority are quite different from modern bureaucracies. Until the end of eighteenth century, charismatic or traditional authority dominated the organization of political and social groups of the feudal classes in Western culture. Society was stratified according to family groups. However, the separation of business from the household that began with the shift from an agricultural self-sufficient economy to an industrial one changed the makeup of the classes. By the mid-nineteenth century, the modern bureaucratic form of organization was prevalent in the industrialized world. The bureaucratic structure, Weber (1968) argues, emerges as an efficient way of organizing humans to achieve a goal. Modern bureaucracy coupled with legal authority required the democratization of government. Rationalization of the society is also strongly associated with democratization. It is this particular aspect of Weber's thesis that this study draws on.

Weber (1968) emphasizes that bureaucratization means intensive qualitative expansion of administrative tasks not just a quantitative increase in the size of an organization. According to Weber, "the fully developed bureaucratic apparatus compares with other organizations exactly as does the machine with non-mechanical modes of production. Precision, speed, knowledge of the files, continuity, discretion, unity, strict subordination, reduction of friction and material and personal costs – these are raised to the optimum point in the strictly bureaucratic administration, and especially in its monocratic form" (1978, p. 973).

Despite the suggestion that bureaucracy possesses a "rational" character, much literature on bureaucracy is grounded in Max Weber's ideal typology. Weber clearly defines the principle of modern bureaucracy as the principle of an official jurisdictional area, which is generally ordered by rules, laws, or administrative regulations. In order to function, the authority to give commands and methodical provisions are needed (Weber, 1968). Bureaucracies are organizations with specific functional attributes: large size; graded hierarchy; formal, rule-based administration; standardized procedures; reliance on written documentation; and clear functional division of labor into specialized tasks (Gerth & Mills, 1946; Olsen, 2006). They are large normative structures in which authority reigns. The rational-legal political order can be enforced by the authority of the state (Olsen, 2006).

Bäck and Hadenius (2008)'s study on the relationship between democracy and state capacity defines the capacity for public bureaucrats to be able do their job in the best way as a criterion for a functioning state. Their statistical analysis uses measurements of bureaucratic quality and corruption control (as defined by the international country risk guide) as variables. However, they fail to provide a full theoretical explanation of either of these variables, to which they give equal weight. In this study, I define bureaucracy as a system in which employees are salaried, technically trained, career appointed, and assigned stated duties that require expert knowledge for them to be able to carry them out (Etzioni-Halevy, 2010) and who advance in the organization according to a principle of meritocracy. Today, as Stephen Miller (1978) notes, bureaucracy has come to stand for all that is wrong with the modern world. It has been made a great target, decried as "headless and soulless," and subject to demands for reform by presidents, public media, citizens, and even academics. Despite negative perceptions of bureaucracy, it is evident that bureaucracy has positive traits: unity and coordination, precision and speed, predictability, obedience, loyalty, impartiality, an institutionalized memory, and continuity across changes in government (Olsen, 2006).

Democracy and Democratization

Like the term "bureaucracy," "democracy" is a difficult word to define. It is of no use defining it in terms of the politics of any particular country (Ryan, 1973), since every country has different political conditions. However, the etymological route is worth pursuing. "Democracy" is derived from the Greek words "demos" and "kratos." "Demo" means "people" and "kratos" can be translated as "power," and so the root meaning of democracy is "power of the people." Here, by democracy I refer to political democracy in a liberal sense. In this conception, people must be the master of their fate and be able to determine their affairs at their will. This contrasts with a dictatorship, in which a single person has absolute power over the people. Therefore, simply put, democratization can be defined as allocating power (or authority) to people. People's sovereignty is the key concept.

David Beetham isolates "the core ideas or principles embodied in the historical conception of democracy as 'rule of the people,' " identifying them as "popular control" and "political equality" (1993, p. 6). Hadenius adopts a similar approach and arrives at the conception of political democracy in which public policy is determined by "the freely expressed will of the people whereby all individuals are to be treated as equals" (1992, p. 9). Lively (1975) describes the norms dictating inclusive citizenship and political equality, while Holden (1988) equates democracy with popular sovereignty (Saward, 1994). Eva Eztioni-Halevy (2010) defines democracy (or a democratic political structure) as the institutional arrangement whereby two or more organized groups of people participate in a contest for power on the strength of their policies or the image of themselves that they project and whereby they secure their position via a free election in which the whole adult population is able to participate. Satori argues that "democracy is a procedure by which leaders compete in elections for power to govern" (1962, pp. 124–127). In the absence of an election process, the government becomes an authoritarian one. However, although most developing countries have institutionalized elections, these elections have not brought about democratization.

Democratization can also be characterized in terms of where the transformation of political power was initiated. Redford (1969) calls the top-down approach model "overhead democracy." He views bureaucracy as an authority that puts policy that has been crafted by democratically elected branches of government, which are supposed to rely on the principle of law, into effect. For Schumpeter (1956), democracy is a political method, a certain type of institutional arrangement for arriving at a political decision. Therefore, people's participation in the policy-making process is important. Democracy, at least in this sense, means that people have the opportunity to accept or reject the individuals who are supposed to govern them. Referendum is a tool to guarantee this minimal power. Transparency is a key to tracking the functioning of democracy.

From a "power" perspective, democracy refers to a change in the way resources are shared. In a participatory democracy, values are shared through citizens' participation. In an electoral democracy, resources are allocated through elections. In a liberal democracy, rights and liberties are allocated to everyone. From a "people" perspective, democracy is about establishing channels for equality. Economic democracy is about equality in the production process. Anyone who participates in this process has a right to a share of what is produced and a say in the decision-making process. In social democracy, the government takes responsibility for providing welfare (social services). In political democracy, the power of the state is equally shared by the citizens.

In a broad context, factors that facilitate the distribution of resources and power and that encourage participation can be considered part of democratization as well. In the South Asian context, this includes the adoption of Western democratic theory, the introduction of local self-government, and e-government.

THE AUTONOMY OF BUREAUCRACY

Bureaucracy takes different forms and play different roles in different cultural contexts (Im, 2014). In a country where democratization has not been fully installed, it can work as a positive driver of economic, political, and social democracy, especially in developing countries where the private sector has not yet wholly developed.

From a Weberian Perspective

For Max Weber, bureaucracy is a neutral tool that serves political power. He presupposes the principle of subordination of administration, that is, bureaucracy, to politics (Timsit, 1991). The division of labor between politicians and bureaucrats is clear; politics takes care of policy formulation, while the role of bureaucrats is limited to implementation, through which they gain knowledge. Such accumulated knowledge becomes a state capacity, a dominant power factor in bureaucratic administration. From this perspective, Larry Preston (1987) argues that bureaucracy supports individual freedom because a structured system creates opportunity in which to make choices, learn, create, and achieve a higher purpose; bureaucracy can serve to motivate bureaucrats. Bureaucrats concretize subgoals in the process of implementing politicians' goals.

Thus, a concept of bureaucratic power arises naturally. Government is where bureaucrats' collected knowledge is concentrated, and it is the agent in the division of labor that can coerce all other agents in society (Dahl & Lindblom, 1953). Governments make crucial contributions to society and are thus "a necessary evil" (Wills, 2000). Paul du Gay contends that bureaucracy allows the democratic state to act forcefully, morally, and accountably; however, as Carl J. Friedrich notes, bureaucracy is "the core of modern government," and the success of democracy itself depends on a successful bureaucracy (1963, pp. 463).

If the power of a bureaucracy expands far enough, we arrive at what is often called the "administrative state." The autonomy of a bureaucracy is problematic in the administrative state and can lead to the kind of dysfunction that sociologists in the 1960s described in which bureaucrats are too busy protecting themselves to serve the people. These days, since knowledge is part of administrative capacity, it is commonly understood that transparency and trust is possible if appropriate public officials are recruited and promoted.

From a Marxist and Neo-Marxist Perspective

In the Marxist model, there is an antagonistic relationship between the bourgeoisie and proletariat regarding the distribution of surplus in society. Because the mode of production in capitalist society is private ownership, commodity production proliferates under it, and labor becomes increasingly fragmented. The bourgeoisie monopolizes the tools of production to maximize its profits by exploiting the proletariat's labor. The surplus enriches the bourgeois class at the expense of the proletariat.

The state from the Marxian perspective is a governing body reflecting the dominant social force of a society. Marxists view the role of the state as uniting the divided parts of the social order by organizing the capitalists and disorganizing the working class. Marx saw the development of bureaucracy in government as the counterpart of bureaucracy in the private sector. The owners of private companies heavily dominate the capitalist state. According to Marx, the bureaucracy is an "appalling parasitic body" for the proletariat, but at the same time, it is the most powerful instrument of administration that exploits class.

From that argument, Neo-Marxists question the classical Marxist assumption that the state is just a tool of bourgeoisie by homing in on the role of bureaucracy. Because the state is more than the "government." Stepan (1978) argues that state is an administrative, legal, bureaucratic, and coercive system. Therefore, the state cannot be understood only in terms of class relations and class struggles. The state is also an independent organization with its own internal structure and its own interests (Skocpol, 1999). According to Skocpol (1999), the state is an organic entity and very much an autonomous unit. Neo Marxists argue that the state's interest is not only classical Marxist's idea of economical class but also expands to various social factors such as gender, age group, and ethnic background which can affect class structure.

Neomarxism sheds light on a new dimension of the state that emerges with authoritarian states across Latin America: the ability of them to be sustained at least partially by the rent-seeking behavior of bureaucrats. Krasner (1984) argues that since the state is an autonomous actor in the political system, public officials act as more than referees. Government institutions do have an autonomous decision-making capacity (Truman, cited in Almond 1988).

Etzioni-Halevy (2010) concludes that bureaucrats around the world not only help politicians make policy but also counter their power and serve as a bulwark against corruption. Evans (1985) argues that the efficacy of the developmental state depends on a meritocratic bureaucracy with a strong sense of corporate identity and a dense set of institutionalized individuals similar to private elites. He also argues that Weberian characteristics significantly enhance prospects for economic growth and that building better bureaucracies is therefore necessary. Evans regards the state as a set of organizations invested with the authority to make binding decisions for people and organizations that are located in a particular territory and to implement these decisions using force if necessary. Again, the autonomy of bureaucracy is an important factor.

BUREAUCRATIC DYSFUNCTION AND BUREAUCRATS TOOLS FOR COUNTERBALANCING DICTATORSHIP

Civil servants are a feature in most developing countries. At first, collaborators with the dictator are most likely to take government jobs, but as time passes, merit-based recruitment is gradually introduced, at least partially. Even though some employees are highly corrupt, some members of this group acquire a level of professionalism that enables them to take action against the dictatorship. Their accumulated professionalism becomes the basis of autonomy.

National planning can thus be a potential tool in facilitating the political democratization of developing countries. For example, economic planning is a prevalent economic growth strategy in developing countries; such planning establishes that a specific level of national economic or industrial development will be reached within a period of five years (or two five-year plans and so on). This method was first used in the Soviet Union (1928–1991), but later other socialist states such as Argentina (1946–1955), Bhutan (1961–), China (1953–), Ethiopia (1957–), India (1947–), Nepal (1956–), Pakistan (1955–1998), Romania (1951–1989), South Korea (1962–1996), Vietnam (1958–), and Malaysia (1956–1960) have used or are still using this method for their economic growth. The success of a five-year plan requires strong government leadership to implement policy.

In the case of South Korea, Park Jung-hee, who led the May 16 military coup in 1961, introduced a five-year plan in order to boost the country's socioeconomic status after the Korean War. It was the first long-term strategic economic development plan in South Korea, and it was renewed until 1996. Before this economic development plan was established, Korea's economy largely depended on U.S. aid and its planning on foreign experts. In the first phase of the economic development plan (1961–1965), 84 percent of total foreign capital was public sector funds in the form of bilateral loans that were directly made to the government. This allowed the government to lead the development rather than the private sector (Stallings, 1990).

In order to implement the plan more efficiently, the president established an economic planning board, which remained in place until 1994. It was a new type of government agency that comprised four bureaus – a general planning bureau, a budget bureau, a material resources mobilization planning bureau, and a statistics bureau – 19 divisions, and 228 employees. The ability of the economic planning board to recruit elites, its power to implement policy, and its adherence to procedure and the rule of law allowed it to facilitate political democracy (Choi, 1987).

Bureaucrats who worked at the board were members of the elite who were selected for the job after having passed a relatively difficult exam. Being guaranteed lifelong employment made them feel secure, which allowed them to assume a long-term perspective on their work. Bureaucrats who worked at other agencies during this time were not fundamentally different from those who worked at the economic board in this regard. This does not mean that there were no corrupt and incompetent bureaucrats. Many of them in fact collaborated with the Japanese colonial regime. These facts do not match as Bäck and Hadenius (2008)'s prediction that a high level of bureaucracy correlates with a low level of corruption.

When bureaucrats acquire power vis-a-vis the regime, they start enjoying a certain autonomy. This power results from the "establishment of a substantive consensus among elites concerning the rules of the democratic game and the worth of democratic institutions" in the democratization process (Burton et al., 1992. p. 3; Grugel & Riggirozzi, 2012). It is natural that once a bureaucracy becomes large bureaucrats come to share a sense of solidarity among themselves and are given to exercise power by bending rules to protect themselves if necessary. Bureaucracy in a democratic country can thus have negative effects.

The most common criticism of Weberian bureaucracy pertains to bureaucratic dysfunction such as is manifested in adherence to rules that lead to delay, red tape, unresponsiveness, avoidance of responsibility, power seeking, and corruption (Dimock, 1959). Many scholars in Western countries have analyzed the negative consequences of bureaucracy, including Selznick, Croizer, Gouldner, Merton, and Blau.

Merton (1940), for example, carries out a functional analysis of bureaucracy and argues that it tends to foster goal displacement, by which he means that strict obedience and conformity to norms and rules may lead to a situation where adherence to procedure becomes an end in itself, inhibiting the ability of the organization to achieve its goals. Merton calls this consequence "latent dysfunction" (Edward, 1975; Merton, 1940, p. 26). Bureaucrats use their capacity as a tool to sustain their position rather than to improve performance.

However, this kind of bureaucratic dysfunction can also have positive effects in developing countries. The main problem of developing countries is how to restrain dictators from exercising arbitrary power, from the politician or dictator (or president)'s perspective, as bureaucracy can be a barrier to their desire to make unpredictable decisions that serve their interests.

Politicians prefer to adopt short-term plans in order to enjoy maximum benefit while they are in office. Several researchers have pointed out that formal bureaucratic procedures, sometimes described as red tape, can act as a safeguard to ensure accountability, predictability, and fairness in decisions (Benveniste, 1983; Goodsell, 1985; Kaufman, 1977; Thomson, 1975). It provides citizens with protection against the arbitrary and capricious exercise of power not only by officials but also politicians and even dictators. Therefore, bureaucratic procedures can serve as a constraint on everyone, including a dictator, which could possibly lead to political democratization. In the following, I explore the principal bureaucratic mechanisms that could promote democratization.

Expertise

Bureaucratic autonomy comes from expertise. Bureaucratic officials have the opportunity to be trained in a field of specialization, and their knowledge of rules of the organization they work for represents a special technical expertise (Weber, 1968). In the case of South Korea, since the task of the Economic Planning Board was to manage foreign aid and capital, they were presented with opportunities to gain financial knowledge. This is the reason why professors of economics were made ministers of the board, while former generals largely made up the ministers in other agencies. The presidents knew that economic policy could not be handled by nonexperts.

However, appointing economists to minister positions on the board was not sufficient to run it. Korea's five-year economic development plan was renewed seven times, and long-term development planning required hiring individuals who would stay in the job for a significant period of time. Bureaucrats also were able to acquire knowledge by studying abroad and attending international conferences or meetings. Well-educated and highly experienced officials, scholars, and business leaders collaborated with the board, contributing to the accumulation of expert knowledge. The board's bureaucrats thus developed an administrative capacity that made them superior to other politicians and stakeholders.

In addition, an open merit system made the organization relatively autonomous and enabled it to avoid becoming beholden to special interests. Therefore, its bureaucrats had the ability to say no to politicians, private economic interest groups, and other stakeholders who lacked their expertise.

The economic planning board was not a special case. Other government agencies in Korea during this period were similarly structured, but the difference between them was the eliteness associated with the economic planning board. Anyone could apply for a public official position, but if an individual earned higher marks on the open examination, he or she could start at a higher level. The recruitment system of bureaucrats relied on the National Civil Service Exam, which was highly competitive, and earning a high mark on it was sufficient to give those who did a sense that they led the country.

In addition, the Korean government allocated a substantial budget and supplied talented and technically trained bureaucrats to support other ministries and academic institutions. Proud to be regarded as experts, Korean elite civil servants, especially those working at the Economic Planning Board, were relatively free from influence from regional interests (e.g., kinship networks and school networks). The examination tested both general ability and knowledge as well as knowledge relevant to a particular job (Wilson, 1989). It was therefore a fair process that resulted in talented people being hired.

Implementation Power

Politicians enjoy announcing attractive policies that may turn out to be talk but no action because their concern is to appeal to voters and supporters. The bureaucracy, on the other hand, is the action-oriented sphere; it secures resources, produces agreement, and coordinates structures. Politicians' policy promises depend on bureaucrats if they are to become reality (Brunsson, 1989). Experienced politicians know that a good policy is useless if it is not implemented and that public opinion will turn against them if it is not. Without the bureaucracy, politicians cannot implement policy.

Bureaucrats are experts at implementing policies, which is a difficult process, since there can be inconsistency among different policies, a lack of legal support, a lack of money, and a lack of cooperation from the citizens. Street-level bureaucrats know exactly what is happening in their field, and they are better able than politicians to tell whether information is distorted or not.

Not only government officials but also professors and other experts also provided recommendations to the board for various economic and planning development projects for the implementation. The main role of elite bureaucrats in the Economic Planning Board was to implement development plans and coordinate with other ministries in order to bring all related government agencies under its jurisdiction and to procure, manage, and allocate foreign capital, since there was not enough domestic capital. The board also held various forums designed to allow it to receive advice and support.

These processes associated with implementation created an opportunity to gather elites who were not part of the military regime. Academic elites were able to perform their planning and budgetary roles under a fair and balanced approach with the overall economic framework in mind and relatively free from the control of the assembly and interest groups who were not sufficiently competent or trustworthy to make economic decisions.

Proceduralism

Democracy requires due process, which is the requirement that the state must respect all legal rights. In other words, a set of "procedures" makes democracy (Castoriadis, 1997). In his incisive critique of Prussian bureaucracy, Max Weber (1958) points out that Prussian politicians used parliamentary inquiries as a means to check on the progress of the administrative implementation of legislation. Such inquiries served as a proving ground for politicians in parliament. They would spar with administrative experts, seeking to show the supremacy of political decisions to an official's use of his education and skill to preserve the technical integrity of an administrative program. In the case of Russia, there is a list of tables containing requirements that must be met for a policy to be implemented. Even if the leader or president wants to implement the policy, if the policy does not satisfy those requirements, it cannot be implemented.

Administrative procedures include processes for making a collective decision inside the bureaucracy and the securing of documents in order to obtain authorizations and licenses. The complexity of these procedures is notoriously referred to as "red tape." Bozeman defines organizational red tape as "rules, regulations, and procedures that remain in force and entail a compliance burden for the organization but have no efficacy for the rules' functional object" (1993, p. 283). In reality, however, red tape can be a positive force. It can protect bureaucrats from arbitrary requests, particularly in semidemocratic countries. "Veto points" allow bureaucrats to resist external pressure.

In the context of an authoritarian regime, collaborators with the dictator always attempt to bypass preset procedures. This is the reason why Van Loon et al. (2016) introduce a two-dimensional construct that includes a compliance burden and lack of functionality in order to measure the effects of red tape. Their findings show that red tape that has a high functionality is likely to produce good results even in developed countries.

The Korean government's economic development plan was not dictated by the president. Each Economic Planning Board project featured a set of procedures that legally had to be followed. Development plans were carried out in three stages: a preparation stage, a sector-planning stage, and a consolidation and finalization stage. During the first five-year plan (1962–1966), the supreme council for national reconstruction, the Economic Planning Board (Overall Planning Bureau), and working-level committees all participated. During the second five-year plan (1967–1971), a series of cabinet council, joint committee, advisory committee, and sector-planning meetings were held. During the third five-year plan (1972–1976), the cabinet council, the deliberation council, the coordination committee, and the sector-planning groups contributed to the economic development planning procedure. For the fourth plan (1977–1981), the cabinet council, deliberation council, and working-level committee meetings were held. These meetings were open to the public to allow a national consensus to emerge. These kinds of procedures prevented influential politicians from capriciously intervening in the process.

Rule of Law

Weberian bureaucracy emphasizes the importance of rules and regulations for simplifying complex procedures and therefore strictly prohibits any action that breaks the law. Adherence to rules allows decisions made at high levels to be executed consistently by all lower levels. O'Donnell (2004) argues that "high-quality democracy requires a truly democratic rule of law that ensures political rights, civil liberties, and mechanisms of accountability which in turn affirm the political equality of all citizens and constrain potential abuses of state power" (p. 32). The rule of law "consists of the enforcement of laws that have been publicly promulgated and passed in a pre-established manner; are prospective, general, stable, clear and hierarchically ordered; and are applied to particular cases by courts independent from the political rulers and are open to all, whose decisions respond to procedural requirements, and that establish guilt through the ordinary trial process" (Maravall, 2003, p. 261).

The essential value of rule of law is its universal applicability. Not only the powerless but also people who are powerful are obligated to follow the rules. In other words, laws are uncomfortable for dictators. More powerful individuals in developing countries are more likely to violate existing rules. For example, the rich and powerful families can avoid paying the income tax they owe, while the middle class is compelled to follow the rules and pay what they owe.

The bureaucrats who are in charge of implementing the law are the gate-keepers who can ensure the rule of law is followed. It is an uphill battle in most nondemocratic countries, but it is possible if bureaucrats are patient and start by applying the principle to the ordinary citizen. Gradually, once following the law becomes more accepted, there will be critical disjuncture between a powerful person and politicians.

CONDITIONS OF BUREAUCRATIC DEMOCRATIZATION

Not all bureaucracies are functional in the democratization of a country. A government bureaucracy can operate in favor of democratization or against it depending on conditions. The first condition for success is a strong bureaucracy. An unorganized bureaucracy in a country run by a dictator cannot democratize the country. The bureaucracy should be relatively big and intelligent. The second condition is the accumulation of its own power. In order to use bureaucracy as a tool for democratization, bureaucrats need to protect themselves from the arbitrary use of political authority and have autonomy (Im, 2007). Bureaucrats' neutral competence, which is their ability to do the work of government expertly (Kaufman, 1956), also can help democratization. Heclo (1975) argues that bureaucrats can pursue neutral competence by bearing in mind the long-term, broader interests of the country and the government.

The bureaucracy should institutionalize red tape. A bureaucracy that operates too simply leaves itself vulnerable to the external pressure. Clear decision-making lines can be another requirement. Also, democratization can be aided when there is relative consensus about the goals government is pursuing and about the legitimacy of the agencies developed to pursue those goals and the laws authorizing agency actions. If tasks are easy to define and lines of authority are clear, bureaucrats can be neutral (Aberbach & Rockman, 1994) (Fig. 1).

Bureaucracy

Strategies of bureaucrats counterbalancing dictatorship
1. Planning
2. Dictators' decision making is usually unpredictable
3. Long-term perspective of dictators

Tools of bureaucrats
1. Expert
2. Implementation Power
3. Proceduralism
4. Rule of law

Conditions for functioning for democratization
1. Big enough to protect themselves from the arbitrary use of political authority
2. Qualification and competency
3. "Take administration out of politics" and political neutrality
4. Red tape
5. Consensus about the good government
6. Having an eye to the long-term, broader interests of the country and the government

Democratization

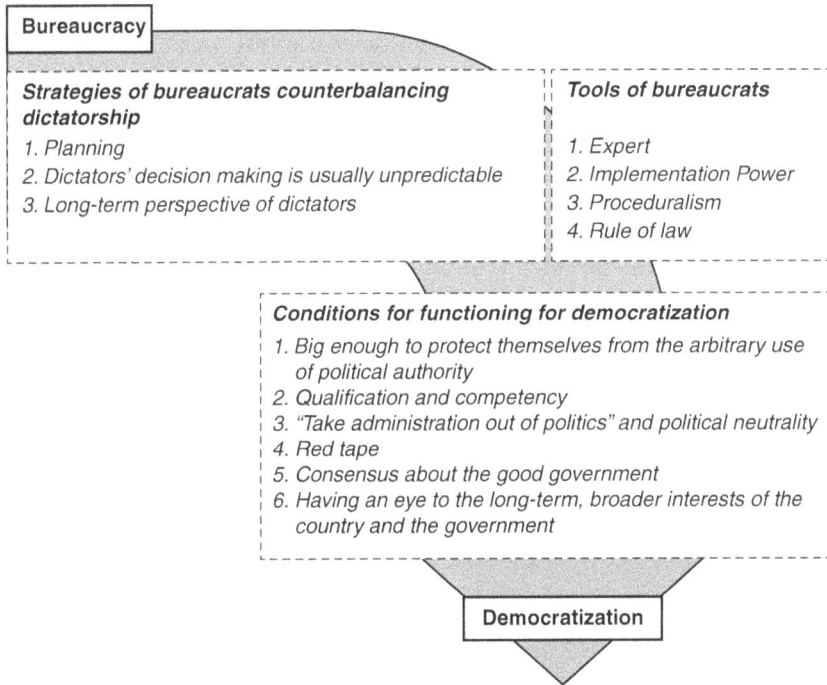

Fig. 1. The necessary conditions for bureaucracy to facilitate the democratization process

CONCLUSION

The main goal of this study is to attract attention to the role of bureaucracy in the process of democratization in developing countries. The suggestion that bureaucracy can contribute to democratization goes against the conventional theory of it, which claims that the chaos that tends to reign in developing countries is the result of politics and that politics in the form of elections can fix the problem, as governance by elected officials, with help from NGOs, will increase transparency and due process.

This idealistic line of reasoning also reflects the Marxist view in a sense, which proposes that after the proletarian revolution, a socialist society can be realized by democratic centralism, a form of government that can be found in China (and that was the form of government adopted by the former Soviet Union as well). However, the conventional view as well as Marxist view cannot explain what is happening in most developing countries. Elections are not the solution to the problem but the cause of the problem itself. The "winner takes all" principle results in the exclusion of various social groups, whose position becomes desperate, intensifying an already undemocratic situation.

This is the reason why this study suggests focusing on bureaucracy. Bureaucracy need not just be a passive and neutral tool of the executive branch but can actively aid in the democratization of a country under certain conditions. Bureaucracy is a double-edged sword to the extent that it can be unpleasant for citizens to deal with, on the one hand, but can also protect them from arbitrary power, on the other.

Since democracy is the process of giving power back to people, the process varies according to the conditions of each country. Bureaucracy on the Weberian understanding of it has the potential to be a force for democracy. Bureaucracy can train people, collect knowledge, predict decisions, share goals, and establish stable institutions staffed by knowledgeable experts that can counterbalance dictators or interest groups. Bureaucratic autonomy allows planning and the efficient implementation of policy in light of a country's unique context. Therefore, bureaucracy can be a positive driver, contributing to political democratization especially in developing countries.

NOTES

1. 'Economy first, and politics second' is the typical development strategy that many developing countries adopt. This implies that government prioritizes economic development over any other issues.

ACKNOWLEDGMENTS

This research is supported by the National Research Foundation of Korea (NRF-2014S1A3A2044898).

REFERENCES

Aberbach, J. D., & Rockman, B. A. (1994). Civil servants and policymakers: Neutral or responsive competence? *Governance*, 7(4), 461–469.
Albrow, M. (1978). *Bureaucracy*. London: Macmillan.
Almond, G. A. (1988). The return to the state. *American Political Science Review*, 82(3), 853–874.

Bäck, H., & Hadenius, A. (2008). Democracy and state capacity: Exploring a J-shaped relationship. *Governance, 21*(1), 1–24.

Beetham, D. (1993). *Auditing democracy in Britain: Democratic audit.* Human Rights Centre Scarman Trust, University of Essex, Colchester.

Beetham, D., & Weir, S. (1999). Auditing British democracy. *The Political Quarterly, 70*(2), 128–138.

Benveniste, G. (1983). *Bureaucracy.* San Fransisco, CA: Jossey-Bass.

Bozeman, B. (1993). A theory of government "red tape". *Journal of Public Administration Research and Theory, 3*(3), 273–304.

Bozeman, B., & Scott, P. (1996). Bureaucratic red tape and formalization: Untangling conceptual knots. *The American Review of Public Administration, 26*(1), 1–17.

Brecht, A. (1954). How bureaucracies develop and function. *The Annals of the American Academy of Political and Social Science, 292*(1), 1–10.

Brunsson, N. (1989). *The organization of hypocrisy: Talk, decisions and actions in organizations.* Chichester: John Wiley & Sons.

Brunsson, N. (2006). Administrative reforms as routines. *Scandinavian Journal of Management, 22*(3), 243–252.

Burton, M., Gunther, R., & Higley, J. (1992). Introduction: Elite transformation and democratic regimes. In J. Higley & R. Gunther (Eds.), *Elites and Democratic Consolidation in Latin America and Southern Europe* (pp. 1–37). Boulder, CO: Rowman & Littlefield.

Bush, G. (1987). Eva Etzioni-Halevy, bureaucracy and democracy: A double dilemma. *Political Science, 39*(2), 198–200.

Castoriadis, C. (1987). *The imaginary institution of society* (Trans., K. Blamey). Cambridge: Polity.

Castoriadis, C. (1997). Democracy as procedure and democracy as regime. *Constellations, 4*(1), 1–18.

Chibber, V. (1999). Building a developmental state: The Korean case reconsidered. *Politics & Society, 27*(3), 309–346.

Chibber, V. (2002). Bureaucratic rationality and the developmental state 1. *American Journal of Sociology, 107*(4), 951–989.

Cho, W., Im, T., Porumbescu, G. A., Lee, H., & Park, J. (2013). A cross-country study of the relationship between Weberian bureaucracy and government performance. *International Review of Public Administration, 18*(3), 115–137.

Choi, B.-S. (1987). The structure of the economic policy-making institutions in Korea and the strategic role of the Economic Planning Board (EPB). *Korean Journal of Policy Studies, 2*, 1–25.

Dahl, R. A. (1963). *Politics economics and welfare: Planning and politico-economic systems resolved into social processes.* New York: Harper & Row.

DeHart-Davis, L., & Pandey, S. K. (2009). Red tape and public employees: Does perceived rule dysfunction alienate managers? *Journal of Public Administration Research and Theory, 15*(1), 133–148.

Dimock, M. E. (1959). *Administrative vitality: The conflict with bureaucracy.* New York: Harper and Brothers.

Du Gay, P. (2005). *Values of bureaucracy.* Oxford: Oxford University Press.

Edwards, R. C. (1975). The social relations of production in the firm and labor market structure. *Politics & Society, 5*(1), 83–108.

Etzioni-Halevy, E. (2013). *Bureaucracy and democracy* (Routledge Library Editions: Political Science Vol. VIII). London: Routledge.

Evans, P., & Rauch, J. E. (1999). Bureaucracy and growth: A cross-national analysis of the effects of "Weberian" state structures on economic growth. *American Sociological Review*, *64*(5), 748–765.

Evans, P. B., Rueschemeyer, D., & Skocpol, T. (1985). *Bringing the state back in*. Cambridge: Cambridge University Press.

Friedrich, C. J. (1963). *Man and his government: An empirical theory of politics*. New York: McGraw-Hill.

Gerth, H., & Wright, M. (1958). Introduction to *From Max Weber: Essays in sociology* (Trans. & Eds. H. H. Gerth & C. Wright Mills). New York: Oxford University Press.

Goodsell, C. T. (1985). *The case for bureaucracy: A public administration*. New Jersey: Chatham House Publishers.

Grugel, J., & Riggirozzi, P. (2012). Post-neoliberalism in Latin America: Rebuilding and reclaiming the State after crisis. *Development and Change*, *43*(1), 1–21.

Hadenius, A. (1992). *Democracy and development*. Cambridge: Cambridge University Press.

Haggard, S. (2004). Institutions and growth in East Asia. *Studies in Comparative International Development*, *38*(4), 53–81.

Heclo, H. (1975). OMB and the presidency – The problem of neutral competence. *The Public Interest*, *0*(38), 80.

Holden, B. (1988). *Understanding Liberal Democracy*. London: Sage.

Im, T. (2007). Bureaucracy, democracy and market: Critique on government reforms over last 20 years. *Korean Public Administration Review*, *43*(3), 41–65.

Im, T. (2010). Does decentralization reform always increase economic growth?: A cross country comparison of the performance. *International Journal of Public Administration*, *33*(10), 508–520.

Johnson, C. (1982). *MITI and the Japanese miracle: The growth of industrial policy: 1925–1975*. Stanford, CA: Stanford University Press.

Kaufman, H. (1956). Emerging conflicts in the doctrines of public administration. *American Political Science Review*, *50*(04), 1057–1073.

Kaufman, H. (2015). *Red tape: Its origins, uses, and abuses*. Washington, DC: Brookings Institution Press.

Krasner, S. D., Nordlinger, E., Geertz, C., Skowronek, S., Tilly, C., Grew, R., & Trimberger, E. K. (1984). Approaches to the state: Alternative conceptions and historical dynamics. *Comparative Politics*, *16*(2): 223–246.

Laski, H. J. (1961). *Liberty in the modern state*. London: Allen & Unwin.

Lasswell, H. D. (1963). *Power and society: A framework for political inquiry*. New Haven: Yale University Press.

Lively, J. (1980). *Democracy*. Oxford, UK: Blackwell.

Maravall, J. M. (2003). The rule of law as a political weapon. *Democracy and the Rule of Law*, *5*, 261–301.

Mauro, P. (1995). Corruption and growth. *The Quarterly Journal of Economics*, *110*(3), 681–712.

Merton, R. K. (1940). Bureaucratic structure and personality. *Social Forces*, *18*(4), 560–568.

Miller, S. (1978). Bureaucracy baiting. *The American Scholar*, *47*(2), 205–222.

Muramatsu, M., & Krauss, E. S. (1987). The conservative policy line and the development of patterned pluralism. *The Political Economy of Japan*, *1*, 516–554.

Nathan, R. P. (1976). The administrative presidency. *The Public Interest*, *0*(44), 40.

North, D. C. (1989). Institutions and economic growth: An historical introduction. *World development*, *17*(9), 1319–1332.

O'Donnell, G. (1982). Reply to Remmer and Merkx. *Latin American Research Review, 17*(2), 41–50.

O'Donnell, G. A. (2004). Why the rule of law matters. *Journal of Democracy, 15*(4), 32–46.

O'Donnell, G., Schmitter, P. C., Whitehead, L., Arnson, C. J., & Lowenthal, A. F. (2013). *Transitions from authoritarian rule: Tentative conclusions about uncertain democracies.* Maryland: JHU Press.

Olsen, J. P. (2006). Maybe it is time to rediscover bureaucracy. *Journal of Public Administration Research and Theory, 16*(1), 1–24.

Przeworski, A. (2016). Democracy: A never-ending quest. *Annual Review of Political Science, 19*, 1–12.

Redford, E. S. (1969). *Democracy in the administrative state.* New York: Oxford University Press.

Remmer, K. L., & Merkx, G. W. (1982). Bureaucratic-authoritarianism revisited. *Latin American Research Review, 17*(2), 3–40.

Rodríguez-Pose, A., & Ezcurra, R. (2011). Is fiscal decentralization harmful for economic growth? Evidence from the OECD countries. *Journal of Economic Geography, 11*(4), 619–643.

Ruostetsaari, I. (2015). *Elite recruitment and coherence of the inner core of power in Finland: Changing patterns during the economic crises of 1991–2011.* Lanham, MD: Lexington Books.

Satori, G. (1962). *Democratic theory.* Detroit, MI: Wayne State University Press.

Saward, M. (1994). *Democratic theory and indices of democratization.* London: Sage.

Schumpeter, J. A. (1950). *Capitalism, socialism and democracy.* New York: Harper.

Sen, A. K. (1999). *Development as freedom.* New York: Knopf/Anchor Books.

Sharp, W. (1927). La Développement de la Bureaucratie aux États-Unis. *Revue des Sciences Politiques, 50*, 394.

Shleifer, A., & Vishny, R. W. (1993). Corruption. *The Quarterly Journal of Economics, 108*(3), 599–617.

Skocpol, T., Evans, P., & Rueschemeyer, D. (1999). *Bringing the state back in.* Cambridge: Cambridge University Press.

Stepan, A. C. (1978). *The state and society: Peru in comparative perspective.* Princeton, NJ: Princeton University Press.

Thompson, V. A. (2007). *Without sympathy or enthusiasm: The problem of administrative compassion.* Tuscaloosa, AL: University of Alabama Press.

Timsit, G. (1991). *Théorie de l'administration.* Paris: Presses universitaires de France.

Van Loon, N. M., Leisink, P. L., Knies, E., & Brewer, G. A. (2016). Red tape: Developing and validating a new job-centered measure. *Public Administration Review, 76*(4), 662–673.

Weber, M. (1946). *From Max Weber essays in sociology.* (Trans., Edited, and with an introduction by H.H. Gerth and C. Wright Mills). New York: Oxford University Press.

Weber, M. (1968). *Economy and society: An outline of interpretive sociology* (Trans. & Eds. G. Roth, C. Wittich, E. Fischoff, et al.). New York: Bedminster Press.

Weber, M. (1976). *The Protestant ethic and the spirit of capitalism* (Trans. T. Parsons & introduction by A. Giddens). New York: Scribners.

Wills, G. (2002). *A necessary evil: A history of American distrust of government.* Simon and Schuster.

Wilson, J. Q. (1989). *Bureaucracy: What government agencies do and why they do it.* Basic Books.

CHAPTER 2

ELECTORAL DEMOCRACY AND THE ROLE OF THE ELECTORAL MANAGEMENT BODY IN SOUTH KOREA

Seon-Gyu Go

ABSTRACT

This chapter explores how the Korean electoral management bodies (EMBs) and the election administration ensure the autonomy of administrative management from political parties and the interior ministry. In particular, the analysis focuses on the role of recognition, rights independence, and professionalism in securing the election administrations in the EMBs. Recent studies have found that the contents of the independent variable, dependent variable, and other parameters influencing fair and autonomous election management system do not differ significantly. Therefore, the institutional independence of the EMBs is not intended to guarantee fairness and impartiality in Korea either. Since 1987, the authoritarian regime collapsed and democracy began to grow in Korea. Also, the role of the EMBs granted by the constitution started to be considered.

The Experience of Democracy and Bureaucracy in South Korea
Public Policy and Governance, 23–52
Copyright © 2017 by Emerald Publishing Limited
All rights of reproduction in any form reserved
doi:10.1108/S2053-769720170000028002

Actively recognizing the role and expanding the rights of the Korean National Election Commission (NEC) has become a decisive factor in the formation of the autonomous and neutral election management system. The scale, manpower and budget of organizations, and personnel have increased. The role of the EMBs has also expanded proportionally. The Korean NEC has enormous authority, such as investigative power and enforcement power that the EMBs of other countries do not have. After all, recognizing the role of bureaucracy and government employees will become a very important factor in ensuring the independence of the EMBs in developing countries. Furthermore, it will be a driving force to develop democracy in developing countries.

Keywords: Election administration; electoral management body (EMB); National Election Commission; integrity; electoral democracy

Recently, there are some events that make us think how election or electoral management is important in a democratic system. Electoral management problems become fatal obstacles to a regime's legitimacy, management ability, or democracy and have happened mainly in developing countries so far. However, this kind of situation happens in developed countries too. The most emblematic case is the Florida election ballot counting issue in the U.S. presidential election in 2000. This incident shows that electoral management can have a significant impact on political processes not only in developing countries where democratic safeguards are insufficient but also in well-developed democracies like the United States.

The incident not only exposed the flaws in American democracy but also a role model for developing countries. Thereafter, there were voting system reviews and various discussions of voter registration. In particular, the possibility that strict voter identification process could make Hispanic voters, who support the Democratic party vote less created political conflict. Sometimes, defects of democracy are exposed in the electoral process as such. Also, the way of voter registration may change the behavior of voters and effect electoral decisions as well.

People began to see that the electoral management problem has not only a technical nature but also a political nature based on the case of the reaffirmation of the residents recall for requiring the dissolution of the Nagoya city council in Japan in 2010. Similar cases have often occurred in recent years, including resident vote demands for an administrative district merger in Shiga Prefecture and re-election of the city mayor of Ahkune in Kagoshima Prefecture. And there was an incident that showed the electoral management procedures are actually complex procedures requiring considerable skills. In Japan in 2011, the east Japan earthquake took many lives. Among the victims were included much of the administrative staff of local governments to manage the elections. The unified local election scheduled immediately after the earthquake had to be postponed, owing to the death of the employees, who know the electoral management practices well. Eventually, the earthquake-affected area election was conducted with the support of unaffected other governments electoral officers. This incident highlights the fact that electoral management is not an easy task that can be given to anyone; it is a complex administrative process that requires a set of skills.

In advanced democratic countries, electoral management has been treated as a technical issue. However, points are clearly emerging that electoral management is not just a matter of administrative and technical management. It is also a matter of politics. In addition, issues about the role of electoral management and organization have recognized that the issues can be raised as a fatal obstacle to the ability of government and democracy. This series of problems in democracy and electoral management can be expressed as "democracy of electoral management." In other words, an election is the minimum condition of democracy. Also, fair and neutral elections are the most critical factor in supporting the democracy.

Therefore, to guarantee elections which ensure fairness and equity, researches for the role of electoral management bodies (EMBs) began to receive attention. In October 2013, the Association of World Election Bodies (A-WEB), which is the international alliance of election-related organizations around the world, was launched in South Korea. It sets the "world democracy to grow together" as a common goal at the inaugural meeting in which 105 countries' election management organizations participated, the United Nations Development Program, and 13 national bodies. Common interests on the type of EMBs that guarantee fairness and impartiality are also growing by launching these international organizations

Studies on EMBs or election management administration are becoming more common. For an election system to carry out a fair and neutral election, it needs autonomy and capacity. Autonomy and capacity of the elections management body are very important factors for stability and legitimacy in a democracy.

Therefore, this chapter explores the process of how Korean EMBs and the election administration ensure the autonomy and administrative management power from political parties and interior ministries with a view of internal factors. The analysis focuses on the role of recognition, rights independence, and professionalism in securing the election administration. Also, the chapter considers the implications of the Korean case to solve the electoral management administration challenges that developing countries are facing.

THE EXISTING RESEARCH ON ELECTORL MANAGEMENT ADMINISTRATION

This section looks at existing studies of electoral management and EMBs. Also, we propose a framework based on previous studies for discussing the Korean case.

First, to define the concept, EMB means the government agency in charge of elections. Electoral management includes vote counting, reporting on Election Day and maintenance of regulations relating to the election campaign as well as the judicial judgment for electoral fraud. The electoral management sector in the interior ministry or administrative court besides the National Election Commission (NEC) is representative. Recently, we have used the term electoral governance. The concept of electoral governance is widely used for referring to the main agent and organizations of nonprofit organizations (NPOs), international observers and nongovernmental organizations (NGO) involved in the electoral process.

Study on the Electoral Management Body as an Independent Variable

Existing studies have a strong tendency to treat EMBs as independent variables. These studies have accumulated for the last 10 years (Mozaffar & Schedler, 2002; Pastor, 1999). As independent variables, most empirical studies dealing with the EMB only pays attention to its autonomy. The reason is that if autonomy is established, the EMB can be fair to manage the election without exhibiting partisan bias. However, this is insufficient. The form, activities, results of the EMB, need to be considered too. Unfortunately, this point has not been seriously discussed in many previous studies yet.

First, is it enough to discuss only autonomy as a form of organization? The answer would be no. The role of the EMB's range of rights is also important. It is because even if the EMB has enough autonomy but insufficient authority, its effect on the dependent variables such as the quality of elections. In other words, it should be discussed who is in charge of the electoral governance besides the EMB. It would be a matter of the sharing responsibilities between the legislature and the judiciary and the relationship between NPOs monitoring the elections, international organizations, and NGOs. The right can even be shared between highly independent EMBs and government agencies. One needs to understand how much central government and local government share power in terms of decentralization. Especially, understanding the distance between the electoral management subject and the people is important.

The reason for studying the EMB is that it eventually exerts a significant influence on the electoral process and results. Then what should be secured in the electoral process and results? Equity is first. The confirmation of the election results should not be biased and voting should not be distorted by political forces being the most basic conditions of democracy. The second is efficiency. Even though the result is fair, if it takes a long time to confirm the result people will lose confidence in democracy. The results should be available as quickly as possible.

What would be required from the EMB in order to satisfy these conditions? One thing is independence or autonomy from political parties. Specifically, the authority for committee staff appointment, the term of office, and the number of members can be used as an indicator. The other is specialization. It will acquire a variety of expertise and practical knowledge about elections. Specifically, an EMB's budget, manpower, and career path can be used as indicators (Kelly, 2007; Van Aaken, 2009). This kind of study which describes whether the independence and expertise achieved the output of efficiency and fairness in the election is rarely done.

Study on the Electoral Management Body (EMB) as a Dependent Variable

A study on the EMBs as a dependent variable examines how the EMB is defined by certain factors. These kinds of studies are very few. Among these studies, Mozaffar tried to quantify the autonomy of EMB as the dependent variable (Mozaffar, 2002). The autonomy of EMB in Mozaffar's study was measured in three steps. Independent variables include institutional heritage and the cleavage of each country. Data was collected from 36 countries in Africa and analyzed. In the analysis, the nations that had British colonial experience and strong nationalism showed a higher level of autonomy in their EMBs. Although this study is valuable as a pioneer in this field, it also has been criticized due to its lack of theoretical support and insufficient clarification of the causal relations.

Next, Gazibo also studied the autonomy of EMBs as a dependent variable (Gazibo, 2006). Gazibo said, the balance of power between the ruling party and opposition parties is the independent variables at the point of democratization. In other words, EMB's autonomy can be established by not only government but also opposition's involvement in designing system (institutional design). This hypothesis was confirmed by the seven African countries cases. The cases of Benin and Ghana were successful in securing EMB autonomy but Togo and Cameroon failed. Burkina Faso, Niger, and Senegal were middle cases.

Ultimately, the criteria to form a fair and highly efficient electoral management system can be summarized as follows. (1) If the opposition believes that elections will be unfair in any case, there is a high possibility of resistance against the authority. (2) The resistance movement causes a very large cost to the authority. It consists of economic losses causing political turmoil and necessary costs to suppress the resistance movement. (3) Benefits from maintaining the power can be almost negligible depending on the costs that a resistance movement against the authority generated. Very important independent variables which influence these criteria include the degree of the winner's power and the opposition's power (great public support, cohesion). In other words, the possible benefits for the authority becomes a strong motivation for securing their power. If the authority believes that they will benefit from maintaining power, the motivation for holding power grows stronger and electoral fraud possibly can be done no matter how powerful is the resistance of the opposition. Conversely, if the benefits for authority are small, they are reluctant to spend much to suppress the resistance of the opposition. On the other hand, when the opposition's power grows, the motivation of the ruling party to commit electoral fraud declines. If the ruling party has the confidence to win fair election, a fair electoral management system does not matter for them.

There is another view that the form of the electoral management system is built in a historic context. Once a system is formed at a critical juncture, the existence of the system is strongly regulated because a system has a high path dependence. Therefore, the EMB system depends on the existence of the former system and transition to the new system from the key turning point in democratization. In this point of view, the form and role of the electoral management system are passively regulated by environmental or historical factors.

After 1987, the attempt to ensure the EMB's autonomy and neutrality became more regularized in Korea. The end of authoritarian regimes through democratization in 1987 is related to the start of a crackdown campaign for illegal elections in 1989. The ruling party's monopoly of power under the authoritarian regime in the past became democratized. The balance of power among the ruling party, opposition parties, and NGOs was maintained and the consultations for a system revision was also provided. After democratization in 1987, changes in the political environment influenced the activities of the autonomous and neutral EMB.

However, in the Korean case, independent self-awareness, establishing roles, and expanding the power of the election administration in the EMBs were important factors. Therefore, in this chapter, we will focus on the EMB as an independent variable. Especially we will focus on capacity of the EMB in terms of its structure, its ability to ensure the neutrality of its members, its budget, human resources, and organization scale. As an explanatory framework, we will give more attention to the subject or to the role of a player from a neo-institutional perspective.

THE ELECTORAL SYSTEM REVISION AND THE PROGRESS OF DEMOCRATIZATION

Adoption of Single-Member District and the Requirement of the Right to Choose Government

Since 1948 when the government was established, the most critical issue in Korean parliamentary electoral reform was the introduction of a fair electoral system. This can be summarized in a guarantee of the free right to choose a government and the realization of voter's choice in correctly allocated seats. Since 1973, the allocation method of the multimember district system and the proportional representative system has brought advantages for securing the ruling party's seats unilaterally in Korea. As shown in Fig. 1, the ruling party of the authoritarian era ensured a higher percentage of seats than votes. It is because multimember district system's institutional effectiveness and the proportional representative system's favorable seat allocation for the ruling party allow the ruling party to secure the extra seats. Even though the percentage of votes or seats in the ruling party dropped to less than half, still the ruling party kept a majority of the seats through the proportional representation seat allocation method. The Yushin regime and the Fifth Republic are prime examples.

Requesting revision of the electoral system maintaining the authoritarian regime was achieved in 1987 with the direct election of the president.

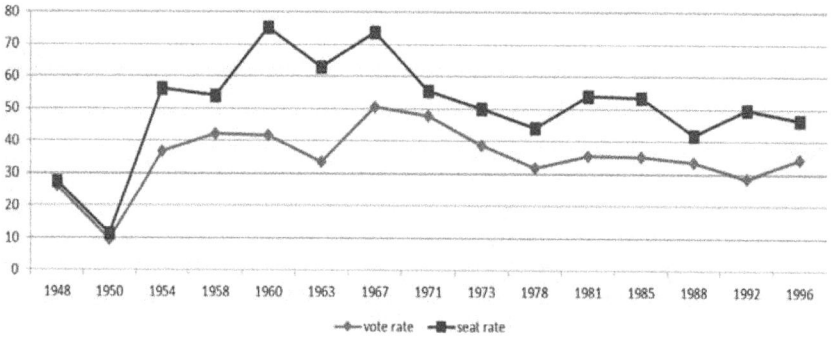

Fig. 1.   Comparison of the Ruling Party's Seats and Vote Rate

At that time, the direction of the electoral system revision was compressed into implementing the single-member district system and the introduction of the proportional representation system based on the vote. Then look at the introduction of the single-member district system and the progress of the reform process after democratization, and also look for the meaning of this electoral system reform.

Requesting of constitutional reform for direct elections of the president drove Korean politics to a new situation in the national assembly election of February 12, 1985. Various measures to ensure the free choice of the government were presented including setting a bipartisan constitutional amendment special committee. In 1987, the constitutional change of the direct election of the president and implementation of the presidential election based on the new constitution was an opportunity for democratic transition. In the presidential election of 1987, the appearance of regional political parties expressed different interests in the process of national assembly election system negotiation. The Democratic Justice Party (ruling party) wanted the mixed-district system that elected one to four persons from one electoral district. In January 1988, The Unification Democratic Party (first largest opposition party) wanted the multimember district system that elected two to four persons from one electoral district. Peaceful and the Democratic Party (the second largest opposition party) blamed the multimember district system for the military dictatorship's stable ruling and insisted the single-member district system and the proportional representation system by turn-out rate (National Election Commission, 2010). The New Democracy Republican Party (the third largest opposition party) also wanted the multimember district system that elected two to four people from one electoral district.

At electoral reform in 1988, the reason each party wanted the multimember district system than the single-member district system was the strategic interests of each party. The purpose of ruling party was to accompany winning and securing a large number of seats but the purpose of Unification Democratic Party (the first largest party) and the New Democratic Republican Party (the third largest party) was also winning. Moreover, using single-member district system could cause the election defeat for the opposition camp into the disunity of opposition parties. Opposition parties were concerned about the possibility of the regional party's appearance, in particular, and excessive competition through the single-member district system. Since then, in electoral system revision, a process of merging opposition parties had focused on the abolition of the multimember district system which is compatible with the authoritarian ruling system. On March 8, 1988, eventually the electoral law led to an amendment required the single-member district system based on people's free right to choose the government and the ruling party also agreed with it.

In electoral reform in 1988, the single-member district system was revived as a pretext to block the authoritarian regime. The multimember district system in the era of the authoritarian regime was undemocratic because it fundamentally blocked the free right to choose the government. However, the introduction of single-member district system was meant to prevent the distortion of the people's will. And the single-member district system adopted in the electoral reform of 1988 ensures the free choice of the people to give power to the ruling party or opposition party. Because of this, the introduction of the single-member district system contributed not only to democratization but also to regional party system.

Realization of Voting and Democracy

One important challenge is the population deviation issue when considering democratic development through electoral reform. Equality of political rights need to be guaranteed by the constitution in order to solidify the democratic electoral system. In order to ensure the equality of political rights, a one person-one vote should be used regardless of education level or property holdings.

Under past authoritarian regimes in South Korea, population deviation significantly undermined the equality of political rights in elections. In particular, the number of districts with a population gap between urban and rural areas was used as the ruling party's means of securing a majority.

After the introduction of the single-member district system in 1988, there was no sign of improvement in the matter of population deviation. From election redistricting of national assembly elections in 1995, the gap between minimum and maximum electoral district was greater than eight times.

Since the introduction of the single-member district system in 1988, population deviation between urban and rural areas has been a serious problem. Electoral redistricting was ruled unconstitutional because of "irrationality" on December 27. The new permitted limit of population deviation was stated as 4:1. In the national assembly election of 2000, electoral redistricting was confirmed based on a population criterion (maximum population: 350,000 people/ minimum population: 9000 people). Again the electoral redistricting exceeding 3:1 was ruled unconstitutional by the Korean constitutional court on October 25, 2000 (National Election Commission, 2010). The court did state that electoral redistricting exceeding 3:1 is beyond the discretion of national assembly so it is unconstitutional (National Election Commission, 2010). Population deviation decreased by 2.83 in the national assembly election of 2004. The ratio of 2.83:1 was maintained in the national assembly election of 2008. On October 30, 2014, the Korean constitutional court did state nonconformity with the decision for electoral redistricting of the national assembly election in 2012 and was ordered to adjust the population deviation below 1.2.

As seen above, safeguards to guarantee the democratic electoral system has made significant progress.

Proportional Representation of Seat Allocation Scheme

The reasons why the Korean electoral system has often changed because the authoritarian regime used the electoral system of the national assembly for the creation of the regime and the long-term seizure of power (Kim Yong-ho, 1993). In particular, the representative case of using an electoral system for the long-term seizure of power is the allocation of seats in a proportional representative system unilaterally by the ruling party.

In 1963, the proportional representation system was launched in Korea. Proportional representation of seats was one-fourth of all seats. Since entering into the authoritarian political system in 1973, the proportional representative system changed the electing format such that the National Council for Unification elects people based on the president's recommendation. Assigning seats was advantageous to the ruling party in 1981 and 1985. Two-thirds were allocated to the first largest party and then rest of one-thirds was distributed by the seat rate of the national assembly.

After parliamentary electoral reform in 1988, the seat allocation of the proportional representation system according to the number of seats by district remained unchanged and acted very favorably to the ruling party. The parliamentary election in 1988 changed in such a way that the allocation of seats for proportional representation was based on valid votes. Allocating the seats in the proportional representation system according to the number of seats or turn-out rate by district was ruled unconstitutional on July 19, 2001. The decision of unconstitutionality led to new proportional representation electoral system allocating parliamentary seats by a turn-out rate of proportional representative. By unconstitutional adjudication, the proportional representative election changed in such a way that the distribution of seats was according to the party share of the vote.

The existing "one-person-one-vote system" went against to the principle of democracy. There is no way that a voter can choose their favor parties and the vote itself hardly affected the election of candidates. Moreover, when voting for an independent candidate, it was not reflected in the voter's decision and it violated the principle of an equal vote in the sense of forcing the inequality of the vote value. The Constitutional Court later ruled that the existing "one-person-one-vote system" was unconstitutional. Because of this, from 2004 a two-vote mixed system was implemented and continues until now. The two-vote mixed system may have contributed to the development of electoral democracy.

And easing the criteria of allocating seats for proportional representation has lowered the barrier to entry for parliamentary parties. When it was introduced in 1963, only those parties getting 5% of the turn-out rate or securing more than three seats in a district were able to receive seats in congress. In 1971, the criteria raised the standard to 5% of the turn-out rate or securing more than five seats in the district to have seats in congress. In the election of 1992, the criteria of more than five seats in a district was maintained but parties getting more than 3% of the nation-wide valid vote even without the regional elected could have one priority seat in congress. In the 2004 election, the appointment of a seat in congress was distributed according to the turn-out rate: more than 3% of valid votes in parliamentary elections or more than five seats in regional assemblymen election by the introduction of the two-vote mixed system. Also, the criteria for seat allocation in the proportion of national assemblymen has changed from a number of seats in local constituencies to the turn-out rate in parliamentary elections. Moreover, changing the seat distribution criteria which is favorable to existing giant parties or the ruling party helped minority parties to enter the congress with fewer barriers.

As we have seen above, various attempts to guarantee the democratic foundations of elections have been conducted since democratization in 1987. A significant degree of democratic systems has been secured. The electoral democracy in Korea has been developed in terms of its institutional aspect. But democratic systems do not mean the development of electoral democracy. Now a fair EMB and operational capacity are required for running the democratic institutional mechanisms.

THE AUTONOMY AND AUTHORITY OF
THE NATIONAL ELECTION COMMISSION

Enhancement of the Neutrality of the National Election Commission

Ensuring high autonomy of EMBs from the bureaucratic power exists to serve electoral integrity in Korea. At the same time having a strong authority is important and required to monitor the election campaign and run democratic elections. Recently, studies about systems maintaining a democratic election system while keeping authoritarian regime in power are under the spotlight.

This political system is called an "electoral authoritarian regime" or "competitive authoritarian regime." The electoral management system in an electoral authoritarian regime ruled by the intentions of the president is not run fairly. Even if the election is not being mobilized by power, election fraud may exist in the election campaign. In this case, EMBs may not be able to stop negative election campaigning and also members of EMBs could be involved in electoral fraud. Therefore, electoral management systems in electoral authoritarian regimes cannot be evaluated as fair and neutral systems.

To conduct neutral elections, the monitoring ability of EMB to stop election fraud is another requirement. Organization and operational methods related to election management systems is determined the law. But the operation of the electoral management system depends on the ability of the EMB, such as manpower, budget, and authority. Even though the election management system is independent of the president, if an EMB's ability is not enough to control the parties, candidates, or election fraud, it is impossible to conduct a fair and neutral election. Therefore a fair and neutral election management system will work only when EMBs are equipped with autonomy and capacity.

First, let us look for the ways to ensure the autonomy of the Korean election management organizations.

The electoral management system in Korea has its origins in the constitution. From 1983, the Constitution states that Election Commissions shall be established for the purpose of fair management of elections and national referenda, and dealing with administrative affairs concerning political parties (Article 114). For keeping neutrality, the NEC shall be composed of three members appointed by the President, three members selected by the National Assembly, and three members designated by the Chief Justice of the Supreme Court. The Constitution also mentions NEC's term and state of a member (Article 114, paragraph 1). The Chairman of the Commission shall be elected from among the members (Article 114, paragraph 2). The term of office of the members of the Commission shall be six years (Article 114, paragraph 3). The members of the Commission shall not join political parties, nor shall they participate in political activities (Article 114, paragraph 4). No member of the Commission shall be expelled from office except by impeachment or a sentence of imprisonment without prison or heavier punishment (Article 114, Section 5).

The NEC may establish, within the limit of Acts and decrees, regulations relating to the management of elections, national referenda, and administrative affairs concerning political parties and may also establish regulations relating to internal discipline that is compatible with the Act (Article 114, Section 6). Election Commissions at each level may issue necessary instructions to administrative agencies concerned with administrative affairs pertaining to elections and national referenda such as the preparation of the poll books and administrative agencies concerned, upon receipt of such instructions, shall comply (Article 115 of claim 1, claim 2).

Public Official Election Act, the Political Party Law, the Political Fund Law, Election Commission Act, and the Local Government Act are also enacted.

The constitution of the NEC has changed several times through the constitutional amendment but the basic framework has been maintained. If the Constitution is not significantly different in the authoritarian regime from now, the possibility of conducting a neutral election by the Constitution itself is very low. In fact, look at the member configuration of the NEC, the limits of neutrality is clearly showed. The NEC is composed of three members appointed by the President, three members selected by the National Assembly, and three members designated by the Chief Justice of the Supreme Court. However, take a closer look, the President appoints three members and the parties select three members. The ruling party can recommend more than one person as a member. Moreover, the Chief Justice of the Supreme Court was originally appointed by a president so the president may influence the selection of the three members designated by the Chief Justice of the Supreme Court. In this situation, it is not possible to maintain a substantially neutral NEC only by the constitutional order. To solve this kind of problem, the operation of self-enforcing institutions is needed to keep neutrality regardless of political intentions.

The Process of Ensuring Autonomy and Expanding Rights

Next, let us look at the process of securing rights relating to securing autonomy. The EMB in Korea continues to manage election administrative procedures within the law. EMB is concerned with the fairness between parties so it is not involved in political issues. EMB believes the electoral administrative management and procedures from the Constitution form the formal (normative, legal) standpoint as an absolute value (Lee, 2015). However, during the Donghae city re-election (1989), the NEC started to actively exercise the rights prescribed by the Constitution or laws and expand its authority.

After democratization in 1987, the Donghae city re-election (1989) was conducted according to the newly introduced single member district system. The parliamentary election in 1988 used the first past the post system. Theoretically, it is necessary to get at least 50% of votes in order to win. Each party illegally campaigned by mobilizing their organizations, human resources, and money to win the election. Under the authoritarian regime, election success is the top priority regardless of means. There were 26 lawsuits for invalid election practices in 1988.

The Donghae city reelections in 1989, despite being re-conducted in accordance with a previous illegal election, had more extreme campaigning. The national party intervened actively, and it became a confrontation between parties, not candidates. As an overheating of the election campaign began, an illegal election was conducted. The Secretary General of the Unification Democratic Party (the first largest ruling party) bought a candidate of another opposition party. To fight this illegal election, the NEC configured the control squad for the first time since it was established. As a result, the control squad of NEC accused all candidates and election campaign managers and the Secretary General of the Unification Democratic party were all arrested. The NEC attempted to block the illegal election by configuring Control squad but was not able to achieve a fair election. Through this election, members of the NEC realized the need of their recognition to change to improve the elections. In other words, NEC members agreed that recognizing the role and powers of the NEC by the Constitution and exercising its authority are very important. A crackdown to block illegal elections was conducted in by-elections, the local election in 1991, parliamentary elections in 1992, and presidential elections in 1992. The NEC tried to stop the illegal elections and plutocracy elections in the political sphere. These demands created the legal basis for the process of the Election Commission Act reform in 1992.

Construction of the NEC election management system through autonomy and empowerment was a major turning point of the Election Commission Act Reform in 1992, the election law Reform in 1994, and election law Reform in 2004. In particular, the Election Commission Act Reform in 1992 strengthened the rights of the NEC. The supervisory authority to crack down on election law violations was stipulated in the Election Commission Act Reform of 1992 (Article 14 2), by setting up the a supervisory group for vote rigging in the Election Commissions at all levels (excluding the Eup/Myeon/Dong Election Commissions), while supervisory authority, organization, manpower, budgetary limits were expanded.

The number of employees in the Korean NEC was 1197 in 1989 (Fig. 2). The number of employees were 2012 in 1997. However, the Korean government had to undergo a restructuring of government employees since the 1997 currency crisis. As a result, the number of government employees was reduced to 1867 people in 1998. The number of employees was 2057 people in 2002.

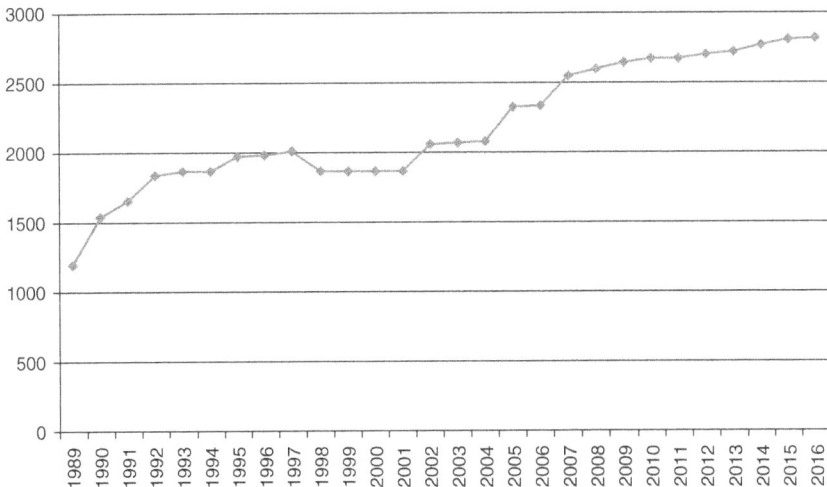

Fig. 2.   Number of Employees in the National Election Commission.

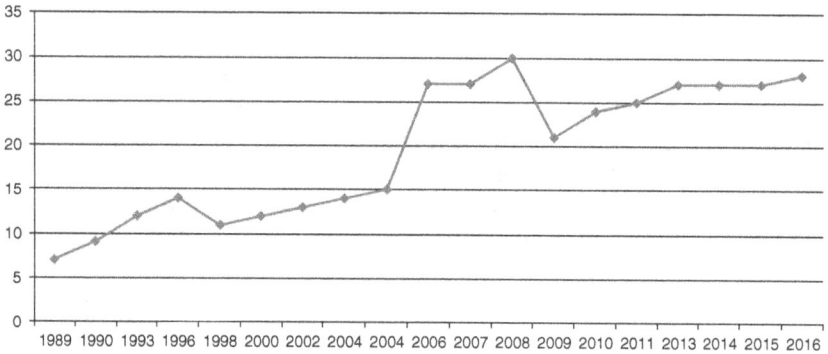

Fig. 3.   Trend of the National Election Commission (Division).

In 2007, it increased to 2549 people and is now at 2816 people in 2016. This figure represents an increase of 2.3 since 1989.

The operating period of the supervisory group of vote rigging was expanded to 10 days prior to the Election Day in the Election Act Reform 2002. Internet campaigns became increasingly popular, and so the cyber supervisory group was established in 2004. The supervisory group of vote rigging has operated constantly since 2008. As the role of the supervisory group expanded, the number of employees at the NEC grew proportionally.

The scale of the NEC has expanded as its role has become more diversified. For instance, the election guidance division was expended (Fig. 3). The political funds division and the public relations department were newly established in 1990. The computer division was newly established in 1992. The electoral training institute was set up in 1996. The investigation division in 2002, the investigation division for political funds in 2004, the overseas voting task force and the electoral cybercrime center in 2008. And the NEC was granted an authentic interpretation power to determine whether the election law is for candidates or political parties. These two rights were not allowed before 1992. In the Election Act Reform of 1994, the Unified Election Law, which is able to apply the same standard, was enacted to manage different elections such as presidential elections, parliamentary elections, and local elections. Applying different election laws restricted the role and authority of the NEC.

By expending the NEC's authority, the organization, manpower, and budget were also increased and the number of elections managed by the NEC increased as well. Presidential elections, parliamentary elections, local elections, referendums, superintendent elections in 2000, local referendums

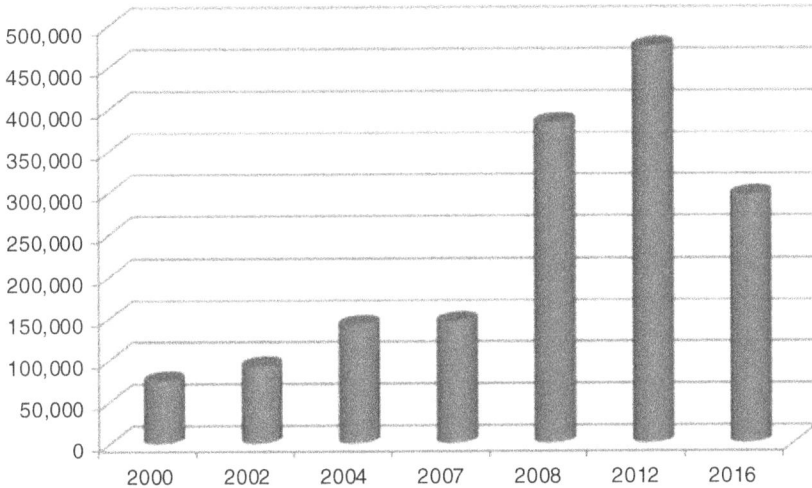

Fig. 4. Budget of the National Election Commission (National Level Election).
Unit: Millions of KRW.

in 2004, primary election in 2005, university general elections, agricultural fisheries union presidential election in 2005, a recall vote in 2006, overseas elections in 2009, House of Commons representative election in 2010, and so on (Fig. 4). The coverage from public elections to local elections and private sector elections has been continuously extended.

As the scope and role of the elections expended, the budget of the NEC has expanded too. The election budget was 750 million KRW in the parliamentary election of 2000 and it increased nearly four times to 2960 million KRW in parliamentary election 2016. When there were parliamentary and presidential elections in 2012, the budget was more than 4700 million KRW.

The supervisory authority of the NEC has been continuously expanding. In order to crack down on illegal elections, there is no distinction between ruling and opposition parties. NEC is able to limit the president's political action. For example, the Uri party (ruling party) occupied the majority of seats in parliamentary elections in 2004. However, by enforcement of the NEC, the ruling party's seats became less than half in less than one year after the election. Also, there was an event to show how the NEC's autonomy is intact. The president elected from the ruling party made a statement to support the ruling party in the process of parliamentary elections in 2004. The NEC judged that this statement violates the Election Act that prescribes public official's political neutrality and warned the president. The warning to this statement became the cause of impeachment and the president suffered politically.

The Factors of the NEC's Role that Are Expanding
Then how has the NEC been able to continue expanding its authority? Moreover, how it was able to have a powerful authority like the police and prosecution to enforce campaigns? Contrary to the police and prosecutors, a strong election task force with enforcement authority could be a threat to politicians. Existing power structures such as the police and prosecution, newly allowing part of the enforcement function to the NEC can be described in two ways.

The first is a mistrust of state institutions that contributed to keeping the old regime from the authoritarian regime (Isozaki, 2012). Under an authoritarian regime, the election is only for the ruling party's gain and a formal procedure for maintaining the regime. Police contribute to repressing the opposition parties in the election process and arrest the students and politicians in the pro-democracy movement. The manipulated election by the government was a routine. The police were at the center of the manipulated election. Police used supervisory power to support the ruling party's win and interrupted the campaigns of opposition parties' candidates in the election. Eventually, due to mistrust of the police and prosecution, people did not want to expand the power of these organizations. Another reason is the expectation to develop democratization through organizations such as the NEC, which required the new role for fair and clean elections after 1989. In the presidential election of 1992, each candidate proposed the end of manipulated elections by the government and political reform as the most important goal. Allowing power in NEC could be disadvantageous for candidates in a shortsighted way but was the inevitable choice to appeal to their politically innovative character.

Consequentially, expanding the power of the NEC is the result of the political history in Korea. As mentioned earlier, the authoritarian regime wanted to maintain the old ways and this experience produced distrust of the police and prosecution. However, the NEC's supervisory power was not just automatically gained by the mistrust of the people, police, and prosecution. The NEC's supervisory power accrued because of the NEC's active commitment and role awareness of fair elections.

Along with manipulated elections by the government, money in elections had been pointed out as a chronic problem in Korea. Not only buying votes but also seats in the National Assembly was frequent. During the election period, money was scattered. Buying a ticket for a nomination or a seat as a proportional representative also occurred. To solve these money-consuming election problems, publicly financed electoral management was introduced in 1994.

The penalties for illegal money election campaign were strengthened in the election law reform of 1994. Candidacy of anyone found to be in violation of the rules could lead to the invalidation of their candidacy. When any election campaign manager or accountant in charge of the election campaign office is sentenced to imprisonment with prison labor or a fine exceeding three million won on account of an excessive disbursement of more than the restricted amount of election expenses is publicly announced, the election of the candidate concerned shall become invalidated.

When any family member, descendant, spouse of the candidate, campaign manager, or accountant committed a crime of illegally giving or receiving political funds, and is sentenced to imprisonment with prison labor, the election of the candidate concerned shall become invalidated. In the process of strengthening the penalties, the NEC demanded more power.

The authority of the NEC was reinforced as one of the measures to eradicate money elections. The strengthening of the enforcement of supervisory authority for illegal election campaigns highly relates to building expertise about election laws and electoral management. The presidential election is for five years, parliamentary and local elections are for four years. Operating the election by police and prosecution with temporary organizations and experts is not efficient. Police personnel are more specialized in criminal cases. In this respect, the improvement of professional skills of the NEC greatly contributes to ensuring the autonomy and authority of the organization.

NEC has been authorized to submit opinions to the National Assembly to legislate in relation to the elections and political parties. In Election Commission Act Reform 1992, the amendment allowing the NEC to submit its opinion in writing to the National Assembly was added (Article 17, Section 2). In accordance with this legal basis, the NEC has continuously presented its opinions in the reform process of elections, political parties, and political finance laws. The NEC's opinions are respected by the National Assembly in the process of legislative discussions. And the legislative opinion of the NEC has the agenda-setting function as reported in the media. Even though the NEC may present its opinion, legislation is decided by the National Assembly alone.

It is difficult to expect that a member of the National Assembly or president promotes an unfavorable amendment to his authority or re-election in Korea. However, presentation of the NEC's various opinions regarding the electoral system supported by people or NGOs increases the chances of pass-ing the amendment. Since 1987, most of the deployment exercises were sup-ported by NGOs and the NECs were successful (Asaba, 2012). A remarkable case is the exclusion of regional parties in 2004. The running of regional par-ties was very costly. The regional parties were abolished for the realization of less cost election and slimming down the size of political parties. This case was proposed by NECs and upheld by NGOs.

COMPARISON BETWEEN KOREA AND DEVELOPING COUNTRIES: THE PHILIPPINES, INDONESIA, AND THAILAND

In the Philippines, under Ferdinand Marcos from 1972 to 1986, the rul-ing party won all elections including parliamentary elections (in 1978, 1984) and presidential elections (in 1981, 1986). The background of election fraud such as the alteration of the voters list, fabrication of the count figure, vote buying by government, and toleration of violence by the Election Commission all aimed to support the authoritarian ruling party's win. In the presidential election 1986, one of the vote counting staff of the Election Commission broke away from the counting room to protest the forced vote rigging (Wurfel, 1988). In the presidential election of 1986, mistrust of election fraud under Marcos, alienation of the army, and street protests of people provided the opportunity of democratization. However, the chief of the Election Commission appointed by President Corazon Aquino had been appointed to another important post in gov-ernment. After that, the other two chiefs of the Election Commission were also replaced in the same way so they never completed their seven-year term at the Election Commission. This kind of involvement by the regimes missed the opportunity to reform the Election Commission. Conclusively, the Election Commission just kept the rampant corruption of the Marcos regime (Calimbahin, 2009).

After the democratization, vote buying, election fraud by threat, and fab-rication of the count figures, all involving Election Commission staff, contin-ued in elections. President Estrada and President Arroyo had appointed their own man as the Election Committee chairperson and committee members. The illegal involvement of elections developed as the political event related to the president. The original recordings of a wiretapped conversation that Arroyo rigged the 2004 national election to maintain her presidency and the political success of her allies between President Arroyo and an official of the Commission on Elections was unveiled. And she was placed under arrest in 2011 for electoral fraud and involvement in the 2007 Mindanao senatorial election. There is not much advantage to reforming the Election Commission, as a president in the Philippines has only a single-term system for the presidency. In a senatorial election, 12 persons are elected by the plural ballot system so there may be a different stance between the candidates who have resources to intervene in the election and those who don't. The House of Representatives is elected by the single-member district system. For them holding power means ruling their district and there is an advantage to becoming involved in election fraud. This advantageous structure made the main political force or activist unwilling to perform the role of extending the autonomy and ability of the Election Commission. Finally, securing the democratic fairness of the Election Commission is made by the NGOs' election monitoring.

There is no transition from a long-term authoritarianism to democracy in Thailand and the country has a history of repeating military coups to transferring power to the people. Since the 1932 revolution of constitutional democracy, elections have been consistently conducted. Until 1980s, prime ministers were elected from among the representatives, who was elected by popular vote, and the multiparty system was formed by the effect of multimember district system. Under the multiparty system, the coalition government was formed and this political system was not that advantageous to people who hold power. However, in the 1997 Constitution, proportional rule using the D'Hondt method and first-past-the-post from single-member constituencies were introduced. Since 1992, the military-civil conflict and subsequent progress of democracy has led to new constitution reform. Right after the Asian financial crisis, a new constitution of Thailand was enacted in 1997. By implementing a new election system and changing the political party system into a two-party system, it also made only one ruling party possible. It made the prime minister has more power and the power produced more advantages (Takeshi Kawanaka, 2013).

At the same time, an independent Election Commission was established in the Constitution of 1997. The election administration was governed by the previous Home Office and has been transferred to the Election Commission. The authority of the Election Commission was strengthened dramatically compared to the previous period. When the Election Commission suspected election fraud, they could issue a "yellow card" to invalidate the election. If the election fraud was clearly identified, the Election Commission could issue "red cards" meaning candidates would not be able to contest the by-elections. The House of Representatives election in 2001, re-election was commended in 62 constituencies and 52 candidates were disqualified from that re-election (Kokpol, 2002). In Thailand, a number of problems involving election ticket brokers frequently occurred and the Election Commission focused on the challenge of vote buying.

The Thaksin regime dominated the elections by winning the majority of the seats in the House of Representatives in 2001. Thereafter, Thaksin had formed the majority party through merging minority parties and he started to expand his influence to the Election Commission. Since the election in 2001, Thaksin appointed his own man on the Election Committee members and the replaced members (Chambers, 2006). Under the Election Commission, which has strong partisanship, the House of Representatives election was conducted in 2005. The Thaksin camp won and took three-fourths of parliamentary seats. However, various forms of electoral fraud allegations were raised and a demand for the resignation of Prime Minister Thaksin Shinawatra was raised too. As a result of this public pressure, Thaksin conducted a re-election in 2006. However, in many constituencies voters used the "abstain" option. Anti-Thaksin Constitutional Court, Supreme Court, and the Election Commission were against one another. As a result, the Constitutional Court later invalidated the House of Representatives election results and recommended the resignation of the Election Committee members. Then the criminal prosecution received the accusing public Election Committee of offering illegal convenience to the candidate of Prime Minister Thaksin's camp so the Election Committee members were sentenced to imprisonment. After that, all Election Commission members were dismissed and Thaksin was expelled from power by a military coup.

Anti-Thaksin people took up the Election Board. In order to prevent the dominance of Thaksin and his followers, a new election board issued the so-called "red cards" and "yellow card" to candidates of Thaksin followers in the House of Representatives election 2007. As a result of the election, the Anti-Thaksin Party won the largest share of the vote and the Democrat Party became the opposition as the second-largest party in the House of Representatives. People believed the Election Commission is generally neutral and unbiased. Based on a survey of The Asia Foundation 2009, nationally, two-thirds (67%) stated that Election Commission is politically unbiased.

Indonesia is a third interesting case. In 1998, a more liberal political-social environment ensued following the resignation of authoritarian President Suharto, ending the three decades of the New Order period. The independent and democratic form of election management committee was set up in accordance with the Election Act Law 1999. For securing the election neutrality, the Election Commission consisted of five independent government representatives including four representatives of a political party. The background of participating political parties' representatives in the Election Commission is for ensuring the legitimacy of the election through participation in political parties. The political party's monitoring in the election was allowed in order to avoid government intervention as the Suharto regime consolidated control of the military, bureaucracy, and the intervention of the election. However, as a result of the political parties participating the Election Commission had failed to produce the intended results. As the members of the Election Committee were actively involved in the campaign to be favorable to the parties, the role of the Election Commission was damaged in the Parliament elections of 1999. The experience in this election was an opportunity to characterize the Indonesian elections. As the presence of members of the Election Committee appointed by the government meant the government monitored the election, this was abolished also. The top priority of the Election Commission was forming a system with nonpartisanship.

The election law was revised in 2000, and the government members and representatives of political parties were abolished. The Election Committees had been constituted by 11 nonpartisanship persons. And the system allowing involvement of the Standing Committee of the National Congress to Election Committee formation was formed. In 2004, the entire Election Commission created a slush fund. In the purchasing process of election equipment, contractors paid money and it became the slush fund for the Ministry of Finance, expenses for the National Assembly chairman, and even private expenses for the Election Commission members. The election chairman and Committee were found guilty in 2005. Eventually, the system reform applying strict accounting procedures for the expenditure of the Election Commission was made. The Election Commission with nonpartisanship and strict accounting procedures for expenditure of Election Commission were strengthened further on the legislation of the NEC law in 2007. The election committee was prohibited from participating and holding any government position. The Select Committee installed by the President recommends candidates for the election committee. The members of the Election Committee were also changed to seven. In the amendment of the law, an election monitoring committee was set up as an organization that specializes in election monitoring in addition to the Election Commission. The powers and functions of the Ethics Committee were strengthened to verify the members of the Election Committee and the election monitoring committee (Go, 2014).

ELECTION BODY PARTNERSHIP FOR DEMOCRACY

Recently, interest in Korean elections, election management and election management bodies is growing in the international community. The "Korea model" of election management has featured not only in the debate in academic research but also in discussions or recommendations of international organizations. "Politics of Election management," published in Japan in 2013, has analyzed the historical formation of the Korean election system, election management body, institutional details of the election administration, political functions, legislative functions, and quasi-judicial functions. This study is meaningful in that they conducted the international comparison of Korea Election mechanisms with Japan, the Philippines, and Costa Rica.

The ACE (Administration and Cost of Elections, Project by IDEA, IFES, and UNDESA) recommends to install EMB (EMBs) as a constitutional institution with a high degree of autonomy from the government and parliament to ensure the legitimacy of the election results.

What is needed for fair and autonomous elections? The international trend strongly appears that the independence of the election management body from the executive authority is most important (Lopez-Pintor, 2000: 27). In this respect, the Korean NEC is to meet a very important condition in terms of constitutional institutions with a high degree of autonomy from the government and political parties. In addition, the Korean NEC is highly autonomous and performs a variety of roles, ranging from the improvement of the electoral system to disclosing electoral crime. These roles would be relevant to the evaluation that these have played an important role in the development of democracy in Korea (Yutaka Onishi, 2013).

Since 2006, the Korean NEC has been conducting the training for government employees in charge of election management in developing countries as part of the foreign-aid business. Election workers from various regions are coming to Korea to learn the know-how of operating the election system. The government employees in charge of election management in 14 countries from Bangladesh, China, East Timor, Mongolia, Indonesia, Nepal, the Philippines, and Uzbekistan in the Asia region, as well as Congo, Egypt, Uganda, Nigeria, Rwanda in Africa region, and Panama, in South America participated in the training in 2006 and 15 countries participated in 2007. In total 105 countries have participated till 2015. The annual average of participating countries is more than 10.

Looking at the number of visitors for training by region (Fig. 5), 18 countries are from the Asian region, 16 countries are from the African region, and 7 countries are from the South America region. Looking at Fig. 5 by

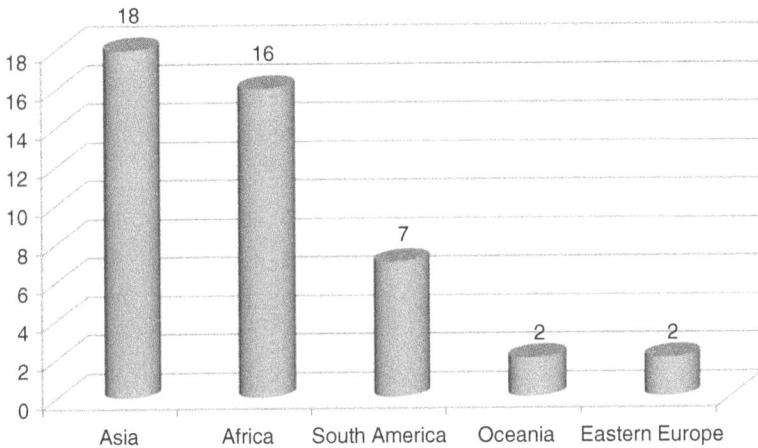

Fig. 5. Regional Distribution of Training Participating Country (Asia/Africa//
South America/Oceania/ Eastern Europe).

county, we can find that many developing countries participated. The countries are divided into annual and one-time participating countries. In the case of Nepal, since 2009, training has been carried out once every year. The Philippines has been regularly carrying out the training every year since 2009. In South America, Peru has carried out the training out in 2007 and 2008, and Ecuador in 2009 and 2010. Mongolia has participated in the training and also invited to be an election adviser for Korea to share Korean election management know-how (KOCEID, 2015)

There is a wide variety of contents in the training. From the introduction of institutional information, such as the Korean electoral system, electoral law, political parties act, political finance law to historical progress of the Korean NEC for ensuring the independence, efficiency, and professionalism. Additionally, the correspondence of the election management system in accordance with social and economic changes, know-how for democratic reform, democratic communication methods among the parties, civic education for voters, electoral manifestos, e-elections utilizing ICT skills and equipment, securing the electoral governance processes are some of the topics included.

The training for international trainees is held during local elections, parliamentary elections, and presidential elections in Korea (Fig. 6). In fact, the system operates through participation in real Korean elections and on-site classes.

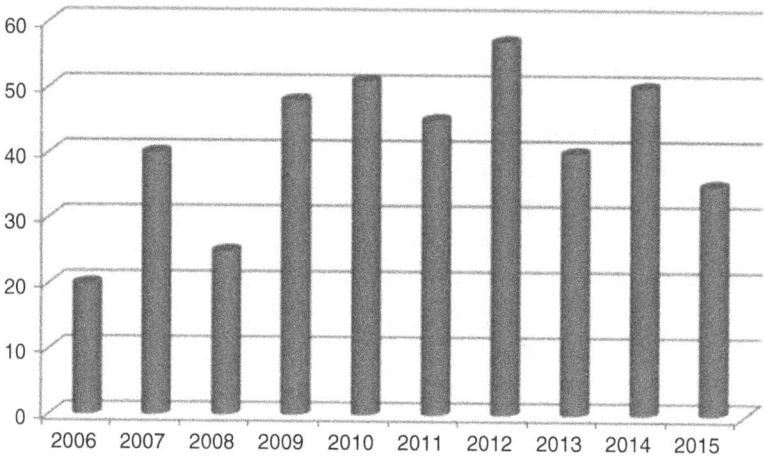

Fig. 6.   The Number of Trainees per Year.

Furthermore, the training includes deep discussions of comparisons between the "Korea model" of election management and other country's electoral management or system. This training focuses on helping the election officials in developing countries to develop, redesign, and create their own electoral management system by taking advantage of the Korean case.

The overseas election officials training is mainly for developing countries. Most officials are in charge of election management practices. However, some countries such as El Salvador or the Dominican Republic sent a Chairperson, Vice Chairperson and Commissioner for the training.

The A-WEB, the International Alliance of election-related organizations around the world was launched in October 2013 and set the growth of democracy as a common goal in the inaugural meeting. The election management bodies from 105 countries, the United Nations Development Programme (UNDP), and 13 international organizations were involved in the meeting. The Korean NEC is responsible for the secretariat. Common interests in the election management bodies that guarantee the fairness and impartiality are growing. To achieve the common goal of "world democracy to grow together," the learning and sharing of experiences, institutions, operational know-how, and the role of each country are required. Therefore, the Korean NEC established ties with A-WEB, and Korea International Cooperation Agency (KOICA) continues the training for developing countries.

CONCLUSION AND IMPLICATIONS

Robert Dahl (1971) emphasized that every country has a different path to reach democracy. The way to create a sustainable democratic system through elections may also be different in each country. The measure to ensure the independence, efficiency, and professionalism of EMBs would also vary from country to country. The Korean case would be unique rather than a generic model.

However, recent studies have found that the contents of the independent variable, dependent variable, and other parameters influencing to the fair and autonomous election management system do not differ significantly. Therefore, the institutional independence of the EMBs is not intended to guarantee the fairness and impartiality in Korean case too. Since 1987, the authoritarian regime has collapsed and democracy began to grow in Korea. Also, the role of the EMBs granted by the constitution started to be considered. Under the authoritarian regimes, the Korean NEC was negative and neutral in order to avoid conflict with the government, the ruling parties and the opposition parties. But the authoritarian regime collapsed and the balance of power has changed, and the NEC has aggressively expanded their role and accumulated their own specialties to establish the autonomous and impartial election management system. These efforts of the NEC were supported by national and other civic organizations.

Actively recognizing the role and expanding the rights of Korean NEC has become a decisive factor in the formation of the neutral election management system in Korea. The scale, manpower, and budget of the organization, and personnel have increased. The role of the EMBs also expanded proportionally. The Korean NEC has enormous authority that EMBs of other countries do not have. After all, recognizing the role of this type of organization has become a very important factor in ensuring the independence of the EMBs in developing countries. Furthermore, it will be a driving force to develop democracy there.

REFERENCES

ACE Electoral Knowledge Network (ACE). Administration and Cost of Elections Project by IDEA, IFES and UNDESA). Retrieved from http://aceproject.org/

Birch, S. (2007). Electoral systems and electoral misconduct. *Comparative Political Studies,* *40*(12), 1533.

Birch, S. (2008). Electoral institutions and popular confidence in electoral processes: A cross-national analysis. *Electoral Studies, 27*(2), 305–320. doi:10.1016/j.electstud.2008.01.005

Birch, S. (2010). Perceptions of electoral fairness and voter turnout (Author abstract). *Comparative Political Studies, 43*(12), 1601–1622.

Bowler, S., & Donovan, T. (2007). Reasoning about institutional change: Winners, losers and support for electoral reforms. *British Journal of Political Science, 37*(3), 455–476. doi:10.1017/S0007123407000245

Boylan, D. M. (2001). *Defusing democracy: Central bank autonomy and the transition from authoritarian rule.* Ann Arbor, MI: University of Michigan Press.

Calimbahin, C. (2009). *An institution reformed and deformed: The commission on elections from Aquino to Arroyo.* Chiba: Institute of Developing Economies.

Carpenter, D. P. (2001). *The forging of bureaucratic autonomy: Reputations, networks, and policy innovation in executive agencies, 1862–1928.* Princeton, NJ: Princeton University Press.

Chambers, P. (2006). Consolidation of Thaksinocracy and crisis of democracy: Thailand's 2005 General Election. *Between Consolidation and Crisis: Elections and Democracy in Five Nations in Southeast Asia, 3,* 277.

Eisenstadt, T. A. (2002). Measuring electoral court failure in democratizing Mexico. *International Political Science Review, 23*(1), 47–68.

Elklit, J., & Reynolds, A. (2005). A framework for the systematic study of election quality. *Democratization, 12*(2), 147–162. doi:10.1080/13510340500069204

Epstein, D. L., Bates, R., Goldstone, J., Kristensen, I., & O'Halloran, S. (2006). Democratic transitions. *American Journal of Political Science, 50*(3), 551–569. doi:10.1111/j.1540-5907.2006.00201.x

Estévez, F., Magar, E., & Rosas, G. (2008). Partisanship in non-partisan electoral agencies and democratic compliance: Evidence from Mexico's Federal Electoral Institute. *Electoral Studies, 27*(2), 257–271. doi:10.1016/j.electstud.2007.11.013

Fukumoto, K., & Horiuchi, Y. (2011). Making outsiders' votes count: Detecting electoral fraud through a natural experiment. *American Political Science Review, 105*(3), 586–603. doi:10.1017/S0003055411000268

Gazibo, M. (2006). The forging of institutional autonomy: A comparative study of electoral management commissions in Africa. *Canadian Journal of Political Science, 39*(3), 611.

Go, S.-K. (2014). Comparative study of Electoral management system in development countries: Philippines, Thailand, Indonesia and Korea. Paper presented at the Korea Association for Public Administration Spring Conference.

Hartlyn, J., McCoy, J., & Mustillo, T. M. (2008). Electoral governance matters: Explaining the quality of elections in contemporary Latin America. *Comparative Political Studies, 41*(1), 73–98. doi:10.1177/0010414007301701

Hood, C. (2002). Control, bargains, and cheating: The politics of public-service reform. *Journal of Public Administration Research and Theory, 12*(3), 309.

Kelly, N. (2007). The independence of electoral management bodies: The Australian experience. *Political Science, 59*(2), 17–32.

Kerevel, Y. (2009). *Election management bodies and public confidence in elections: Lessons from Latin America.* Washington, DC: International Foundation for Electoral Systems.

Kokpol, O. (2002). *Electoral politics in Thailand. Electoral politics in Southeast and East Asia.* Singapore: Friedrich-Ebert-Stiftung, Office for Regional Co-operation in Southeast Asia. Electronic edition.

Korea National Election Commission. (1994). *The history of national election commission (1963–1993).* Korea National Election Commission.

Korean Civic Education Institute for Democracy. (2015). *Annual report 2015*. Seoul: KOCEID.

Lee, J.-W. (2015). *The development of Korean election*. Seoul: Pakyongsa.

Lehoucq, F. E. (2002). Can parties police themselves? Governance and democratization. *International Political Science Review*, *23*(1), 29.

Lehoucq, F. E. (2003). Electoral fraud: Causes, types, and consequences. *Annual Review of Political Science*, *6*, 233–256. doi:10.1146/annurev.polisci.6.121901.085655

Lopez-Pintor, R. (2000). *Electoral management bodies as institutions of governance*. New York: UNDP. Retrieved from http://www.undp.org/governance/docs/Elections-Pub-EMBbook.pdf

Magaloni, B. (2006). *Voting for autocracy: Hegemonic party survival and its demise in Mexico*. Cambridge: Cambridge University Press.

Majone, G. (2001). Non-majoritarian institutions and the limits of democratic governance: A political transaction-cost approach. *Journal of Institutional and Theoretical Economics*, *157*(1), 57–78.

Manin, B., Przeworski, A., & Stokes, S. (1999). Elections and representation. *Democracy, Accountability, and Representation*, 29–54. Cambridge University press.

Massicotte, L., Blais, A., & Yoshinaka, A. (2003). *Establishing the rules of the game—Election laws in democracies*. Toronto: University of Toronto Press.

Mozaffar, S. (2002). Patterns of electoral governance in Africa's emerging democracies. *International Political Science Review*, *23*(1), 85–101.

Noriyo, I. Judicial function of EMB in Korea. In *Politics of electoral management: Comparative study of Korea model of electoral governance and Japanese Electoral Management* (264–294). Tokyo, Japan: Yubigak.

Nye, J. S., Zelikow, P., & King, D. C. (1997). *Why people don't trust government*. Cambridge, MA: Harvard University Press.

Ockey, J. (2008). Thailand in 2007: The struggle to control democracy. *Asian Survey*, *48*(1), 20–28. doi:10.1525/as.2008.48.1.20

Omotola, J. S. (2010). Elections and democratic transition in Nigeria under the Fourth Republic. *African Affairs*, *109*(437), 535–553. doi:10.1093/afraf/adq040

Pastor, R. A. (1999). The role of electoral administration in democratic transitions: Implications for policy and research. *Democratization*, *6*(4), 1–27. doi:10.1080/13510349908403630

Przeworski, A. (2000). *Democracy and development: Political institutions and well-being in the world, 1950–1990* (Vol. 3). Cambridge: Cambridge University Press.

Przeworski, A. (2005). Democracy as an equilibrium. *Public Choice*, *123*(3), 253–273. doi:10.1007/s11127-005-7163-4

Rosas, G. (2010). Trust in elections and the institutional design of electoral authorities: Evidence from Latin America. *Electoral Studies*, *29*(1), 74–90. doi:10.1016/j.electstud.2009.09.006

Schaffer, F. C. (2008). *The hidden costs of clean election reform*. Ithaca: Cornell University Press.

Schaffer, F. C. (2002). Might cleaning up elections keep people away from the polls? Historical and comparative perspectives. *International Political Science Review*, *23*(1), 69–84.

Takeshi, K. (2013). *Establishment of electoral management system in East Asia*. Tokyo: Asia Institute.

Takeshi, K., & Yuki, A. (2013). Comparative electoral system of Korea and Philippines. In *Politics of electoral management: Comparative study of Korea model of electoral governance and Japanese electoral management* (pp. 86–101). Tokyo, Japan: Yubigak.

Van Aaken, A. (2009). Independent electoral management bodies and international election observer missions: Any impact on the observed level of democracy? A conceptual framework. *Constitutional Political Economy, 20*(3), 296–322. doi:10.1007/s10602-008-9070-4

Vibert, F. (2007). *The rise of the unelected: Democracy and the new separation of powers.* Cambridge: Cambridge University Press.

Wall, A. (2006). *Electoral management design: The international IDEA handbook.* International Institute for Democracy and Electoral Assistance.

Wurfel, D. (1991). *Filipino politics: Development and decay.* Ithaca: Cornell University Press.

Yuki, A. Process of reforming electoral district in Korea. In *Politics of electoral management: Comparative study of Korea model of electoral governance and Japanese electoral management* (pp. 233–258). Tokyo, Japan: Yubigak.

CHAPTER 3

REDISCOVERING KOREA'S LOCAL BUREAUCRACY: THE UNSUNG PLAYERS IN THE NATION'S DEMOCRATIZATION PROCESS

Shi-Chul Lee

ABSTRACT

Korea is a highly centralized country where most administrative functions are carried out by the central government in Seoul. Increasingly, however, local governments have been given greater autonomy in their operations. This chapter examines how the ideal values of political decentralization have interacted with the country's local bureaucracy, which inherently has dark side in itself. The focus is on how local government employees have contributed, or responded, to the democratic change of their communities, particularly since the 1980s. At the outset, the experiences of Korea's decentralization and local autonomy are briefly reviewed. It is then examined how the bureaucrats have played in the process of democratization in terms of three features: bureaucratic power, scope, and culture. Institutionalizing competitive local bureaucracy contributed to reduce the disparity between capital regions (Seoul and its surrounded area) and noncapital regions (locals). Empowering local bureaucracy to

The Experience of Democracy and Bureaucracy in South Korea
Public Policy and Governance, 53–82
Copyright © 2017 by Emerald Publishing Limited
doi:10.1108/S2053-769720170000028003

allow own localized decision-making process was the first move of Korean governance.

Keywords: Local bureaucracy; decentralization; political decentralization; administrative decentralization; autonomy

The Capital Area, Seoul, has been home to a Korean capital for around 2000 years. Its geographically advantaged central location and relatively gentle landscape have given it a central role in the country's affairs. The concept of "local" means "outside of Seoul," but unconsciously "local" has been hierarchically annotated as all regions other than Seoul where all administrative power is concentrated. Due to that, "local (*Ji-Bang* in Korean)" generally denoted the periphery, rural, and distant from the center. From the perspective of traditional Korean bureaucratic culture, the perception of "local" still possesses the meaning of a punishing location due to "the culture of exile."[1]

Local regions (other than Seoul) have been continuously underestimated and controlled by central government. This particular situation led to economic disparity between capital regions (Seoul and its surrounded area) and noncapital regions (locals). Therefore, the process of adding power to local regions to compete with the central region is a process of political democratization. Regional democratic governance ultimately refers to local autonomy and decentralization that have been included in the list of vital items for realizing democratic development since the 1970s (Kim, 2014).

In that sense, not surprisingly, the term "local bureaucracy" usually implies something negative. While "bureaucracy," say, at the federal or central government level, is often criticized as being slow, rigid, inefficient, and money wasting, local bureaucracy is considered to reflect an abridged, and sometimes a worse, version of everything aforementioned. Bureaucrat bashing has been a pastime for the press, and sometimes for academia, in this nation as well. The local news media being no exception, a number of gloomy illustrations appear in newspapers and on TV—most of them are negative and some are cynical at best.

Meanwhile, even in such a traditionally hierarchical society as Korea, the central government would suffer from practical or procedural difficulties in changing anything without the support of local bureaucrats. We believe that the Korean local bureaucracy has actively played a role in, or at least supported, the overall progress of development as well as democratization, helping design the institutional system linked with the decentralization of political power. That said, however, it should come as no surprise that local bureaucracy in this nation still has a great deal of challenges, both inside and outside of its own organizations.

This chapter primarily examines how the process of political decentralization and effort to gain local autonomy, raised largely by academia, have been realized through the support of the Korean local bureaucracy. This chapter views reducing disparity between capital regions (Seoul and its surrounding area) and noncapital regions (locals) as democratization. The focus will be on how local government employees, as a group or as individuals, have contributed, or responded, to the democratic change of their communities, particularly since the 1980s. An underlying question would be whether democracy is compatible with bureaucracy at the local level.

THEORETICAL CONSIDERATIONS

The subject of bureaucracy and democracy is neither new nor fully explored, particularly when it comes to bureaucracy's impact on democracy, or the other way around. No shortage of critics would unleash their weaponry if it were only argued that public bureaucracy contributed directly to the growth of democracy in such a country as Korea. Rather, the prevailing wisdom is that it has not played any significant role in the country's democratization process for the past decades. Furthermore, it is sometimes argued that bureaucracy, being "soulless and heartless," has been an obstacle to the expansion of citizens' freedom and participation in state affairs.

Bureaucracy is often contrasted with politics; the former embraces commitment to passion and partisan interests, while the latter is more about impersonalism and impartiality (Aberbach & Rockman, 1987). Additionally, politicians attempt to interact aggressively and flexibly with "voters," while unelected public officials are inclined to be defensive and inflexible when facing "taxpayers." In pluralistic societies, as in most western democracies, various actors, including the public bureaucracy, come into play in managing a society. Korea has traditionally been considered a hierarchical society, at least up until the late twentieth century, so for the past decades its localities have become both an exemplary case and a cautionary tale of various actors and players competing and collaborating in making public decisions.

On the basis of long-existing literature, it is worth examining how local bureaucracy works in the Korean setting, mainly focusing on three critical dimensions: bureaucratic power, bureaucratic scope, and bureaucratic culture (Aberbach & Rockman, 1987; Downs, 1967). Each of these reflects the structure, function, and actors of bureaucracy, respectively. Additionally, on the basis of the time-honored discourse of Etzioni (1968), we can juxtapose two more elements: control and consensus. These two features of a society provide a useful tool for deeper discussion of how bureaucracy and democracy interact with each other. In the Korean setting as well, one can draw practical implications from the control-consensus viewpoint and decide how each local bureaucracy has responded and contributed to the democratic changes of the community in its respective jurisdictions.

Conventional wisdom proposes two key dimensions of discussion about bureaucracy: variance in bureaucratic control "over state policy" and variance in bureaucratic control "over society" (Fried, 1990: 329). The former could refer to the extent to which local bureaucrats can disagree with elected leaders, while the latter refers to the overall regulatory/distributive power over local residents. Additionally, Aberbach and Rockman (1987: 482) suggest an analytic framework in the context of comparative public administration, using three key units: structures, functions, and actors. All these features appear to be useful when taking into account Korea's local bureaucracy as well. The overall framework of discussion is presented in Fig. 1.

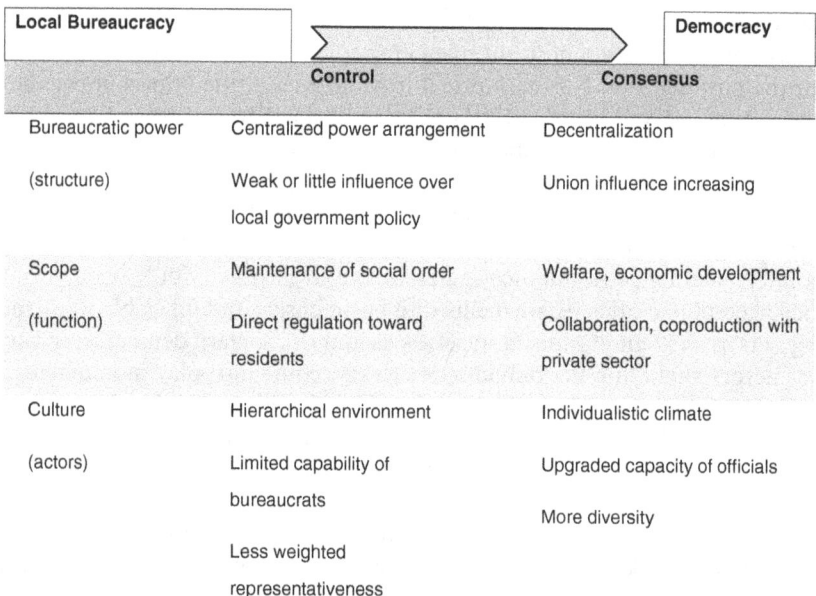

Local Bureaucracy		Democracy
	Control	Consensus
Bureaucratic power	Centralized power arrangement	Decentralization
(structure)	Weak or little influence over local government policy	Union influence increasing
Scope	Maintenance of social order	Welfare, economic development
(function)	Direct regulation toward residents	Collaboration, coproduction with private sector
Culture	Hierarchical environment	Individualistic climate
(actors)	Limited capability of bureaucrats	Upgraded capacity of officials
		More diversity
	Less weighted representativeness	

Fig. 1.   Framing Korea's Local Bureaucracy for Democracy.

Some other critical issues are also to be noted, for instance, decentralization, local autonomy, administrative capacity, etc. As will be discussed later, the term "local autonomy" was once considered a synonym of "democracy," especially during the Korean military dictatorship in the 1960s and the 1970s. Naturally, decentralization, however widely its academic or political meaning is expanded, did and still does embrace a variety of features of democratization in Korean society.

Generally speaking, Korean society, considered as a nation or a collection of local communities, has been evolving from control focused to consensus weighted. The former emphasizes efficiency, while the latter is more about democracy. In addition, in order to gain a better understanding of the role of local democracy in the democratization process, it would be suitable to go over three important features of local bureaucracy: bureaucratic power, scope, and culture.

PRECEEDING ISSUES: DECENTRALIZATION AND LOCAL AUTONOMY

The issue of local bureaucracy in Korea cannot possibly be discussed in its full terms without first examining how the trend of local autonomy and decentralization has evolved in this highly centralized country. Despite strong central government in Korea, simply understanding the central administrative organization is not enough to know the entire administrative organization of the state. One of the reasons is that central administrative functions are often performed by local administrative organizations. In that sense, the change in the functional relationship between central government and local government was normally understood as a decentralization process.

The term "Decentralization" can be understood in at least two ways (Pollitt et al., 1998: 7); political decentralization and administrative decentralization. Political decentralization is transferring centralized authority within the central government to elected representatives in the "local government." Conversely, administrative decentralization is transferring authority to appointed public officials (through the merit system) who are recruited by central government. Both political and administrative decentralization is the transferring process of de-concentration. However, political decentralization is more focused on the concept of the local self-government as the system of central-local government relationship, rather administrative decentralization more toward local autonomy as the relationship perspective between central public officials and local public officials, which are bureaucracy (Im, 2014).

In fact, from a wider perspective, we can take both into account as important dimensions of democracy.

Political Decentralization: Local Government Elections and
Forming Local Councils

In the Korean political context, political decentralization is generally considered as a synonym of local self-government. In the 1980s, people believed that restructuring the centralized power of the decision-making system through "elections" is the only way to create a democratic environment. At that time, reformers wanted to support left-wing parties for a balanced political environment by voting. From that perspective, discussions on the implementation and methods of local autonomy and its outcomes have been going on in the same trajectory as the process of democratization of Korean politics since the establishment of the official government in 1948. The goal of the democratization movement aimed to re-distribute concentrated power.

Local autonomy is often called the "school for democracy," and nowhere might the saying fit better than in modern South Korea. While this young nation, liberated from Japanese occupation, went through turbulent times in the 1950s and the 1960s, i.e., war, poverty, authoritarian governments, etc., local autonomy was indeed considered as a synonym of democracy. This perspective had a number of supporters, including those in academia, in large part because the political regime since the 1961 military coup had forced local elections to be suspended.

Under the first Korean constitution in 1948, the earliest local council members were popularly elected in 1952, which happened to be in the middle of the Korean War, to form the first local councils. Eight years later, "local governments were established in full as mayors and governors were all directly elected by the people" (Ministry of the Interior homepage, 2016). However, the new experiment hit a roadblock when the military coup led by the late President Park Chung Hee took place in 1961. Local councils were dissolved; mayors and governors were once again appointed by the President for the next 30 years.

As the military dictatorship began waning in the 1980s, a long-awaited political challenge emerged in Korean academia as well as in the political arena: local autonomy. The Constitution of Korea still stated that local authorities were entitled in principle to legal rights within jurisdictions to take care of their businesses for "the well-being of local residents" and to establish "rules and regulations regarding local autonomy." In that regard, there were no officially stated legal obstacles to introducing local autonomy at that time—except a supplementary provision in the constitution stating that local autonomy is delayed until "the time of reunification of the motherland." Hence, based on dubious political grounds and an unclear national consensus, no mayors or governors were elected, let alone local councils. Thus, no local autonomy was in practice until the early 1990s.

The election of President Rho Tae Woo in 1987, which resulted from a well-known nationwide civil resistance movement at the time, marked a turning point toward the democratization of the country. The next civilian governments, led by the late Presidents Kim Young Sam and Kim Dae Jung, respectively, contributed to the institutionalization of local autonomy. Unlike their predecessors, both Kims showed pride in being civilian presidents directly elected by the popular vote, making conspicuous efforts to distribute centralized power to local citizens.

As is widely known, South Korea's government organization can be called a three-tiered system composed of national-, regional-, and elementary-level governments. As of January 1, 2015, there were 243 local governments: 17 regional governments and 226 elementary governments, of which all the heads and the council members are now elected by the general public.

Local autonomy is presently in practice in Korea. Aside from a variety of difficulties and challenges, as illustrated later on, one cannot overemphasize how significant it is for this country to restore local autonomy after a 35-year absence. As a high-level official in Daegu Metropolitan Government argued, the active role of local bureaucrats in the democratization process of Korea is believed to have started in the mid-1990s with the launch of local councils and the inauguration of mayors and governors elected by voters. Before then, the whole group of public servants in this nation, national or local, may have served as "agents" of the regime, not as "servants" of the people (interview on August 4, 2016).

How its hard-won fruit can go hand in hand with democracy, another critical national value, can be a different story. As a matter of fact, it remains doubtful whether revived local autonomy can indeed usher in decentralization or democracy. That said, the general assessment on the achievement of this nation's local autonomy for the past three decades appears to be positive. A 2015 national survey (Table 1) reports that about 31% of the general public has a positive view, while 26.5% has a negative view. Policy experts, mostly professors, tend to have much more encouraging opinions: more than half gave a "good" sign, four times as many as gave negative views (Ministry of the Interior, 2015).

Seoul's administrative control over localities remains in various fashions, mostly based on current laws, despite their independent status as "juristic

Table 1. How People View 30-Year Local Autonomy in Korea.

(%)	Positive	Neutral	Negative	Dominance Ratio (Positive/Negative)
General public	31.2	42.3	26.5	1.18
Policy experts	56.3	29.5	14.2	3.96

Source: Drawn from Ministry of the Interior (2015).

persons." The very same law clearly states that the 17 regional governments "shall be under direct control of the Government" (Article 3-2, Local Autonomy Act), even though the heads of all local governments are elected by the people. Additionally, the relevant law and presidential decree mandate that vice governors of provinces and vice mayors of metropolitan cities are appointed by the central government, as national public officials, not local ones.

National control or influence does not become weaker when it comes to the matters of organization, audit, finance, etc. While local governments can have a limited degree of discretion with their own organizations, the establishment of administrative organizations and the maximum number of local public officials within their jurisdictions are to be "in accordance with" the standards and personnel expenditure ceilings prescribed by Presidential Decree. Therefore, most of the management of administrative resources is under the control of the Ministry of the Interior.

Local councils, together with the heads of local governments, can be a symbol of local democracy. Yet in reality, it may be one of the most controversial fields where scholars and practitioners can argue that democracy is in danger of being hampered for various reasons. For example, a dictatorial governor or local council, though directly elected by taxpayers, is less likely to contribute to long-term democracy or civic happiness, instead showing a greater interest in short-term publicity or personal gains. From a slightly different point of view, a certain political party may dominate the whole community, resulting in a twisted, detrimental form of democracy.[2]

It is reported that, on top of their regular and fair job practice, a number of local council members exercise unfair, arbitrary pressure on the local officials mostly for their personal interests. These behaviors are not only illegal but will most likely impede sustainable development of local democracy. In this vein, there appears to be room for local bureaucracy to resist individual unfair council members; if that is the case, public officials at the local government level ought to have the ability to "say no" to some crooked politicians and should be encouraged by the general public as well as scholars.

On balance, local autonomy since the 1990s, and the general decentralization trend in the 2000s, would be likely to lead to a paradigm shift in light of local governance and the distribution of administrative authority in this nation. With some exceptions, most of the local leaders elected by voters started showing a great deal of interest in shifting their policy focus, methods, and mode of managing local bureaucracy. As for high- and mid-level local bureaucrats, they began adapting themselves to the changing environment. Among other things, according to a former high-level local official, they came to understand who were their real bosses. For example, before the first mayoral and gubernatorial election in 1995, they simply "looked up" to the Ministry of the Interior before making decisions on important matters or big budgetary projects, because the ministry had sole authority to appoint and fire mayors or governors. The local election indeed changed everything; local bureaucrats began listening to the elected leaders and the local voters.

Administrative Decentralization: Reforming Governing System

Comparing to political decentralization, administrative decentralization received less attention and has even been neglected in the democratization discourse. The main reason was that people had doubt about the legitimacy of the appointed local public officials. Despite the merit system of personnel administration in local government being realized in the career civil service in 1963, regionalism and familism was still a serious barrier for the political modernization. Furthermore, from a functional perspective, central administrative functions are often performed by local administrative organizations. The performance of local public officials matter significantly for the overall image of government.

The past decades have witnessed "the Miracle of the Han River" not only in Seoul but also throughout the nation. Yet it would not be fair to state that the world-renowned accomplishments in both economic development and political democratization have taken place without significant substantive challenges, including inevitable spatial variation. It may be the case as well when it comes to the role of local bureaucracy in the development process.

Although it is not entirely necessary here to delve into the issue of decentralization per se, one can easily notice that decentralization or devolution can take a variety of forms from one country, or political arrangement, to another. A common theme on the subject would be whether or not a centralized form of government is more effective, more efficient, or in some cases more democratic than a decentralized arrangement. Obviously, the question remains to be further explored, inviting more arguments and challenges from both academic and practical perspectives. The criteria for the evaluation count first; for instance, by what specific means would you assess which is more democratic? It will be worth examining the two arrangements' key features, rationales, and implications for Korea's local bureaucracy.

Existing literature states that, as a recurring subject in political science or public administration, decentralization can be categorized into two comparable phases: the territorial distribution of economic resources, or de-concentration, and the institutional arrangement of administrative power, or devolution (Denhardt, 1993; Kodras, 1997; Lee, 2007). The focus in this manuscript is undoubtedly placed on the latter. That said, it is to be noted that spatial redistribution of economic values has also been a critical issue recently in light of both public policy and national politics, at least during the Roh Moo Hyun Administration (2003–2008). (See Table 2 for two dimensions of decentralization in Korea.)

Once a national mantra, particularly in the 2000s, was that the deconcentration campaign in Korea is not quite as noticeable these days as it was before, but it was strongly initiated by the national government as lately as a decade ago. For example, special laws were enacted in 2004 largely based on political consensus to address both issues, which were followed by a series of relevant policy measures such as the construction of the New Administrative City, the relocation of public bodies from Seoul to provincial regions, and creating Enterprise Cities in the provincial regions (Lee, 2007).

Traditional systems aside, an impetus to centralization in Asian countries, particularly since World War II, might first come from political and economic necessities. A number of developing countries in this region, for instance, have experienced rapid social changes such as wars, independence from imperialism, nation building, military coups, etc. It is obvious then that centralized

Table 2. Two Features of Decentralization in Korea.

	De-Concentration	Devolution
Main issues	Distribution of economic resources and values	Political/administrative power arrangement among governments
Dimension	Horizontal, space	Vertical, institution
Values	Equity	Self-autonomy, competition
Key players	Politicians, national government	Bureaucrats, national & local governments
Relevant legislation	Special law governing balanced national development (2004)	Special law governing decentralization (2004)

Source: Modified from Lee (2007: 16).

governance and economic planning appeared more effective and efficient, at least in the short term. As Dahl and Tufte (1973) maintain, Jacobin thought, by which a nation's general will should prevail over the particularistic local wills, appeared to make sense. That was particularly the case in Korea, then a young developing country that had been just liberated in 1945 from a 35-year Japanese occupation and suffered from the devastating three-year Korean War in the early 1950s.

As in other similar contexts, Korea's governing system was undoubtedly inclined toward a centralized political and administrative pattern. The military's influence remained, at least until the first direct presidential election system was revived in 1987. Oftentimes, an arbitrarily defined "public interest" dominated society as a whole. Governors and mayors were all appointed by the President through the Ministry of Interior Affairs, a strong arm of the national government. Arguably, Korea's world-famous economic achievement over the past decades is attributable to its centralized decision-making system. It is still suggested that Korea's national bureaucrats, some from the military, had been more able, more efficient, and, even, more patriotic than their civilian counterparts. Not everybody, nor all scholars, agree on that. In fact, the "tragic excellence of bureaucracy" had been repeatedly noticed in numerous cases.

At any rate, local bureaucrats in general had not been given much attention. It is believed that any incapacity of local bureaucracy has a lot to do with how administrative authority is distributed between the national government and local authorities. Korea's local authorities, constitutional and legal guarantees notwithstanding, had been practically considered as field agencies of the central government, and specifically of each ministry, until the historic revival of local autonomy in the early 1990s. With no elected governors, mayors, or council members, local bureaucracy was nothing but an implementing arm of Seoul.

Even after the restoration of local elections more than 20 years ago, the disproportion in power between the national government and local ones was noticeable. For instance, as of 2005, when the newly launched Roh Moo Hyun Administration began the devolution campaign, one can see some of the contrasting indicators as follows (Hong et al., 2006; Lee, 2007; Ministry of the Interior, 2016):

- Local government fulfills only 27.6% of overall governmental functions;
- Ratio of national public servants to local public servants is 63.7 to 36.3;
- Central government's field agencies from 24 entities total about 6500;
- Ratio of national tax revenue to local tax is 77.5% to 22.5%.

While there were certainly grandiose plans in 2004, such as The First Five-year Comprehensive Plan for Devolution and 47 different projects, most notably financial measures, the general assessment is not as favorable as it could be. The financial imbalance remains intact; the number of special administrative agencies has not been reduced much. It is to be noted that resistance from national bureaucrats was so strong that a number of delegation efforts were hindered in the process (Lee, 2007). It is widely agreed that succeeding administrations—of the former President Lee Myung Bak or the recently deposed President Park Geun Hye—have not shown as much enthusiasm in either de-concentration or devolution.

Basically, the reason why neither de-concentration nor devolution is working well lies with current laws and regulations, although one can argue that it still stands on dubious legal ground. For instance, the Local Autonomy Act, the law governing local autonomy and devolution, has ambiguously stated since its enactment that the national government shall "guide and supervise" (Article 167) most of the basic functions including personnel affairs.[3] Not surprisingly, the central government, through a few strong arms, controls and exercises its power over local authorities in critical areas such as financial matters. In the early months of each year, the Ministry of the Interior issues an annual fiscal guidance memorandum to metropolitan and provincial governments, which by law is the beginning of the local government budgeting process. All bond issues are required to proceed to the Ministry for a final approval. The central government supervises even the training process of the public officials, including establishing a comprehensive plan for training, based on the Local Public Officials Act, with localities being allowed limited discretion in this matter.

Yet there exists a good sign, although limited. Despite less-appreciated efforts, devolution appears to have democratic benefits in the long term. Adams (2009) argues—based on empirical evidence from cases of South Korea and the U.S.—that administrative devolution to local governments promoted resident participation and government responsiveness, making policy decisions happen closer to them.

INTERACTION OF KOREA'S LOCAL BUREAUCRACY WITH DEMOCRACY

It is useful to review how the dynamism of Korea's local bureaucracy has evolved by using the frame suggested in Fig. 1: bureaucratic power, bureaucratic scope, and bureaucratic culture. As mentioned earlier, the general tendency appears to have been to shift the weight from control/efficiency to consensus/democracy.

The Re-Battle within the Local Bureaucracy: Local Elected Bureaucrats vs. Local Career Public Officials

Rationales
As mentioned earlier, Fried (1990) argues that the two primary dimensions of bureaucratic power we can examine are (i) control over state policy, and (ii) control over society. Traditionally considered double-faced, Korea's local bureaucracy did not show much resistance against, let alone control over, the local boss or his policies while he reigned over the general public, often harshly. For the past decades, however, particularly since the revival of local autonomy, public officials appear to have shown an increased influence over the local government's policy in general.

The government sector is obviously not the only authoritarian institution in a city or a province; not surprisingly, even "governing without government" could exist theoretically in a community (Peters, 1996; Rhodes, 1996; Stoker, 2003). As shown in many areas around the world, local communities can be run by combining a variety of public and private entities, including local governments, firms, NGOs, universities, and individuals. That said, it is fair to say that local governments and local bureaucrats still play the most important role in the public decision-making process within their jurisdictions, at least in Korea.

Special attention should be paid to the sustainability of local democracy, particularly in developing countries or even pluralistic societies in their early stages; the ostensible democratic process may harm medium- or long-term democracy as well. Reforming local bureaucracy for democracy is important, but it should not be allowed to end up with both bureaucracy and public interest falling to ruin. In other words, you do not cut off your nose to spite your face. In this vein, Im (2007) discusses the impact of the bureaucratic reforms of the Korean government on the basis of the "democratization criterion of bureaucracy," one of which reforms is to protect bureaucrats from the arbitrary exercise of political power. That should also be the case at the local level.

Challenges
There is no shortage of reports illustrating the inefficient use of local resources, or "moral hazards," inflicted by elected officials. The dark side of

the local bureaucracy occasionally involves large-scale construction projects such as a light-rail transit in Yongin[4] and casino development in Jeongseon, which are easily pledged in an election; a variety of local festivals simply "created" for short-term publicity; overall local finances that sometimes verge on bankruptcy (MK, January 28, 2015). In these cases, local bureaucracy may as well be the last bastion of a sustainable city or county. However, can the career officials possibly resist, or even reject, elected mayors or governors? A recent empirical study (Park, 2014) argues that it would be challenging; high-level local officials do have normative "policy ethics," but in reality they tend to become much less confident in opposing the elected officials' improper decisions.

Out of more than one million public officials in this nation, the local bureaucrats' share is only 36.3%, or 372,000 as of 2014. Union membership among public officials is much stronger than that within the private sector in general.[5] Based on the size and cohesiveness of their membership, Korean local bureaucrats, while having actively pursued their interests, appear to have contributed to democracy within their own boundaries. In other words, the unions have, arguably, played a key role in the democratization of both government and society at the local level. Public employee unions have been legal in this country only since 2006 and have evolved in their own fashion, now forming multiple national organizations. One of them, the Korean Government Employees' Union, an affiliate of the Korean Confederation of Trade Unions (minju-nochong), is considered comparatively radical. At the local level, the unions or the branches tend to become more conservative, focusing on practical matters of local officials. For instance, the public officials union of Gyeongbuk Province appears to have paid more attention to pragmatic issues and has consistently had its voice heard on matters of personnel, organization, working environment, etc. (www.gbnojo.or.kr, accessed on July 21, 2016).

As the six-decade-old Parkinson's Law has now become a convenient reference point around the world for self-satisfying and uncontrolled organizational growth, bureaucratic power, most likely together with the expansion of administrative outfits, tends to grow if not seriously checked. Hence, some controlling mechanisms are necessary for local democracy in its ideal form. This should be particularly the case if local bureaucracy becomes compromised by local politics, or, on the contrary, elected officials become "captured" by local bureaucrats.

Public officials had not been used to listening to lay citizens during the rapid economic growth of this nation, let alone in the Chosun Dynasty or during the Japanese occupation (1910–1945). It is difficult to entirely deny that Korean bureaucrats still tend to be a "pedantocracy" when facing residents as though they were on a higher moral and professional ground. Democratization since the 1990s, following the earlier economic success of this young nation, has changed just that, whether in Seoul or in any local community.

Responses

Generally speaking, there are certain measures in Korea's legal and institutional system for residents or local government to take in case local democracy does not work well or is in danger of being wrecked. For example, the heads of local governments can directly put some important policy measures to a vote. Although politically risky, this is often used to avoid policy limbo or to score political points in critical areas. Residents may file a request for inspection when they find the local government's business violates laws or substantially undermines public interests (Article 16, Local Autonomy Act). The Citizen Referendum Act in Korea was enacted in 2004. It was brought into play in multiple cases, notably, for example, when locating sites for radioactive waste, a critical issue still fully unsolved. The Citizen Recall Act of 2006 provides a checking mechanism to "recall" inappropriate mayors or council members (Lee, 2007). Since then, there have been 81 recall attempts, but only two local council members lost their jobs on account of collective resident actions. Additionally, other tools of this nature, like resident lawsuits, are also provided for by, and actually used based on, relevant laws.

When juxtaposed with the aforementioned decentralization issue, it appears to be the central government or the national bureaucracy, not local ones, that might hinder further democratic development in Korea. Ever since the restoration of local autonomy in the mid-1990s, local bureaucrats have continuously witnessed and had hands-on experience in grass-roots democracy. In virtually all administrative processes, including enacting ordinances, budget appropriations, and building and implementing policies/programs in various local fields, local officials engage in participatory democracy in the field. Elected mayors or governors feel much closer to them than to the country's President. Local council members are likely to be much more familiar with local issues than members of the National Assembly. Audits, inspections, and hearings have become routine in local areas compared to Seoul. The local on- and off-line press aside, public servants are easily checked and balanced.

In relation to bureaucrats' power or the previously mentioned policy ethics, it is not unusual that electoral pledges by local politicians are considerably modified, or in some cases, cancelled altogether, after professional technocrats go over each promise after the election campaign. Legal constraints and financial feasibility come into play. Local officials' expertise, or knowledge of specific matters, can prevent mayors from planning fiscally infeasible projects. Institutional mechanisms, such as a preliminary local financial alert system that is operated by the local officials together with the Ministry of the Interior, can also hold them back from beginning irresponsible projects.[6]

Sometimes a bureaucrat's personal interest comes into conflict with the elected official's political will. In a recent controversial case, a high-level official, who holds a legal guarantee of official status, was illegally transferred by a district mayor to another local government against his will. In a lawsuit filed after the official's retirement, he won in an abuse of power case, making the district mayor pay 10 million won, or about US$9000 (Naeil Shinmun, August 29, 2013). In short, local bureaucrats' professional influence over the community has changed significantly over the past decade.

Within the local government, the unions, apparently with some variations, have taken part in the "checks and balances" process; they urge and nudge mayors and governors to discuss organizational matters of their interest beforehand with the union, for instance, over personnel affairs, organizational restructuring, and other morale support activities. Unions issue statements to keep "political neutrality" in personnel affairs, pay visits to their elected bosses to show opposing views, and sometimes lead open-air rallies. Unsurprisingly, there are actual cases in which the politicians' earlier selections for certain positions were withdrawn mainly due to the union's strong opposition. The union sometimes preemptively negotiates with elected officials on sensitive personnel matters (Citizens' Voice of Yangpyong, July 24, 2016). According to an anonymous interview with local officials in Daegu and Daejeon, some appointed officials were notified to shun or delay, if not flatly reject, implementing decisions by elected officials. In rare cases, elected politicians and local bureaucrats show sympathy to each other, when facing serious legal challenges, and collaborate in finding temporary solutions (Yonhap News, October 22, 1999).[7]

With so big a change, one can easily say that local bureaucrats' power has been greatly weakened or compromised, but it is also true that the quality and legitimacy of their work has been noticeably upgraded. An illustration of "participatory budgeting" would be a fitting example. Obviously, the local council, with the final authority to approve the annual budget, does not usually like to share its power with other entities in the local area. Yet a "citizen participatory budget" system imported and further developed by local officials allows citizens to get involved in the budget appropriation process during the early stages, before any funding plan gets to the local council. A recent local newspaper story in Daegu reports that 413 local programs in need of about 11.8 billion won, or US$10 million, were suggested in the civilian budgeting process with the assistance of City Hall experts (Maeil Shinmun, August 19, 2016). Experience shows that a number of these propositions will likely survive the council's official review process.

Rising the Importance of the Community Level

Rationale

Overall government activities are a critical part of the "authoritative allocation of values," in David Easton's terms. It is not easy to correctly measure the relative amount and extent of what bureaucrats do, but there are some useful parameters, such as the size of local finances and the government share of employment (Fried, 1990). In South Korea, with the strengthened legitimacy of local government, the range of responsibilities within bureaucratic structures has expanded significantly since the mid-1990s. Although the sheer scale of local budgets or the size of a bureaucratic body might not be as big as those of some other advanced nations, the role of bureaucrats in each community did matter. That was particularly the case until the 1960s, when there had been neither trained professionals nor officially accepted mechanisms in local communities other than local bureaucracy.

It would be useful to categorize bureaucratic range into horizontal and vertical dimensions. The former can refer to the nature of services or activities bureaucracy engages in, or how broadly bureaucrats should shoulder the burden for the public. The latter has more to do with the capacity of any bureaucracy to attend to certain jobs or responsibilities. Today's bureaucracy might not be the most efficient, rational way of organizing human activity, as Max Weber (1922) once suggested, but the scope or the range of what public officials are entitled to do has definitely expanded and is still in the process of transforming. This phenomenon is sometimes more easily witnessed in local areas than in Seoul.

Meanwhile, history shows that innovation often takes place in the periphery; outsiders take initiative in creating something new for a community or a society. That may also be the case in Korea. Particularly since the revival of local autonomy about 20 years ago, a number of creative policies and programs have been fashioned by local governments or local officials. Most recently, for instance, several welfare programs initiated by local governments of Seoul and Seongnam created many political complications for the national government (Korea JoongAng Daily, August 4, 2016).[8] Apparently, the experimental measures are understood to have been initiated largely through the political will or leadership of the two cities' mayors, both of them now considered as future presidential candidates, rather than through ordinary local bureaucrats. Yet a message can be drawn in this dynamic country: localities can provide national leadership.

Challenges

Until the 1980s, no matter what one might have thought of bureaucracy, it was difficult to argue that the group had been anything more than a simple tool of the political regime. In an extended context, what local bureaucrats did was mostly keep order in the community and provide basic services under the supervision of national bureaucrats.

It is to be noted that there are no significant differences or variations between national officials and local counterparts in Korea. The Local Public Officials Act largely follows the State Public Officials Act in terms of the legal status, classification, appointment, rank, payment, etc., of local public officials. One noteworthy exception is the system of Senior Civil Service Corps, a pool of high-level national officials, to which the group of local officials has no equivalent. It is clarified (Article 2, State Public Officials Act) that career public officials, either national or local, are referred to as those "who are appointed based on their performance and qualifications, whose status is guaranteed and who are expected to serve as public officials for all their life."

The capacity of bureaucracy is a recurring topic to which scholars pay attention to with respect to the range of bureaucracy, rather than its power. Back and Hadenius (2008) maintain that a country's democratization can have a meaningful effect on its administrative capacity in general. It is further argued that democracy's impact on state capacity is "negative at low values of democracy, nonexistent at median values, and strongly positive at high levels." What happens the other way around, that is, how a strong and able bureaucracy influences democracy, is seldom studied, understandably.

Perhaps local bureaucracy, facing so many challenges, has really reached "the point of myopia," for even for an advanced country like the United Kingdom, where local autonomy originated is often criticized (*The Guardian*, May 23, 2012). In Korea, too, one can easily cast doubt on the capacity of bureaucracy, or perhaps on the government sector in general, to meet voters' ever-changing demands, especially compared with that of the private sector. There is no doubt that also at the local level "government failure" is frequently used interchangeably with "bureaucratic failure." The firms, the market, and civil society in a community often appear to work better than the local government or officials, resulting in a variety of outsourcing and privatization of public services.

A general consensus in Korea is that during the authoritarian administrations of the 1960s and 1970s, and perhaps even through the 1980s, the overall competence of government bureaucrats used to be higher than that of the private sector (furthermore, the Army's policy and administrative capability has sometimes been used partly to justify the Military Coup in 1961). The national government, represented by the well-known Economic Planning Board (EPB), took the initiative in establishing a series of Five Year Plans for Economic Development, largely based on the advanced skills and knowledge of the bureaucracy. Those plans appear to have contributed to the fast economic growth rarely seen elsewhere in the world, making South Korea the first "recipient-turned-donor" nation, especially after the Korean War in 1950 devastated the entire country.

Communication with the outside has also become critical. In the process of carrying out tough projects, such as locating waste dumps or facilities for the disabled, many of them called NIMBY (Not In My Back Yard) projects, frequent dialogue is required and attempted, mostly by local officials. Developing and presenting persuasive rationales to the relevant residents has become necessary. A benefit in return, or WTA (Willingness To Accept), is occasionally negotiated for many public projects around the nation. Now the process comes first, before the outcome, which is a reflection of the growing importance of local democracy.

Responses

The rags-to-riches story has taken place in provincial areas as well. While there should be a number of factors to explain the world-renowned economic success, including political leadership and the aforementioned national government plan, it can also be argued that local bureaucracy has played an important role, particularly in relation to Saemaul Undong, or the new community movement. The national campaign launched in the early 1970s, and which has recently received global attention (Lee & Lee, 2014: 240–241), is believed to have been an important driver for the development of the countryside and was largely implemented by none other than local officials.[9]

While the argument that government bureaucrats, as a "soulless and heartless" group, were an obstacle to the expansion of citizens' freedom and participation in state affairs may hold true in part, there are many cases illustrating that local bureaucracy played a more active role in the process of democratic development. So (2014: 5) assessed the nationwide movement especially during the 1970s and 1980s with a view to reinventing local administration. As the current President of the Korea Saemaul Undong Center (Saemaul Joongang-hoe), he reviews how local governments and bureaucrats interacted with people in their communities in terms of function, structure, and culture. In the process, it is argued that local officials played a vital role by building "local governance" and accumulating "social capital" at the village level. In a similar viewpoint, Uhm (2011: 115–117) reviews the role of local officials in rural Saemaul Undong in the 1970s, concluding that they functioned as moderators or buffers in the process, using both soft power (persuasion, communication) and hard power (coercion, inducement).

There are compelling reasons to believe that local bureaucracy has not just been compromised but has found a way to work together with the community as a whole, perhaps in a better fashion. Korean localities too have been pressured to "outsource" their nonessential services to private companies, mainly since the mid-1990s. The assistance from outside has consistently expanded over recent decades in this rapidly changing environment. For instance, a number of committees consisting of scholars, practitioners, and experts in various fields have been formed to address ever-changing challenges. Research and technological support, particularly in advanced fields like information and telecommunications, is everywhere. Experts prevail in local meetings as outsiders or as contract workers inside City Hall.

Table 3 shows how the general range of local bureaucracy has shifted for the past two decades. In short, the range, not only the power, of local bureaucracy in this country has substantially broadened since the 1990s, along with the democratization of the entire society.

Table 3.   A Paradigm Shift for Korea's Local Bureaucracy.

	Before Local Autonomy, until the 1980s	After Local Autonomy, since the 1990s
Focus	(Basic) service provision	Economic development
Policy emphasis	Supply-side, "Hardware" provision	Demand-side, "Software" planning
Methods	Hierarchy and control	Partnership and cooperation
Mode	Managerialism	Entrepreneurialism
Bureaucratic orientation	National government (Ministry of the Interior)	Head of the local government and voters

Source: Modified from Lee and Park (2007).

Culture: Becoming More Flexible and Transparent

Rationale

According to Wildavsky (1987), one decides important choices in one's life based on one's culture, or one's way of life, particularly with respect to political features. Illustrating how a certain political culture is defined, Lane (1992) presents four basic dimensions: an individual's supposed qualities, an individual's relationship with the group, the group's structure, and the duties and rights that attach to an individual's social position. Bureaucratic culture can be defined as "a generally shared psychological orientation" toward government or bureaucrats themselves. Two important aspects of bureaucratic culture would be acceptance of authority and the extent to which each official seeks his/her own interests (Downs, 1967; Peters, 1984).

Shin et al. (1989) argue that Koreans' political preferences are determined largely by their preferred culture. If those views hold true, the orientation of local bureaucracy should also rely on the preferred culture and personal interests of each individual or the group; for instance, an individualistic culture would be more supportive of democracy than a hierarchical culture.

All told, what if political culture or the administrative climate change over time? The environment surrounding local bureaucracy under the authoritarian regime of the 1960s and 1970s is quite different from the current political climate. Despite some suggestions that cultural patterns are stable (Hofstede, 1980), that appears to be less convincing, especially in as rapidly changing a society as South Korea, as we have previously shown in light of the decentralization and democratization process.

The group of local officials is in fact among the most influential local opinion leaders themselves. They have been well educated and are ready to accept a new world. Naturally, they are in a good position to have their voices heard and represented through any local democratic mechanism. Within their organizations, they learn, experiment, and evaluate various mechanisms of democratization, a typical example being unions, as mentioned previously. Yet "the principal-agent problem" exists in City Hall as well as in a firm (Jensen & Meckling, 1976). Local officials in Korea, as in many advanced countries, are urged as "the trustworthy agents" to change the general attitude, the speed, and the quality to attend to what "the principal" wants, even though the two sides would find it difficult to share exactly the same goals or interests.

Challenges

As noted earlier, acceptance of authority matters in any bureaucracy; the sources of authority originate from, as is well known, tradition, charismatic personality, and rationality (Peters, 1984). The overall trend of modernization and democratization in Korea has shepherded local governments and local bureaucracies toward a rational process of decision making. Yet a number of challenges remain.

Certain pathologies frequently criticized in local bureaucracy are not foreign to Korea, either. For instance, "trained incapacity," resulting largely from "over-conformity" (Merton, 1957), has been an easy target for bureaucrat bashing in this country. Aside from criticism against bureaucracy as a whole, Korea's local bureaucracy is often compared with its counterpart in Seoul. It is easy to condemn the group, "captured" or compromised by local elites of the private sector, for relying solely on existing regulations, customs, or precedence, while defending or actively seeking their own interests instead of positively acting to benefit the community, customers, or even their own organization.

On the other hand, recent news shows a continuing trend over the past decade: the popularity of the profession. About four out of ten college graduates seeking jobs in Korea at least attempt to prepare for the civil service examination. This year more than 222,000 individuals applied for about 4,000 entry-level jobs in national government; in an extreme case, there were about 14,000 applicants for seven new positions (YTN, July 22, 2016; Chosun Ilbo, August 2, 2006). Entrance exams for local officials show little difference. Despite the expansion of the quality private job market, comparatively low salaries for "public servants," and continuing "bureaucrat-bashing," this unique phenomenon illustrates not only how the current economic struggles but also that civil service jobs are still in high demand.

It is only natural to imagine that the overall environment within Korea's bureaucracy, both at the national and the local level, should be decent. The general mindset could be expected to have now changed greatly, in a more democratic and flexible direction. Public servants would be more kind and caring toward their primary customers: taxpayers. While City Hall is becoming more transparent, the corruption still found in many developing countries would more likely diminish in one of the fastest-growing OECD members. The composition of bureaucracy would likely be getting more diverse than ever. Many of these statements appear to turn out to be true, but not all.

Bureaucratic corruption has been considered one of the greatest causes of national and local instability. It would obviously be a significant barrier to democracy in many developing and developed nations as well, because it hinders routine government work and undermines residents' fundamental trust in public officials. As Korea's local bureaucracy witnesses a great deal of transformation, the concern for corruption appears to remain largely intact. For instance, the number of disciplinary actions against local bureaucrats has been steady at between 2000 and 3000 from 2008 through 2015 (Ministry of Personnel Management, 2016). The Improper Solicitation and Graft Act, a radical piece of legislation recently enacted and effective in September 2016, aims at preventing corruption in the entire society, the public sector included.[10]

Responses

Together with the overall transformation of Korean society, especially since the 1990s, its local bureaucracy has also experienced many internal changes. The young officials obviously tend to be more individualistic, if not egoistic, which makes them more likely to fit into a consensus-oriented democratic society, when compared with a traditional hierarchical environment. The local bureaucrats, certainly with the support from the elected bosses, have greatly increased intra-organizational communication. For instance, a "masked" (anonymous) meeting is often held in the Gyeongbuk provincial government to allow low-level officials to voice their messages openly and candidly to the governor; the program itself was awarded the "National Government Innovation Model" prize. Additionally, it is occasionally recommended to low-level officials under Grade 7 that they attend a directorial meeting, once allowed only to directors and above, to become exposed to the organizational issues and to advance their opinions (Kyunghyang Shinmun, December 3, 2015; January 12, 2016).

Perhaps, one of the most striking examples of the rapidly changing climate facing local bureaucrats can be found in the civil affairs office in City Hall. When civil petitions, complaints, or any civil affairs documents are filed, it is now required to record them, notify every stakeholder, and finally respond to the petitioners. "One-Stop Service," for example, which can be seen in most local offices, requires relevant officials to get together in a place at a certain time to take care of a complicated petition solely in order for the petition to be responded to quickly. In most cases, each level of official or related office is notified by text message, SMS, or intra-network from the very beginning of the petition to every stage of document handling.[11] A number of petitions can be filed and responded to even by SMS these days. The number of online civil affairs documents continuously expands; additionally, the entire process of petition or complaints is made public through online procedures, with virtually no exception in entire localities (Edaily, October 10, 2014; Maeil Shinmun, August 1, 2016).

A number of residents and high-level local officials interviewed (in July 2016) agree that the speed, the process, and the quality of response to civil petitions have unquestionably been upgraded. This is believed to be not only because of a legal mandate but also thanks to the less-appreciated change in local bureaucrats' general attitude not only in the civil affairs office but wherever they face residents. In short, local bureaucrats have themselves adjusted to the changing environment as individuals, thereby making local bureaucracy as a group less vulnerable to the perennial pastime of bureaucrat bashing.

One solution against corruption would be securing more transparency in the government sector. A good example of Korea's bureaucracy being made more transparent is the "Government 3.0" initiative, which was launched in 2013 based on previous president Park Geun Hye administration's pledge for government innovation. Sometimes argued to have been initiated mostly by the national government, and partly as political rhetoric, the initiative seeks as much transparency as possible from government and bureaucracy. In large part originating in the digital government movement, the policy seeks to go further. For instance, City Hall is required to make most of its public documents public in the original form. Apparently, local bureaucrats who had not initially shown any great enthusiasm appeared to accept its benefits for themselves: public support and long-term effectiveness (Lee, 2013; Nam, 2013).

One other important feature to be noted in relation to bureaucratic culture is representativeness in the local context. The subject of representative bureaucracy, or, in more detailed form, affirmative action, is not new at all in some advanced countries as well as in Korea. The efforts to change the civil service to become more diverse in terms of gender, class, region, professional field, etc., have been incessantly made for the past few decades, with particular emphasis during the Participatory Government, or the Roh Moo Hyun administration, in the 2000s. Under the State Public Officials Act, all national and local governments are obliged, or strongly urged, to "give preferential treatment to the disabled, those who have majored in science and technology, low-income people, etc. in terms of conducting personnel management, such as hiring, promotion, and transference, and to effectively achieve gender equality." There is wide agreement that the representativeness of bureaucracy, both national and local, has greatly been improved during the first decade of the twenty-first century.

A striking change is found in gender composition in this traditionally Confucian, conservative country. Namkoong (2006) finds that the share of female officials Grade 5 and over, which was only 3.0% (378 persons) in

1996, increased to 7.4% (1203 persons) and that the Roh Administration's affirmative action policies, together with other relevant policies like enhanced childcare leave and training programs were attributable to the change. As of December 2014, about 49%, or 310,000 officials, of the entire bureaucratic body in the Executive Branch are women.

Yet it is to be noted that there are significant variations when it comes to localities. When a woman breaks a glass ceiling, not everybody appears to applaud the falling of another barrier so that the world is more fair and equitable. The female share of officials in all local governments was 33.7% in 2015, with Daegu showing the lowest level, 31.2% (Ministry of the Interior, 2016). In short, there have been significant achievements, but room for improvement remains.[12]

CONCLUSION

A great deal of literature has examined the relationship between local decentralization and democratization and argued about the matter of strong central government, the military regime, local elections, and bureaucratic expansion. However, implementing local autonomy in a centralized country implies a fundamental change in the country's decision-making system (Im, 2002). Decentralization is the redistribution of the point of decision making to the local level in that it aims to rationalize the decision-making process, which is undoubtedly a process of democratization.

At the outset of this chapter, the experience of Korea's decentralization and local autonomy was briefly reviewed. We then examined how the nation's local bureaucracy has played a meaningful role in its process of democratization, let alone economic development. In retrospect, the revival of local elections was a milestone of political decentralization in South Korea to distribute political power to localities. The ideas of systematic decentralization and local autonomy, on top of the aforementioned constitutional provisions, have been forwarded by various social scientists; those ideas were later officially accepted by the political leadership and the government.

Just as with bureaucracy in general, Korea's local bureaucracy has certain inherent and undeniable constraints. We might call them the "trilemma" of local bureaucracy: (i) they are appointed, not elected; (ii) they characteristically tend to be oriented toward a closed system rather than an open one; and (iii) they are situated in "the periphery" in terms of their spatial context. Each of these seems to be difficult to reconcile with democracy.

The textbook says that as "the agents" are asked to respond to "the principal" to carry out their business as efficiently as possible, "information asymmetry" occurs, leading to something undesirable for taxpayers; the agents are more likely to seek their own interests. Yet Korea's recent experience allows us to conclude that local bureaucracy can be and has been compatible with sustainable democracy.

No doubt, bureaucracy may still be a good mechanism with which to carry out public business in an efficient fashion. Does it also contribute to democracy in the long term? Perhaps, we have to get back to the basic questions of whether bureaucracy exists for democracy or the market, which can be in conflict with each other. Most of Korea's public officials unions oppose the "spoils system," which can actually be compatible with political democracy in a sense. What is wrong with a newly elected mayor bringing some of his fellows into his administration in order to initiate bureaucratic innovation? How should the bureaucratic interests be reconciled with the idealism of local politics?

Even Max Weber, an early admirer of bureaucracy, saw the system as a potential threat to individual freedoms, cautiously warning that society might fall into a "polar night of icy darkness," with too much bureaucratic, rule-based, rational control (Weber, 1922). Although we do not have to wholly believe in this gloomy prospect, there ought to be every possible effort to address the concerns. As implied previously, the two biggest negative prospects are an overly powerful local bureaucracy and, paradoxically, one that is too weak and too compromised by democratically elected officials. Both failures must be addressed.

From a different perspective, Confucius once said, "Raise the straight and set them above the crooked, and you will win the hearts of the people. If you raise the crooked and set them above the straight, the people will deny you their support" (The Analects Discourse of Confucius, 479 B.C.).[13] Modern bureaucracy, whether national or local, will win people's support only when the group shows integrity and conforms to democratic, pluralistic norms in present times.

In conclusion, Korea's local bureaucracy interacted with democratization within inevitable limitations, partly contributing to the progress of political democratization, and partly helping design and implement the institutional system in the local jurisdictions. However, with a number of challenges and inherently dark features remaining, it is to be seen whether Korea's local bureaucracy continues to support the country's democracy. Local bureaucracy does not carry the whole city or province upon its shoulders; its limited capacity aside, it should not even attempt to. I hope that this chapter can serve as an invitation to further discussion in both academia and in the practical world on how democracy and local bureaucracy can embrace, reconcile, and work together for mutual benefits.

NOTES

1. The exile (*Guihyang*) is one of Korea's traditional penalties. When the central bureaucrat was guilty of sin, he was deprived of the status of government and descended to local regions. It was the type of punishment which restricts the place of residence by keeping sinners in distant areas; the farther from the center (currently Seoul), the higher the punishment.

2. As a matter of fact, this kind of phenomenon has happened for the past decades in a few jurisdictions in South Korea as well. For instance, in Daegu and Kwangju, both metropolitan cities, the same political party has taken both the mayor's job and the ruling position in the city council.

3. Article 81, Local Autonomy Act: "The Minister of Education or the Minister of the Interior shall guide and supervise the personnel affairs of the City/Do in order for the City/Do to administer its personnel affairs in accordance with the Act."

4. "Yongin residents file lawsuit over wasteful rail project." Posted on: October 11, 2013. http://english.hani.co.kr/arti/english_edition/e_national/606689.html

5. The exact size of union membership in Korea's public sector, local government included, was not available; however, according to unidentified statistics, it is about 50%, compared to 9%.

6. The Ministry, based on the relevant data submitted online by local officials, regularly monitors the overall fiscal conditions of local governments, with particular attention to "at-risk" localities. Those authorities in trouble are mandated to establish a master plan for a sound fiscal system and disclose it to the residents; any loans or bonds are strictly prohibited until the risk factors are solved (Ministry of the Interior homepage. http://www.moi.go.kr/eng/a01/engMain.do (accessed on August 14, 2016)).

7. In a widely reported case in 1999, an elected district mayor in Daejeon City who was thought to be very active and political wanted badly to impose local taxes on powerful research institutions in a science town, was met with vehement opposition from the metropolitan government. Facing a rare state of limbo due to the inaction of his own bureaucrats, many of whom were directly under the personnel supervision of the Daejeon Metropolitan government, the district mayor reportedly created the relevant paperwork by himself, allowing them to avoid the administrative burden.

8. The Seoul Metropolitan Government decided to dole out 500,000 won, or about US$450, in cash to each of 3000 young unemployed or underemployed citizens, based on certain criteria. The city government argues that the policy is not just about money itself but about providing them with time to find jobs. Yet the Ministry of Health & Welfare, provoked by this bold experiment not approved beforehand by the Ministry, strongly opposes this locally led youth support program on the basis of legal barriers, moral laxity, political complexities, and other procedural matters (for details, see *Korea JoongAng Daily*, August 4, 2016).

9. It is to be noted that there have been both positive and negative opinions regarding the *Saemaul Undong* movement. While it is argued that the national campaign achieved a great deal of development in the countryside, partly contributing to Korea's economic growth, the opposing views are that it was nothing but a political means to manipulate the general public. (An anonymous referee for this manuscript raised the question, too, mentioning that the national movement is not entirely appropriate to discuss in relation to the scope of Korean bureaucracy.) That said, it would be fair to say that the community development campaign contributed at least partly to eradicating the then prevailing poverty in provincial areas until the 1970s.

10. The Act, also known as Kim Young-ran Law, prohibits public officials, teachers and press members from receiving gifts over 50,000 won, or about US$45, or being treated to food for over 30,000 won, or US$27.

11. Daegu, Korea's fourth-largest metropolitan city and a well-known conservative area, has an integrated system for civil affairs called "Dudeuriso." The moment a petition or complaint is filed, it is notified right away to the petitioner, the manager, the team leader and the division director. Within a designated period, like seven days, the result is also required to be notified back; afterward, the level of satisfaction is evaluated by the original petitioner (dudeuriso.daegu.go.kr, accessed on August 10, 2016).

12. In a similar vein, other underrepresented groups within the government, including the physically challenged, scientists and engineers, have also been given more opportunities to serve on the basis of the Korean version of affirmative action. Other related, women-friendly programs like extended maternity leave and work-life balance assistance also help make local bureaucracy more diverse, better accessible and more widely available to all members of society.

13. 擧直錯諸枉 則民服, 擧枉錯諸直 則民不服 <論語 爲政篇>(originally written in Chinese).

REFERENCES

Aberbach, J. D., & Rockman, B. A. (1987). Comparative administration methods, muddles, and models. *Administration & Society, 18*(4), 473–506.

Adams, B. E. (2010). The democratic benefits of devolution: A comparison of South Korea and the United States. *Korea Journal, 50*(2), 182–206.

Ahn, C.-S. (2002). *Local governance and democracy in Korea.* Seoul: Nanam.

Bäck, H., & Hadenius, A. (2008). Democracy and state capacity: Exploring a J-shaped relationship. *Governance, 21*(1), 1–24.

Bozeman, B. (1993). A theory of government red tape. *Journal of Public Administration Research and Theory, 3*(3), 273–304.

Cho, S.-J., & Im, T. (2016). *2015 Theory of Korean public organizations*(2nd ed.). Paju: Bobmunsa.

Chosun Ilbo. (2006, August 2). One out of 1997 applicants, Civil service exam becoming a lottery.

Citizens' Voice of Yangpyong. (2016, July 14). County to accept union's request, ending conflicts on personnel affairs.

Dahl, R. A., & Tufte, E. R. (1973). *Size and democracy* (Vol. 2). Stanford, CA: Stanford University Press.

Denhardt, R. B. (1993). *The pursuit of significance: Strategies for managerial success in public organizations.* Belmont, CA: Wadsworth Publishing.

Dimock, M. E. (1959). *Administrative vitality: The conflict with bureaucracy.* New York: Harper and Brothers.

Downs, A., & Corporation, R. (1967). *Inside bureaucracy.* Boston, MA: Little, Brown.

Edaily. (2014, October 10). Seoul City to expand the number of online civil affair document to 60.

Eom. S.-J. (2011). Between mobilization and participation: A study on the roles of public officials in local administrations during the Rural Saemaul Undong in the 1970s. *Korean Public Administration Review, 45*(3), 97.

Etzioni, A. (1968). *The active society: A theory of societal and political processes.* London: Collier-Macmillan.

Evans, P., & Rauch, J. E. (1999). Bureaucracy and growth: A cross-national analysis of the effects of "Weberian" state structures on economic growth. *American Sociological Review,* 748–765.

The Guardian. (2012, May 23). Local government has become bureaucratic to the point of myopia.

Hong, J.-H., Ha, H.-S., & Choi, Y.-C. (2006). Development of decentralization indicators to measure the degree of decentralization. *Korean Journal of Local Government Studies, 10*(2), 7–30.

Im. T. (2000). Special issues: Power relations between politics and administrations in France. *Journal of Governmental Studies, 6*(2), 103.

Im, T. (2007). Bureaucracy, democracy and market. *Korean Public Administration Review, 41*(23), 41–65.

Im, T. (2010). Does decentralization reform always increase economic growth?: A cross country comparison of the performance. *International Journal of Public Administration, 33*(10), 508–520.

Jensen, M. C., & Meckling, W. H. (1976). Theory of the firm: Managerial behavior, agency costs and ownership structure. *Journal of Financial Economics, 3*(4), 305–360.

Keun, N. (2007). Civil service reform in participatory government: Civil service system in transition. *Korean Journal of Policy Studies, 22*(1), 19.

Kim, S.-E. (2014). Regional policy and national development in Korea. *Korean Journal of Policy Studies, 29*(1), 101–122.

Kodras, J.E. (1997). Restructuring the state: Devolution, privatization, and the geographical redistribution of power and capacity in governance. In *State devolution in America,* 79–96. Thousands Oaks, CA: Sage.

Korea JoongAng Daily. (2016, August 4). Seoul gov't gives cash to unemployed youth.

Kyunghyang Shinmun. (2015, December 3). Masked discussion awarded a government innovation model.

Kyunghyang Shinmun. (2016, January 12). Low-level officials attend directorial meeting in Youngcheon.

Lane, R. (1992). Political culture: Residual category or general theory? *Comparative Political Studies, 25*(3), 362–387.

Laski, H. J. (2014). *Liberty in the modern state.* Abingdon, UK: Routledge.

Lee, E., & Lee, S.-C. (2014). Challenges of Saemaul ODA in African region. *The Korean Journal of Local Government Studies, 18*(2).

Lee, S.-C. (2005). Decentralization and local governance: A discussion on current mismatches and issues to be addressed. *Korean Journal of Local Government Studies, 9*(1), 185.

Lee, S.-C. (2006). Recent decentralization challenges in Korea: Repertoire, reality and reshaping. *International Review of Public Administration, 11*(2), 15–27.

Lee, S.-J., & Oh, Y.-G. (2013). *Citizen happiness and Government 3.0.* Seoul: Hakjisa.

Maeil Kyungje. (2015, January 28). Five critical issues for 50 years of local finance.

Maeil Shinmun. (2013, August 29). District Mayor sentenced to pay 10 million won in a personnel affairs case.

Maeil Shinmun. (2016, August 1). Dudreeso, Daegu's online civil affairs office visited 6,600 times.

Maeil Shinmun. (2016, August 19). 413 programs suggested for 11.8 billion won as citizen participatory budget.

Merton, R. K. (1957). *Social theory and social structure* (Rev. ed.). New York: Free Press. Retrieved from http://psycnet.apa.org/psycinfo/1959-00989-000

Ministry of the Interior. (2016, August 14). Homepage. Retrieved from http://www.moi.go.kr/eng/a01/engMain.do

Ministry of the Interior. (2015). A survey on 20 years of local autonomy.

Ministry of the Interior. (2015, December 31) Statistics for female officials in local government.

Ministry of Personnel Management. (2016). Personnel affairs statistics for public officials.

Nam, T. (2013). Government 3.0 in Korea: Fad or fashion? Paper presented at the Proceedings of the 7th International Conference on Theory and Practice of Electronic Governance.

North, D. C. (1989). Institutions and economic growth: An historical introduction. *World Development, 17*(9), 1319–1332.

O'Donnell, G. A. (2004). Why the rule of law matters. *Journal of Democracy, 15*(4), 32–46.

Olsen, J. P. (2006). Maybe it is time to rediscover bureaucracy. *Journal of Public Administration Research and Theory, 16*(1), 1–24.

Peters, G. (1996). *The future of governing: Four emerging models*. Lawerence, KA: University of Kansas Press.

Peters, G. (2002). *Politics of bureaucracy*. Abingdon, UK: Routledge.

Rhodes, R. A. W. (1996). The new governance: Governing without government. *Political Studies, 44*(4), 652–667.

Rousseau, M. O., & Zariski, R. (1987). *Regionalism and regional devolution in comparative perspective*. Westport, CT: Praeger Publishers.

Shin, D. C., Chey, M., & Kim, K.-W. (1989). Cultural origins of public support for democracy in Korea: An empirical test of the Douglas-Wildavsky theory of culture. *Comparative Political Studies, 22*(2), 217–238.

So, J.-K. (2014). A study on reinventing local administration through Saemaul Undong in Korea. *Korea Local Administration Review, 28*(4), 3.

Stoker, G. (2003). *Transforming local governance: From Thatcherism to new labour*. Basingstoke, UK: Palgrave Macmillan.

Weber, M. (1922). *The nature, conditions, and development of bureaucratic Herrschaft*. (translated into English from German)

Wildavsky, A. (1987). Choosing preferences by constructing institutions: A cultural theory of preference formation. *American Political Science Review, 81*(01), 3–21.

Yonhap News. (1999, October 22). Disputes over taxation unsolved: Daejeon Metropolitan City vs. Youseong District.

YTN. (2016, July 22). A nation where public service is a dream job. Four out of ten job young seekers preparing for civil service exam.

CHAPTER 4

BUREAUCRACY, REGULATORY MANAGEMENT, AND KOREAN DEMOCRACY

Hyukwoo Lee

ABSTRACT

Regulatory authority officials in Korea have been considerably strong enough to affect citizen's intentions and alter their incentives to take new challenges. But, from the result of steady regulation reform, absurd bureaucratic interventions have been sharply reduced. Corruption in the process of rent seeking has decreased too. It is impossible to exercise regulatory authority that infringes on the essence of the freedom of the people because people who live in a democratic society would not accept these absurd practices.

This chapter introduces some key features of the regulatory management system in South Korea as well as the challenges that need to be overcome. In particular, the bureaucracy has worked hard to chip away at past regulations that produce rents for various private interest groups but provide little to society at large. Regulatory quality is tied closely to democracy as maintaining a fair and even playing field for entrepreneurs is a key freedom. Introducing checks and balances into the regulatory system

The Experience of Democracy and Bureaucracy in South Korea
Public Policy and Governance, 83–111
doi:10.1108/S2053-769720170000028004

can be an important way to facilitate this goal. The Regulatory Reform Committee (RRC) facilitated to strengthen the logic of regulatory neces- sity and the logic of improving regulation which increased the level of its institutionalization.

Keywords: Regulatory management; bureaucracy; democracy; Regulatory Reform Committee; bureaucratic rent seeking; Sinmungo

In a democratic state, public officials tend to design regulation carefully and consider whether its enforcement works properly. They know that the regula- tions are one of the key factors of the country's prosperity. The more public officials make high quality regulations, the more feasible their intervention in the private sector and market is likely to appear. The autonomy of the people will be higher in this type of regulatory system. And the autonomy of the people is a key element for the functioning of democracy (Dahl, 1998, Held, 1987). Democracy is a system that secures fundamental freedoms like expressing opinions on public issues and the opportunity of everyone in soci- ety to participate. Democracy is also the system that does not accept any kind of institutionalized privileges guaranteed by the state. These kinds of institutionalized privileges have usually been made from unreasonable regu- lations that impose restrictions on new challenges and activities (Tullock, 1967). So, only countries that pay attention to the prevention of such privi- leges can develop and realize democracy in which people should not be unfairly treated (Lee, 2014).

The Korean government has guaranteed equal political rights to all citi- zens since its independence from the Japanese in 1945 and has established a system to ensure the freedom of expression of political opinions among the people. Since then, South Korea could escape from its oppressive condi- tion of pre-modern tyranny that controlled the rights and freedom of citi- zens with absurd regulatory controls. However, after its independence, the Korean government and its public officials have not seriously thought about the importance of regulatory reform, but rather made use of regulations as a means of correcting the social state and intervening in various private sec- tor affairs arbitrarily for about 30 years. They have also not paid attention to the establishment of a well-structured regulatory management system. In short, at that time, democracy was just considered a norm and a formality but did not function, and regulatory intervention was routine and widespread by government in the private sector. Due to the existence of this kind of regu- latory intervention, the substantive democratic transition in Korean society was delayed for a long time. In this respect, it is just recently that the government and its officials understood that regulatory oversight is directly related to the realization of democracy.

The full-scale realization of democracy in South Korea took place in the late 1980s with the end of the authoritarian government. At that time, the government and its officials came to properly understand the meaning of regulations to individuals in society and the whole nation and took a strong interest in regulatory reform. They have abandoned the previous approach that took regulatory remedies for social problems for granted. They also understand that regulations can be a set of constraints on autonomy, may reduce the individual's chances to overcome new challenges, and give rise to negative effects in the private sector. In this situation, if this kind of constraint is absurd and overburdens enterprises and individuals, people cannot accept this kind of absurd regulation. People have learned that unreasonable regulations do not solve social problems and also add to the burden of the private sector and are the cause of the loss of the social democratic and autonomous problem-solving skills.

South Korea has begun to have an interest in regulatory controls and successfully achieved the state where democracy can be implemented practically through regulatory oversight.

Bureaucratic regulatory management has impacted Korean society in a big way. Most of all, the nature of Korean society changed from the bureaucratic economic and social control to the habits of democratic civil society-led operations principally due to the respect of individual freedom and responsibility. With reasonable government intervention, government corruption was significantly reduced, and there has also been reduced rents created by regulation. The equality and equal opportunities in the private sector have increased due to decreasing protection and privilege by unreasonable regulation. The official practice of arbitrary and unilateral intervention also disappeared and patriarchal bureaucratic correction of social problems also changed with the transition of the role of public officials from regulators to social providers of public services. This is a dramatic change that has affected almost everything in Korea for the past 20 years. And it plays an important role in changes like the bureaucratic way of regulation, the promotion of unreasonable regulatory reform, and the introduction of a regulatory management system.

This study was designed to analyze regulation and its enforcement, and the impact of bureaucrat's regulatory management on Korean democracy. To this end, in the second section, there will be a theoretical discussion about the relationship between democracy, regulation, and bureaucracy. In the third section, I will analyze the implementation of democracy through the lens of bureaucratic regulatory management in Korea. In the fourth section, how this regulatory management may impact the consolidation and implementation of democracy in Korea is described. Finally, in the fifth section, it will discuss the challenges for public officials who have the responsibility to increase the level of democratic consolidation with more appropriate regulatory management.

Li (2005) investigates the determinants of regulatory reforms during 1990–1998 in 50 developing countries. The author finds that the reforms are attributable to differences in the configurations of interest groups and in the political structure—in particular, the decision-making mechanisms and the ideology of the legislature. Regulatory reforms are more likely in countries with strong pro-reform interest groups (e.g., a larger financial sector and a greater proportion of urban consumers) and less likely in countries where incumbent operators have already made large investments and hence have strong incentives to oppose reforms. Democracy facilitates the actions of interest groups.

DEMOCRACY, REGULATIONS, AND BUREAUCRATS

Regulation: The Rules of the Game That Determine Democracy

Regulation and Human Behavior

Regulation is government intervention into people's behavior. This intervention not only restricts the rights of citizens (including foreigners subject to Acts of the Republic of Korea), but also institutions both in the private and public sectors. In any country, people must make decisions, subject to government regulation (Baldwin, 1999; Choi, 1992; Lee, 2009; Meier, 1985; Stone, 1988; Vedung, 1998). The government's actions constrain the scope of individual behavior, but their intention is to secure public order and welfare for a better distribution of resources. Therefore, the performance of a society depends on whether the regulation is designed reasonably or not. In a regulatory system that guarantees the creativity of the people, a country can be prosperous, but if poverty and disorder are rampant, government regulation could be a threat, but also a barrier to democracy.

Regulations have a significant impact on democracy. Democracy does not allow the use of arbitrary decisions of the regulatory authorities (Held, 1982; IM, 2014).[1] And it is a system that respects basic human rights as a prerequisite of democracy. When public officials can make regulation transparent when it is designed according to a predefined procedure of agreement between members. Regulations, which survive this process, can have validity. Regulation gives rise to inevitable benefits for certain groups, and burdens or costs for other groups (Wilson, 1992). Without legitimacy in the process of regulation design, they may be an infringement on democracy. People are burdened or experience costs from the regulation will not submit to this situation without legitimacy in regulation and enforcement. When arbitrary judgment or decision is combined with politics, it can become a source of power to the wrong people.

For this reason, a government needs to re-evaluate previously designed regulations and check whether it constrains citizen autonomy excessively and irrationally. These reflections are critical to democracy. If the government complies with the applicable procedures and sets a reasonable level of regulation necessary for the survival of the community, government may protect and promote democracy (Ahn & Jung, 2007; Etzioni-Halevy, 1983). In developed countries, an agency is established for evaluating, improving, and monitoring both newly designed and existing regulations for democratic control on the bureaucracy and society. Therefore, a country equipped with more democratic procedures reasonable enough to consider the interests of citizens is more likely to design better regulations. In addition, when a government installs parallel institutions to analyze the effectiveness of regulations to improve their validity, it could heighten the possibility of achieving more reasonable regulations according to the principles of checks and balances. Under this scheme, a regulatory designer is less likely to have arbitrary powers to insist only on regulatory effects or side effects. Thus, a regulation is likely to be made to reflect the reasonable demand of ordinary people to solve social problems.

Excessive Social Regulation

For this reason, countries that try to develop and design regulations to protect and uplift democracy become developed countries, whereas countries that suppress democratic regulations remain undeveloped in the end (Dahl, 1998; Lee, 2014). In developed countries, democracy is realized in daily life with the freedom of the people. On the contrary, countries that fail to control arbitrary intervention by the state power like North Korea has serious restrictions on these rights. In developed countries, they admit different backgrounds and different ideas and do not control how or where people live. Whenever government tries to introduce burdensome and unreasonable regulations which prevent people's basic rights like freedom of residence, assembly and argument, democratic regulatory control systems automatically begin to filter out the irrational elements of that regulation. But in North Korea, people who have loyalty to the leader can live in the capital Pyongyang.[2] In a word, there is no freedom in North Korea. These absurd regulations cause strange behaviors such that people have to praise their political leader in the morning and evening to live in Pyongyang. This system of social discrimination is again being strictly protected by regulation. As a result, those who have privileged rights and only belong to a specific class will continue to enjoy a better life compared to most of the ordinary people.

Regulation Is Not a Fixed Entity
The quality of regulation is also an important distinction between developed countries (Worldbank, 2004). Even if regulation is equipped with procedural legitimacy and was made following an examination of possible adverse effects at the introduction stage, the demand for improvement is continuous because discomfort and new social problems occur constantly in any society due to new technologies and trends among the people. Thus, no matter how relevant a public official make regulation, regulation is likely to become uncomfortable and unreasonable with time. Due to the vested interests created by regulation, someone will take a loss in his property or rights. A regulatory framework for the automotive era will not work when vehicles are primarily drones and unmanned vehicles. Regulation for wired communication is also difficult to operate when online social networks become a universal form of communication. Existing regulatory frameworks protect vested interests and impose disadvantages on a number of invisible people who try to find new opportunities. This kind of regulation is intended to protect a particular person or group of people and will not satisfy the conditions of democracy. So, countries with continued interest in improving their regulatory system have a higher level of democracy among developed countries.

Bureaucrats: Designers, Executors, and Managers of Regulation

Regulation from the Bureaucrat's Perspective
Bureaucracy can be defined as the means to implement policy. The bureaucracy usually carries out policy decision making in accordance with established rules from a neutral point of view. It must not involve any emotional or subjective judgment during the bureaucratic regulatory process. Bureaucrats' behavior can be understood as the exercise of legal authority (Sager & Rosser,

2009; Weber, 1978). This is the ideal form of bureaucracy proposed by Max Weber. Government has appointed bureaucrats who are experts to perform public tasks and complex social problems fairly and objectively. If officials perform their tasks and decision making faithfully, their works may serve as a means for implementing democracy.

However, it is impossible to work out such a bureaucratic system fully and in reality. Officials, as human beings, also inevitably have a subjective point of view and values and the authority to create rules to intervene in business processes (Crozier, 1964; Downs, 1967). So, the neutral and objective character that bureaucrats are expected to have is easily contaminated in the process of exercising their rights. Moreover, the larger discretion bureaucrats have, the more they are likely to misuse, abuse, and make discretionary judgment (Crozier, 1964). In many cases, bureaucrats are selfish rather than objective as is originally intended. There are also countless cases identified in previous analyses of bureaucracy. Bureaucrats trying to maximize their budget (Niskannen, 1995), and pay attention to the interests of their own department first (Down, 1967). Unlike the ideals of the original bureaucratic model, bureaucracy may cause damage to democracy in this way (Etzioni-Halevy, 1983; Jung, 2011; Han & Jung, 2014; Lindbloom, 1977; Park & Joo, 2007).[3]

But Bureaucrats are core principal officials who design and enforce regulations. They constantly produce the basis of the provisions of the regulation and decide the content of those provisions (Appleby, 1949). This means that regulations are likely to reflect the interests of the bureaucrats and not the interests of the public (Etzioni-Halevy, 1983; Krueger, 1974; Tullock, 1967). And it means that depending on how the bureaucrats do in regulation design and enforcement, democratic values can be created and enhanced. Otherwise, the opposite state may arise. Whether an official's interpretation and implementation of regulations are made properly is the basis upon which those regulatory decisions can be justified or not. But from the bureaucratic perspective, regulation is a means of influence and a symbol of authority. Regulations are also the basis for any meaningful role in the presence of government officials and government needs. Bureaucracy is an organization that is operated based on the work area generated by regulation.

In fact, from the perspective of the bureaucracy, regulation is important because it is the source of the rationality of the regulatory authority and it influence. However, it is also important to bureaucrats because regulation is the means to maintain and expand their influence so they can have control over the market and civil sector. Regulation is not easily improved because there are unreasonable restrictions. Regulatory influence tends to rarely be reduced for this reason. It is not easy to find regulatory officials reduce their own authority through correcting unreasonable regulations. No matter how absurd the bureaucratic regulations are, bureaucrats have an incentive to avoid corrections as they may result in a reduction of their influence (Kaufman, 1991; Mitnick, 1980). When bureaucrats confront unreasonable regulations, they tend to scale their own influence rather than regulatory quality. Of course, in the situation that regulatory authority is rampant and bureaucrats' power is expanded excessively, democracy is weakened.

It is important to understand how officials see and take advantage of regulatory measures. In the design and operation stage, bureaucrats may recognize regulatory authority as a means of active intervention or they may they consider the social impact of such regulation as decisive to determine the quality of regulation and exert reasonable control on democracy.[4] When officials are only aware of the regulatory restrictions as a means of solving social problems, they are likely to overlook the adverse impact of social regulations. Due to regulatory action generating benefits and damages at the same time, it is necessary to review regulations carefully to see whether they cause privilege or excessive discomfort and social loss. Otherwise, democratic values will be infringed.

The Role of Bureaucracy in Regulation

Bureaucrat as Designer.
The role of such officials may be classified as a regulatory designers, executors, and managers. Regulatory designers play a role in developing regulatory alternatives and confirming final regulations. During the regulatory design period, there usually occurs debate and compromise on the level of regulatory rent between public officials and stakeholders. The groups who may have the possibility to get benefits from new regulation try to access and impact bureaucracy to make regulation according to their own interest. In contrast, the other groups bearing the burden and cost often attempt to minimize their disadvantage and collapse the original governmental intentions. The irony is that bureaucrats in the regulatory process often come a little closer to the perspective of stakeholders from the original regulation's intention to represent a particular group rather than the perspective of public (Sherman, 1980; Stigler, 1975). In the case of individual departments which have their own customers like the department of gender equality, the department of agriculture, forestry and fisheries and the department of employment and labor, this phenomenon will arise very frequently. As it may give rise to a burden for the majority of the people and adverse effects to society in the long term, it

is a universal phenomenon that the department of gender equality has only focused on women and family-specific regulations, the department of agriculture, forestry, and fisheries is interested only in the regulation for farmers or fishermen. And the department of employment and labor tends to attempt to introduce regulation for the protection of workers, not shareholders. In this regard, officials are often said to oppose deregulation or regulatory reform that lowers their influence on their task sectors (Mitnick, 1980).

Bureaucrat as Executer.
Bureaucrats are also regulatory enforcers. Bureaucrats apply regulation, and feel the effects of regulation on the street level (Lipsky, 1980). No matter how reasonable the design of the regulations established, without a proper enforcement phase, they cannot achieve the intended effect. But at this step in regulatory enforcement, officials have a lot of discretion. Compared to uniform regulations, bureaucrats have always confronted various policy environment conditions and different regulatory target groups. Debates on regulatory interpretation will always occur, too (Bardach et al., 1992). This means it is natural for regulation to exist unreasonably in the regulatory enforcement stage. The situation and targets of regulation change ceaselessly, but regulation, once introduced, is not easily altered. So, it cannot be overemphasized that, in the introduction of regulation, one should be as cautious as possible. In regulatory enforcement, corruption may occur in the arbitrary utilization of regulatory discretion in return for bribes (Choi & Sagong, 1996; Worldbank, 2004). While debating the specific issues related to regulation, the interests of the entire people and the interests of the community are diminished and competition to protect the interests of specific groups emerges. Like most of the side-effects of regulation, corruption tends to be presented as a result of the abuse of regulatory authority in regulatory enforcement process (Lim, 2014; Myrdal, 1971). Therefore, it is important to prevent the abuse of authority in regulatory enforcement to disconnect it from corruption. In the enforcement phase, bureaucracy has such a tremendous influence that it is urgent to make a device to check the official's behavior and continue to look at whether this device is working properly.

Bureaucrat as Manager.
Finally, a bureaucrat is also the individual assigned to keep regulations in a good condition. Public officials are appointed to design and enforce regulations, but also serve to review regulations to check whether they are valid

or not. They have a mission to maintain good quality in government regulations. To achieve this mission, they must review the rationality of present regulations and reduce the absurdity of regulations. In a word, they must have a completely different perspective on regulations compared to the bureaucrats who architect and enforce regulations. The former focuses on the problems of regulation, while the latter must have an interest in the necessity of the regulations. Regulatory officials as managers play a role in checking the validity of the regulatory work that regulatory designers and enforcers carried out.

In fact, regulation is an important means to solve social problems, and also the basis of bureaucrats' influence, bureaucracy has an incentive to improve unreasonable regulation, which may shrink their grip on the private sector or market. In this manner, officials will focus more on the role as designers and enforcers than as managers. It is very important that government does not damage the ability of bureaucrats to gain even bureaucratic responsibilities in the regulatory management process (Park & Joo, 2007; Wood & Waterman, 1994). The more bureaucrats faithfully serve as regulatory managers, the higher the rationality of the regulation overall. In this situation, it is likely to reduce the failure of democracy due to unreasonable regulations. The arbitrary exercise of regulatory authority by officials and special interests in conjunction with the introduction and application of regulations and unnecessary interference in the private sector can be reduced in this way. So, in developed countries, regulatory management is established as a dedicated organization separate from the government department which tends to be the regulatory designer or enforcer. Unlike bureaucrats who need to address immediate social problems through regulations, it is necessary to analyze whether the regulation is as relevant as they expected to this objective, and whether it is neutral and professional.

Democracy-Friendly Regulatory Requirements: Regulatory Design and the Behavior of Bureaucrats

The Definition of Democracy-Friendly Regulation
To discuss democracy-friendly regulations, we must derive a minimum agreement from the various concepts of democracy. Democracy has diverse interpretations, so the concept is sometime confusing. Therefore, to the response of how regulation could enhance democratic values, extremely contradictory opinions can be found at all times. In the debates on the concept of

democracy, there exists various views of scope from the freedom of the people to the well-being of citizens. However, speaking of democracy, at least there is a common assumption that it will be based on the maintenance of a representative system, a guarantee of public freedom, respect for property rights, and the necessity for the legal basis for the intervention of individuals. And it is not allowed to exclude someone's universal values in the community, or to give privileges to certain groups or individuals except in exceptional cases that community has agreed upon. This can be understood, in a democracy, as public officials having to work to break bureaucratic authoritarianism based on arbitrary authority of the bureaucracy and its regulations (Held, 1982; IM, 2014). Regulatory management has also focused on how to restrict bureaucratic arbitrariness. And officials have acknowledged the importance of citizen participation and communication in regulatory procedures and that adequately reflect the will of the people (Bozeman, 1987).

Then how can officials meet these minimum standards of democracy? First, officials must carefully use the regulatory authority given to them as much as possible. They should also consider whether the regulations that they want to introduce meet the requirements of procedural justice. If there is a space to improve the procedural validity of regulations, and they should strive to equip the system to solve the problem. Of course, they should identify the validity of legal basis of any regulation over and over again. Most of all, public officials themselves should not make judgments about which regulation can be a panacea to solve social problems. Regulation is a means of solving social problems. But it has also caused a reallocation of resources. As a result, regulation means a cost to someone and a benefit to others. In the regulatory processes of changing in the arrangement of the allocation of social resources, if there has emerged excessive benefits or unreasonable burdens to someone, it is not democratic. In a democratic society, there must be a legal justification based on an agreement with the community for the privileges and benefits that are distributed among the people.

Therefore, bureaucrats who implement policy goals with regulations need to work in a system in which designers, enforcers, and managers of regulation play a proper role to solve social problems. In other words, within the bureaucratic structure, government should establish the substantive and procedural devices and operate properly to ensure the freedom and rights of the citizens in a democracy (Han & Jung, 2014). Through bureaucratic structures and procedures, bureaucrats should be expected to perform their tasks without any resistance to regulatory reform considering the benefits to society as a whole. At the same time, they should guide themselves on how to control their own regulatory influence on the private sector. Developed countries have continued to revise regulatory management systems to meet the minimum requirements of democracy. In these well-designed regulatory management systems, officials must work and perform their tasks by formal rules and procedures which justify the validity of regulation at any time. They should analyze the causes of social problems, explore the various regulatory alternatives to address them, compare these alternatives, and finally choose the best alternative. Of course, they take stakeholder's opinions to improve the quality of regulation. So, whether a country establishes these well-designed regulatory management systems or not, they are closely linked to the realization and maintenance of the level of democracy because they can curb arbitrary bureaucratic discretion from unreasonable regulations.

On the other hand, the OECD takes the presence of a formal regulatory management system as an important indicator measuring national capacity. The reason that each country is concerned about the institutionalization of regulatory controls is because formal regulatory management systems are a key element to secure democracy both inside and outside of government. Proper regulation control cannot be achieved through normative and ethical requirements alone that call do not curb the abuse of the regulation authority. A strict regulatory review system for newly designed regulation is a representative example of regulatory management. By introducing detailed regulatory review guidelines and reviewing the validity of regulations, bureaucrats should closely examine the impact of regulation on the regulated. Government also pays attention to existing regulations, whether they may be subject to improvement with changes in the situation. Furthermore, governments in the world compete to establish a separate body from official government departments and cast regulatory expertise as regulatory managers to manage regulation more systematically. It is meaningful that government equips itself with such a system to oversee regulatory validity and control its social influence.

Also, if government establishes a system of checks and balances and reduces exclusive bureaucratic power, it can help the government to become free from corruption (Williams, 1987). From historical experience, we know that if one lacks the authority to regulate the rights of officials, their regulatory discretion leads to undemocratic results eventually. Due to this reason, it is often a huge contribution to democracy to provide a device to check the powers of regulatory officials in government.

DEMOCRACY THROUGH REGULATORY OVERSIGHT BY THE BUREAUCRACY

The Emergence of a Regulatory Reform Body and
a Democracy-Friendly Bureaucracy

Regulatory Reform Committee
In South Korea, since the 1960s, until a President was elected through a direct election in 1987, has experienced an authoritarian system of government. During this time, government is separated from citizen and exercises its authority strongly for the nominal purpose of national development. In the process, there has been a practice that officials have autonomous rights to intervene in the private sector based on a high degree of professionalism (Han & Jung, 2014; Park & Yun, 2014). This system may have contributed to the achievement of economic development. On the other hand, excluding the various groups in policy formulation, this structure that doesn't reflect the democratic value and interests of individuals in the private sector (Ahn & Jung, 2003). Government could have always realized it's will in the suppression of civil participation. Bureaucrats at that time could also use regulatory authority in the name of national development or social order. Officials lead the private sector and this structure caused bureaucratic corruption. Of course, the arbitrary use of regulatory power was the primary source of this kind of corruption.

Since the advent of democratic government in 1988, in order to solve this problem, government had promoted regulatory reform in earnest. But in many cases, there was no significant effect to curb the arbitrariness of bureaucrats' regulatory activities. It was acknowledged as the behavior of the bureaucrats to resist to regulatory reform (Hong, 1996; Sagong, 1998). Bureaucrats took a passive stance toward regulatory reform that could diminish their social influence. At that time, officials were worried about the collapse of the organization and its influence in their business areas protected by regulatory authority (Lee & Lee, 2002). The OECD (1997) also regarded the low performance of regulatory reform in the Kim Young-sam government (1993–1997) as bureaucrats' conscious structure to favor government intervention and obsession with fame and power. During the Kim Dae-jung administration (1998–2002), there was also the diagnosis of the adherence to the administrative convenience of bureaucrats which was the cause of regulatory reform that did not work properly (FKI, 1999).

In this respect, in Korea, regulatory reform began in earnest since the Framework Act on Administrative Regulations was enacted in 1997 and the

Regulatory Reform Committee (RRC) was established on the basis of this law. Government also made regulatory control procedures. This action can be interpreted as a regulatory oversight structure wherein management, are not designers and enforcers, emerged to lead regulatory reform in government. In a word, the Korean government was not able to produce a systematic mechanism for the review of the reasonableness of regulation until RRC had been installed. On the basis of this formal system, regulatory officials were able to take control of the exercise of their own regulatory authority. Government could also promote regulatory reform officials who worked in that organization where were dedicated to the regulatory reform of the government.

In particular, the RRC was installed in 1998 as a body to review the validity of new and strengthening regulations and to check the problems of existing regulation. With the regulatory review processes, it monitored the irrationality of new and strengthened regulations. It also has performed a periodic review of the validity of existing regulations within a regulatory sunset period. It is important that government established a provision of a systematic checking device and started to have an interest in restricting its own regulatory authority which may cause adverse effects in the private sector. For example, if some officials made a regulation in the interests of their agencies or customer groups, it will be reviewed as an overall social cost in the review process by the RRC. In this process, even if the introduction of regulation was proper to some people, if it extracts a high level of social cost, that kind of regulation could not be accepted in government. In this system of the RRC and the regulatory review, bureaucrats who intend to design regulations must consider the costs and benefits of the regulation and try to make costs and reduce the regulatory burden. They have no choice but to devise the various regulatory alternatives and have an interest in designing more reasonable regulations in accordance with the discriminatory nature of the regulations.

In this sense, it is important that government installs a mechanism that is dedicated to improving unreasonable restrictions, such as the RRC. It also means that the RRC can join forces with regulatory reform within the whole government system. In particular, in the regulatory review process, 22 members of the RRC play a key role in reviewing and reforming new and existing regulation. The committee is composed of 22 members including the Prime Minister (chairman), a chairman from the private sector, 14 civilian committee members, and 6 government members. The 14 civilian committee members are experts from academia, business, and citizens' groups. The six government members are ministers from central government ministries. This makes it possible to reflect the views of experts in the private sector, not government, on regulatory reform. So, with the installation of this institution, public officials should pay attention to meeting the criteria presented by the RRC that includes civilian members. When they create a new regulation, the problems related to existing regulation can emerge. As a result, the regulations that distort democracy are likely to be improved.

Moreover, the installation of the Regulatory Reform Committee can be advantageous as it allows the emergence of bureaucrats who understand the necessity and philosophy of regulatory reform. Such regulatory reform is a cornerstone of democracy. In 2016, there are 60 officials working in the Regulatory Reform Office, which is the Secretariat of the RRC. The bureaucrats in the RRC, unlike the bureaucrats in other government apparatuses which have interests in the necessity of regulation to solve social problems related to their own department, may have no choice but to be interested in the problems and side effects of regulation. So, they are likely to be interested in the appropriate role of government, the nature of the market, the costs and benefits of regulation, and the feasibility of regulations. Of course, the officials belonging to these organizations will be trained in their career as bureaucrats friendly to regulatory reforms and have accumulated expertise in this field. For systematic regulatory management, it is essential to have such regulatory reform mechanisms in government, and, as a result, regulatory reform officials in government may have an appropriate voice against unreasonable regulation that are usually designed and implemented by universal government departments.

The Regulatory Management of Bureaucrats for Democratic Transition

Establishment and Application of Regulatory Management Procedures
South Korea has established a regulatory management device to prevent arbitrary bureaucratic regulatory design. In particular, according to the Framework Act on Administrative Reform, Article 4, regulations must be based on law, and, in detail, regulations shall be directly provided for by Acts, and the specific details of the regulations may be determined by Presidential Decree, Ordinance of the Prime Minister, Ordinance of the Ministry, or Municipal Ordinances and Municipal Rules, as entrusted by Acts or higher Acts and subordinate statutes by fixing the specific scope.[5] And no administrative agencies may limit the rights of citizens or impose duties on citizens pursuant to regulations that are not based on Acts. With this institution, government is able to control the establishment of regulations that do not have a legal base.

According to the guidelines for regulatory review, officials should analyze the costs and benefits of regulation and the validity of regulation should be reviewed by the Regulatory Reform Commission. In addition, through the Legislative notice, regulatory proposals have to be presented to citizens to collect the opinions of the public. The RRC will eventually review the feasibility of regulation and decide the regulatory validity and if there is found problems related to regulation, and it will request commentary from them. For this end, the Framework Act on Administrative Regulations, Chapter 2, presented the various tools to manage regulations properly, such as Regulatory Impact Analysis (RIA), regulatory survival period specification, gathering opinions about regulation, regulatory review requests, preliminary examination of regulations, regulatory review, and improvement of recommendations on regulations. Officials must comply with these requests in order to make regulations and various regulatory issues are presented and discussed in this review process. As a result, if regulation is judged to cause undue benefits or an overburden to certain groups, it must be complemented in a designated period. It is also a prerequisite for the realization of democracy that regulation should be put in these monitoring devices.

The significance of the procedures and devices in introducing regulations can be clearly understood when it is compared with the regulatory procedures introduced by the National Assembly. In South Korea, the National Assembly does not have any system to monitor the validity of regulation, whereas the administration is equipped with a very systematic regulatory review mechanism as discussed above. For this reason, paradoxically, the National Assembly has been establishing more undemocratic regulations to defend the vested interests of certain groups than the administration has. In May 2016, the National assembly passed amendments to the Medical Technicians, ETC. Act Article 12 Clause 5, which bans purchasing foreign glasses and contact lenses on the Internet. If this kind of entry barrier regulation is presented to the administration, reviewed as to its validity, it might never be adopted. This is a typical regulation to create a regulatory rent and protect the interests of optometrists at the expense of most people. With this regulation, Korean people must buy glasses and contact lens at off-line glasses stores which are about five times more expensive than on the international market. On the other hand, since 1998, in the establishment of the regulatory management system, there have been few examples that regulation has been passed to ensure the excessive profits of a particular group, or the regulatory burden of the people.

Sinmungo System.

Meanwhile, apart from regulatory review on new regulation, South Korea is equipped with a procedure to check and improve the absurdity of the existing regulations. Sinmungo is a typical regulatory scheme in this sense. Historically, Korean society has a long tradition of hearing people's voice as a way of preventing corrupt acts and protecting people's basic rights. For instance, Sinmungo (meaning a big drum in Korean) was hung outside of the royal palace in early fifteenth century during the Chosun Dynasty in an effort to resolve people's complaints directly and stabilize their lives. By beating the drum, people suffering from injustice could voice their complaints. For a long time, Sinmungo had served as a channel for the government to listen to the people's complaints and solve them. Its tradition has been kept in many aspects of public administration. This continues in the era of digital governance such that an e-Sinmungo is the official pathway for citizens to request the Government to improve the absurdity and inconsistency of regulation applied improperly to them. When one files a petition to the Sinmungo, an officer in charge of matters must respond to the petitioner within 14 days specifying whether they accept the petition or not. If the petition is not accepted, the ministry must explain in detail why it is not acceptable within three months. The last step of the regulatory petition process is that the RRC can recommend regulatory changes to the relevant ministry if its explanation is not sufficiently justified. By filing the petition, one can not only observe the whole review process, but also can have his or her voice heard. Finally, the RIA Reports are made available to the public online as well. Since their introduction, as of April 2016, a total of 34,901 regulatory reform cases were processed through the system, of which 21,538 were general civil complaints and 13,201 cases that received feedback, while the rest were still in the midst of the application and review process. As a result, some unreasonable restrictions on citizens' autonomy have been removed. In this sense, Sinmungo can be called a democratic-friendly regulatory reform system, because it is the system that evaluates the inconvenience caused by unreasonable regulations directly from citizens, and it corrects government's mistakes in regulatory design and enforcement. Democracy can be achieved in such an environment where government listens to public opinion more actively.

Review of the Adequacy of Regulation

Regulatory Impact Analysis.
In addition to the provisions of the regulatory process, it is also important to review the adequacy of the regulation which leads public officials to induce rational use of the regulatory authority. This means that a regulation that does not ensure content validity is subject to improvement or supplementation. With this concern, the Framework Act on Administrative Regulation regulates for RIA to be administered for any regulations either established or

reinforced since 1998. Based on such a foundation, the government enforces RIA to examine the following evaluation categories—the necessity of the regulation, the comparison of multiple alternatives, the Regulatory Cost-Benefit Analysis of alternatives, the results of the analysis of alternatives, and stakeholders' views of preferred alternatives.

Regulation should be designed for the specific sector in which people cannot solve public problems in the market. There is no reason to bother the government to intervene in areas that are functioning normally in the private sector, and if government intervenes in this area rashly, it can lead to confusion and inefficiency by relying on the government. Of course, democratic decision-making mechanisms, which are based on civilian's autonomy, are damaged. The more government intervenes in the private sector, the less people have autonomy and accountability to their own deals. Civilian autonomy and accountability are the key elements to realize democracy in any society. In Korea, officials must prove they regulate only market failures.

After admitting the necessity of regulation, it needs to search and analyze various regulatory alternatives to solve regulatory problems. To lessen the damage to the autonomy of private actors, it is required to adopt an alternative approach to reduce the regulatory burden as much as possible. It is an obligation to conduct comparative analysis on proposed regulation, existing regulation, less regulatory alternatives, and nonregulatory alternatives (subsidies, economic incentives, campaigns, self-regulation, etc.). To promote quality control, the guideline on drafting a RIA Report requires a review process for at least three alternatives when newly establishing a regulation by comparing the costs and benefits associated with each option. So, officials should consider co-regulation and self-regulation that use and trust the capacity of the private sector first. It has also provided a device to determine the regulation effect before full-scale implementation. The RRC also has reviewed the validity of the regulation in this stance. With this consideration, government has tried to reduce the arbitrary use of regulatory authority.

Officials should analyze the costs and benefits of regulatory alternatives and choose the most reasonable alternative. In this process, officials determine the target groups that are affected by the regulations and estimate the costs and benefit of the regulation. The regulatory targets and measures must be set in a minimal scope for maximum effectiveness. Officials shall also conduct additional analysis such as a small business impact assessment, and a gender assessment, too, because, even if it is the same regulation, this can have a discriminatory impact according to its size or character. So to speak, relatively small groups or females have often experienced a greater regulatory burden compared to other regulatory groups. In this case, it is necessary for differential regulation design according to the state of the regulated group with consideration of the gaps. Also, the director of the central administrative agency is responsible for making a RIA Report open to the public during the pre-announcement of legislation.

Regulatory Reform Task Force Team (RRTFT): A Better Regulation Task Force.

The Roh Moo-Hyun administration tried to focus on improving the quality of regulation rather than on reducing the number of regulations through large-scale short-term regulatory reform. The Regulatory Reform Task Force Team (RRTFT) was established within the office for government policy and coordinated under the Prime Minister's Office in August 2004. The TF team extensively handled bundled and essential regulations. Headed by the Deputy Minister for Regulatory Reform, the RRTFT was focusing on reforming existing bundled regulations that reach several ministries. The Regulatory Reform Task Force is composed of approximately 50 persons comprising a total of three teams: the planning supervision team, regulatory reform Team 1, and regulatory reform Team 2; 12 of the members are from enterprises, 2 are from economic organizations, 10 are researchers, and 26 are public officials. As such, it attempted user-centered reform. The director-level public officials or nongovernmental experts could serve as team leaders. The organization has been restructured since and the member count of 20 was raised to 35. The three teams in the original plan were changed to a total of five teams, with the society and culture team and implementation management team added. The Prime Minister was the chair of the discussions and decisions were made at the Ministerial Meetings. The Regulatory Reform Task Force set up 54 plans for improving key regulations in seven sectors. The Roh Administration tried to reform 1473 individual tasks and improved 954 cases.

Regulatory Openness and Consultation with Stakeholders.

South Korea also takes a positive attitude to listen to regulatory inconvenience and feedback from private stakeholders. According to the Framework Act on Administrative regulation, if the head of a central administrative agency intends to establish a new regulation or reinforce existing regulations, he/she shall sufficiently hear the opinions of administrative agencies, civic groups, interested parties, research institutes, experts, etc., in such means as public hearings, a pre-announcement of legislations, etc. So, officials must listen to a formal opinion from the stakeholders, in particular groups who bear the costs. He should take a description and explanation of the need for regulation to ensure regulatory compliance. Public consultation can be a powerful tool to improve regulatory quality by acting as a quality check on draft proposals and by providing input and data to the policy-making process. The Framework Act on Administrative Regulation establishes a legislative basis for public consultation mechanisms.

The major of elements in the consultation process are as follows: ministries are expected to consult with affected parties prior to drafting new regulatory proposals; and drafted regulations must be available on a notice and comment procedure for a minimum of 20 days. In the case of new or revised regulations, the government requires heads of agencies to "… gather sufficient evidence of public opinion through public hearings and public notices on legislation by administrative agencies, civic groups, interested parties, research institutes, and experts." Public and stakeholder perspectives can also be voiced through their representatives on various regulatory reform bodies and committees. The key central government body, the RRC, provides an important channel through which a range of views can be expressed. In addition to the formal committee structures for stakeholders to express their views, the government has made use of a range of consultation mechanisms including a greater use of the Internet to facilitate an exchange between government and society. Especially, the RRC helps stakeholders have easy access to the lists and content of regulations by registering all regulations, making them public on its website.

With increased interest, participation by the public, and firms in regulatory reform, the demand for greater access to regulatory information and reform processes has increased as well. In 2014, the Regulatory Information Portal (www.better.go.kr) was created to provide an open communication channel for people to freely express their opinions toward regulatory reform. To ensure free participation, the government does not collect personal information so that citizens can freely discuss their opinions on regulatory reform. The Regulatory Information Portal publicizes information on regulatory proposals and the revision process.

These devices are guaranteed by the democratic behavior of officials (Kim, 1988; Redford, 1969). If the government tries to introduce any regulation, it can get new ideas about regulatory design and feedback on any unexpected results of regulation based on stakeholder consultation.

Behavioral Changes in Regulatory Officials for Democracy

In Korea, the bureaucratic behavior of regulatory designers has been continuously improved. Government officials in South Korea have experienced a steady transition from a patriarchal bureaucracy to more democratic friendly bureaucrats who consider specifically the strengths and weaknesses of the regulatory restrictions at the design stage. As a result, it seems to be formulated with a common opinion that government must be careful in the creation or strengthening of regulation (Ju, 2004). It is recognized that the state must respect the freedom of the people and admit the participation of citizens in the policy process in the democratic era (Park, 1994). Regulation is still an important means for officials to create influence in the community; at least it has had a lot of progress in diminishing the arbitrariness of bureaucrats' regulatory authority. It is mainly because government has established the RRC to make each department of government constantly check the validity of regulation.

The graph in Fig. 1 shows the statistics of reviews of the RRC and shows the trend of bureaucrats' diminishing regulatory power. The regulatory review from 1998 to 2012 showed that the acceptance of ministries' drafts equal 376 cases (47.5%), recommendations to modify equal 251 cases (31.7%), judgment pending equal 108 cases (13.6%), partial judgment pending equal 9 cases (1.1%), and rejections equal 47 cases (5.4%). Overall, even if the acceptance of a ministry's draft is the largest portion, it does not exceed the 50% of the total. This means that the RRC has played a critical role in improving the quality of regulation. Without these efforts, Korea would be a country with a much more complicated and unreasonable regulation burden than is the case in the current situation. Citizens may endure more rights

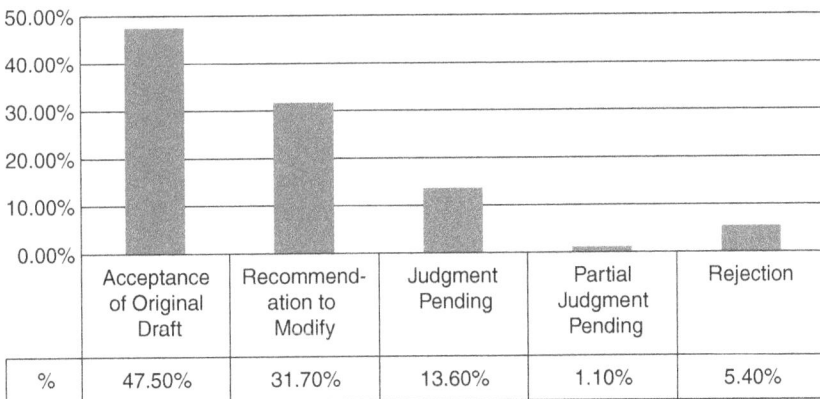

%	Acceptance of Original Draft	Recommendation to Modify	Judgment Pending	Partial Judgment Pending	Rejection
%	47.50%	31.70%	13.60%	1.10%	5.40%

Fig. 1. Results of regulatory review of Regulatory Reform Committee in Korea 1998–2012. *Source:* Lee(2013, p. 28).

infringement and absurd regulatory discrimination. As a result, we would not realize democracy at the current level.[6]

When government has come to pay more attention on the various difficulties and costs, the confusion from unreasonable regulation can be reduced. The autonomous decisions of private actors can be respected. It can be clear that the resolution of social problems is the responsibility of the individual and government is likely to take more careful posture to intervene into the private sector and limit their own regulatory authority. In this situation, democracy that guarantees individual rights is likely.

Regulatory management of the Korean government has also induced changes in bureaucrats' behavior as regulatory enforcers. Changes in regulatory behavior can be found in reductions of bureaucratic corruption, especially at the executive level. Actually, the Bureaucrats corruption in government has been dramatically diminished in Korea by regulatory reform. For example, in Korea, when a government official had tremendous discretion in the distribution of governmental resources in the 1960s to 1980s, corruption was rampant, and people usually bribed government officials to exercise regulation in their own interests. But since the 1990s, government has had an active interest in regulatory reform, and this kind of bad habit declined sharply in the government sector.

In addition, improvements in regulation will encourage transparency in the public sector. For example, to apply the principle of competitive contract with electronic contract systems in procurement, a fair regulatory system in selecting right operator can emerge. Realization of transparency in regulatory policy is also a key prerequisite for democracy. In Korea, in efforts to simplify administrative procedures, the E-Government system was launched in 2003 and most of administrative services became available online. In 2010, the central government established the Administrative Investigations Management Plan for the purpose of decreasing administrative burdens from business and citizens. This plan is based on Framework Act on Administrative Investigations which has purposes like definitions and basic principles (administrative agencies shall prevent the repetition of administrative investigations, for example) of administrative investigations. Through the plan, government is aimed at classifying administrative burdens into several types and reduce the burdens systematically.

Construction of regulatory management systems in South Korea highlighted the importance of bureaucrats as managers who strive to improve the quality of regulations as much as possible. For example, the cost in, cost out system, which is the typical tool the Park Geun Hye Government designed, can be the typical case. In this system, when a ministry wants to introduce a regulation, the ministry must submit evidence of previous performance of regulatory reform. So, with this system, government cannot help keeping an interest in regulatory reform. And in the regulation design stages, each ministry may have incentives to reduce the regulatory burden as much as possible. Without this effort, it has to do more effort to save and accumulate regulatory reform to meet the cost in, cost out rules. It can be helpful to realize democracy when bureaucrats themselves become interested in regulatory reform. Lots of unreasonable regulations which unduly constraint autonomy of private sector or create unfair benefits to someone can be diminished.

REGULATORY MANAGEMENT OF THE BUREAUCRATIC IMPACT ON DEMOCRACY

Changes in Bureaucratic Roles: From Regulator to Service Provider

In Korea, the constant interests of bureaucrats in regulatory reform have transformed the character of public officials from regulators to service providers. In fact, South Korean government had strongly controlled the civil society by strict regulations. For example, the Park Chung-Hee government (1962–1979) had once regulated the content of the lyrics of pop songs, the length of hair and further restricted freedom of assembly and association. People did not go out of their house after 12 p.m. Bureaucrat's regulatory power had invaded in every aspect of people's daily lives. Government was thought of as the corrector of the social disorder and creator to make a neat country with various strict commands. But sometimes, public officials call for bribes in return to the regulated at the expense of closing his eye at the regulatory violations. As a result, people naturally regard the public officials as regulators, not public service providers. Public officials no doubt have a strong authority to intervene into every aspect of the life of citizens. They would think that government has to correct every evil of society to maintain the social order. But in these situations, the autonomy of citizens is reduced. People have to meet government standards, even wearing skirts and writing song lyrics.

Continued regulatory reform in Korea entails that government makes public officials reconsider their role as regulators. As a result, public officials are becoming an entity to serve public needs from a regulated entity. Bureaucracy is not the group that regulates the citizen but the subject to provide adequate services to the public. In Korea, it is hard to find ridiculous regulation such as the regulation on skirt length. Officials as service providers should have always been interested in the relevance and ease of service delivery to the people. Satisfaction for administrative services is evaluated annually and reflects the results of the compensation system of bureaucracy. Officials would have an interest in enhancing the convenience of citizens.

Regulations aimed at all citizens are greatly reduced and government started to learn that it is much better that it applies strict regulations to a small number of offenders. For example, in the past, people have been checked whether they have a ticket before boarding the train, but now people do not have to do this kind of pre-inspection. As a result, government efforts to abolish or improve these kinds of unreasonable regulations have transformed social habits like depending on government to make a more democratic society in which people take responsibility for their own problems. Citizen's responsibility is the key element for realizing democracy.

The Significant Reduction of Bureaucratic Corruption

In Korea, Bureaucratic corruption and misuse of public authority has dramatically declined as the result of the constant pursuit of government to reform unreasonable regulations. Regulation was essentially regarded as one of the major sources of authority and influence of the bureaucrats in Korea. Public officials have the authority to make new challenges in the private business possible or not and sometimes they can promote certain behaviors that were regarded as a breakthrough to social problems with regulatory tools. With this authority and discretion of regulatory officials, persons in the private sector have good reasons to access the regulatory bureaucrats confidentially. From a private point of view, it can be a much preferred strategy to access public officials and request a favorable decision to struggle to survive in a competitive market. According to public choice theory, the profits generated from regulation are called rent and the effort of the private sector to influence regulatory officials is called rent-seeking behavior. The more rent-seeking behavior exists, the lower the possibility of a society that can achieve democracy. So, in nondemocratic countries, it is apparent that bureaucratic influence is large enough to make citizens in general consider rent-seeking behavior as a tool to solve their own problems.

Official corruption is a rampant phenomenon in the course of private sector rent-seeking behavior. Officials set up unfair practices such as giving some profits or benefits to a particular business or private entity. According to Sagong's (1996) research, the analysis of causes of corruption in the construction sector, the amount of bribes are affected even by rent as well as its discretion. In addition, individual corruption cases are occurring in the construction sector, the rent which is created from regulations may be the root cause of the massive bribery scandal which take place in the relentless and systematic, sometimes in unethical way. The fact that rampant corruption of officials is due to unreasonable regulations would also be already identified repeatedly by multiple studies. Of course, in Korea, the government has continued to reduce constantly rent created by regulation. This means that government influence decreased and people have to compete in their business in a fair mode. When people confront and fail in some projects, they attribute it to themselves, not government aid or authority. Naturally, bureaucratic corruption can be sharply decreased.

An Increase in the Democratic Autonomy of Society

In the steady realization of rational intervention, deregulation or improvement of unreasonable regulation, to the private sectors in bureaucracy, naturally the autonomy of society will increase. In Korea, the autonomy of the private sector has been steadily increasing. People have come to try to do new challenges to realize their own creative ideas. Reduction of the regulatory authority for the media has increased the autonomy of the media and secured the freedom of criticism and sharing of ideas. It is very important for the realization of democracy to allow society to criticize the bureaucracy of government. It makes it recognize that government and the role of the bureaucracy is not a Leviathan which almost does everything to correct social absurdity, but a subject to serve public goods to society. If officials are unreasonably exerting regulatory authority, the media has been able to capture such practices and freely criticize them. This starts a virtuous cycle to control the exercise of regulatory authority absurdity and make bureaucratic intervention more democratic.

EPILOGUE: REMAINING CHALLENGES

So far, this chapter looked at the impact of the regulation management of the bureaucracy for democracy in Korea. In sum, the regulatory authority officials in Korea have been considerably strong enough to affect citizen's intention and alter their incentives to take new challenges. But, from the result of steady regulation reform, absurd bureaucratic interventions were sharply reduced. Corruption caused in the process of seeking the rent decreased too.

Increasing the autonomy of society, public officials cannot seem to utilize fully the patriarchal behavior of their own regulatory authority. It is impossible to exercise regulatory authority that infringes on the essence of the freedom of the people, because people who live in a democratic society would not accept these absurd practices.

However, in Korea, the improvement of democracy and the proper use of bureaucratic regulatory authority are still ongoing tasks for the government and community. Increasing the autonomy of society had created a pluralistic society and this pluralistic society also has contributed to the realization of democratic pluralistic society. In this process, conflicts between interest groups have intensified. Paradoxically, the regulations which protect special interests are being applied in massive ways. It is very difficult to fix regulation related to strong interest groups, no matter how absurd it is. Of course regulations to protect these interests are guaranteed to give the rent for these groups, and other groups have to take the burden and inequality from these absurd regulations. In this situation, democracy still is being practiced imperfectly. There are lots of absurd regulations to reform before consolidating democracy. If any country wants to maintain and conserve democracy, regulatory management must be an everlasting job to any government.

Because of this reason, the Korean government still has an interest in regulation reform and its impact on the community. Government intervention is monitoring its costs and benefits to be regulated. The government has committed itself to continuous efforts to enhance its capacity for the design and management of government regulation. Like Sinmungo, it operates a system that responds immediately to the difficulties of regulation that arose from the private sector. This is not the only effort to improve unreasonable regulation, but also action to reduce inefficiency and nondemocratic society that might result from unreasonable restrictions. So the Korean government should still pay attention to the regulatory management of its system and has to work systematically because of the necessity of improving regulation. There is also a need to establish a checks and balances system in regulatory management between the logic of regulatory necessity and the logic of improving regulation which has focused on the side effects of regulation. It is necessary to strengthen the authority of the RRC and increase the level of its institutionalization.

Last but not least, government itself has to separate the problems that need to be solved by government intervention from the tasks that can be solved by the market mechanism. In a democratic state, government tries to produce the regulations which are essential to maintain society, but it has an obligation to improve unnecessary regulations constantly once they've been found.

NOTES

1. In fact, there are many misunderstood concepts in democracy. People always insist or argue the necessity of democracy in a way that they understand. Sometimes, conflict occurs among a variety of concepts and arguments around democracy. The interesting thing is that democracy can tolerate many individual ideas and arguments. In a more democratic society, there are high levels of social conflict, people raise more individual opinions and finally make compromises. Even freedom does not compromise the end is recognized. But democracy is also the system that admits determined tasks. Many things in the world that are a lot of work are done by luck rather than a precise calculation. So, it is also democracy that respects and even accepts this decision under the influence of luck. Although, the democratic opposition to this decision is subject to free criticism, it will not change the fact that people must comply with comprise.

2. North Korea has adopted the Democratic People's Republic of Pyongyang Act with the Presidium of the Supreme People's Assembly ordinance the arcs 286, on November 26, 1998. In the Pyongyang Act, chapter 429, Pyongyang residency is discussed. In this provision, citizens who want to live in the province of Pyongyang are subject to the approval of the appropriate authorities. Even Pyongyang citizens are differentiated and separated from the center and surrounding areas. In addition, in Article 30, it said that if Pyongyang citizens have severely violated the law and order of the country, national authority has the right to deprive them Pyongyang citizenship. In a word, it means that they can be expelled out of Pyongyang. Food distribution is usually cut off from Pyongyang citizens.

3. It also explains the paradoxical situation of these bureaucracies as the dilemma of bureaucracy and democracy. Bureaucracy is inevitable to realize democracy, is also a threat as well. Officials must be politically neutral, yet adhere to participate in policy formation. They have to be deviated from those of political control (Etzioni-Halevy, 1983).

4. Bureaucrats who define themselves as fixers of social problems are referred to as paternalistic bureaucrats.

5. The hierarchy of laws in Korea is oriented by the constitution and the laws passed by the National Assembly to implement constitutional ideologies. National agencies and local governments undertake legislation-related tasks in accordance with the constitution which is prior to all other laws. Presidential decrees seek to run government regulations effectively, executive legislation such as ordinance of the Prime Minister, ordinance of the Ministries, and regulations of local governments are fulfilling part of the overall legal system.

6. One of the interesting phenomena is that people rarely considers the cost of regulation prior to its inconvenience presence. Even if they might think the cost in the stage of regulatory design, they tend to underestimate the level of burden. But in reality, it is important to carefully avoid the discomfort with a systematic device

in advance. In this sense, regulatory review by Regulatory Reform Committee has greatly contributed to the regulatory streamlining and makes our society more free and open state.

REFERENCES

Ahn, B.-Y., & Jung, M.-K. (2007). Democracy, equality and administration: Towards theoretical and empirical implications for the studies of the Korean public administration. *Korean Journal of Public Administration, 41*(3), 1–40.

Appleby, P. H. (1949). *Policy and administration.* Birmingham: University of Alabama Press.

Baldwin, R., Cave, M., & Lodge, M. (2012). *Understanding regulation: Theory, strategy, and practice.* Oxford, UK: Oxford University Press.

Bardach, E., & Kagan, R. A. (1982). *Going by the book: The problem of regulatory unreasonableness.* Philadelphia: Temple University Press.

Bernstein, M. H. (2015). *Regulating business by independent commission.* Princeton, NJ: Princeton University Press.

Bozeman, B. (1987). *All organizations are public: Bridging public and private organizational theories.* San Francisco, CA: Jossey-Bass.

Choi, B.-S., & Sakong, Y.-H. (1996). Corruption and governmental regulation. *The Korea Public Administration Journal, 5*(4), 49–71.

Crozier, M. (1964). *The bureaucratic phenomenon.* Chicago: University of Chicago Press.

Dahl, R. A. (1998). *On democracy.* New Haven, CT: Yale University Press.

Downs, A., & Corporation, R. (1967). *Inside bureaucracy.* Boston, MA: Little, Brown.

Etzioni-Halevy, E. (2013). *Bureaucracy and democracy* (Routledge Library Editions: Political Science Vol. 7). Abingdon, UK: Routledge.

Han, S.-I., & Jung, S.-Y. (2014). Bureaucracy and administrative democracy: Institutional design to embody public value in Korean text. *Journal of Governmental Studies, 20*(2), 3–33.

Held, D. (2006). *Models of democracy.* Cambridge, UK: Polity Books.

Ju, H.-J. (2004). Analyzing the street level bureaucrats' cognition types toward the regulatory reform. *Korean Policy Sciences Review, 8*(2), 194–213.

Jung, M.-K. (2011). Administrative democracy and the publicness. *Journal of Social Science, 50*(2), 33–80.

Kaufman, H. (1991). *Time, chance, and organizations: Natural selection in a perilous environment.* London: Chatham House Publishers.

Krueger, A. O. (1974). The political economy of the rent-seeking society. *The American Economic Review, 64*(3), 291–303.

Kim, Y.-P. (1988). Bureaucratic decision modes and the democratic epistemology: An epistemological understanding toward the democratic bureaucracy. *Korean Public Administration Review, 22*(2), 373–392.

Lee, H. (2013). *Regulatory review of Regulatory Reform Committee, activating method about regulatory review for reinforcing regulatory reform.* Research Paper 2013-06. Seoul: Korea Institute of Public Administration.

Lim, S.-B. (2014). A study on public official's the trend analysis of the corruption & policy issues. *Korean Corruption Studies Review, 19*(1), 29–50.

Lindblom, C. E. (1977). *Politics and markets: The world's political-economic systems.* New York: Basic Books Publishers.

Lipsky, M. (1980). *Street-level democracy: Dilemmas of the individual in public* services (30th Anniversary Expanded Edition). New York: The Russell Sage Foundation.

McChesney, F. S. (1999). Of stranded costs and stranded hopes: The difficulties of deregulation. *The Independent Review, 3*(4), 485–509.

Meier, K. J. (1985). *Regulation: Politics, bureaucracy, and economics.* Basingstoke, UK: Palgrave Macmillan.

Mitnick, B. M., Quirk, P. J., Agencies, C. R., & Brown-John, C. L. (1980). *The political economy of regulation: Creating, designing, and removing.* New York: Columbia University Press.

Myrdal, G. (1969). *An approach to the Asian drama: Methodological and theoretical.* New York: Vintage Books.

OECD. (1997). *Annual report on competition policy in Korea 1995.* Paris: OECD

Park, C.-O., & Joo, J.-H. (2007). Government bureaucracy and democracy: In search of reconciliation by methods of controlling bureaucracy. *Korean Journal of Public Administration, 45*(1), 221–253.

Park, J.-M., & Yun, G.-S. (2014). Three traditions of the state bureaucracy in South Korea. *Korean Public Administration Review, 48*(1), 1–24.

Redford, E. S. (1969). *Democracy in the administrative state.* New York: Oxford University Press.

Sager, F., & Rosser, C. (2009). Weber, Wilson, and Hegel: Theories of modern bureaucracy. *Public Administration Review, 69*(6), 1136–1147.

Sakong, Y.-H. (2002). Articles of general interest: Discretion, rent-seeking and corruption. *The Korea Association for Policy Studies, 11*(4), 75–100.

Sherman, L. W. (1980). Three models of organizational corruption in agencies of social control. *Social Problems, 27*(4), 478–491.

Stigler, G. J. (1975). *The citizen and the state: Essays on regulation* (Vol. 720). Chicago: University of Chicago Press.

Stone, D. A. (1988). *Policy paradox and political reason.* Boston, MA: Addison-Wesley Longman.

Tullock, G. (1967). The welfare costs of tariffs, monopolies, and theft. *Economic Inquiry, 5*(3), 224–232.

Vedung, E., Bemelmans-Videc, M., & Rist, R. (1998). Policy instruments: Typologies and theories. *Carrots, Sticks, and Sermons: Policy Instruments and Their Evaluation, 5,* 21–58

Williams, R. (1987). *Political Corruption in Africa.* Brookfield, VT: Gower.

Wood, B. D., & Waterman, R. W. (1994). *Bureaucratic dynamics: The role of bureaucracy in a democracy.* Boulder, CO: Westview Press.

CHAPTER 5

CHANGE AND CONTINUITY IN POLICE ORGANIZATIONS: INSTITUTION, LEGITIMACY, AND DEMOCRATIZATION*

Wonhyuk Cho

ABSTRACT

This chapter analyzes how institutional pressures have allowed for continuities as well as brought about changes in modern police organizations in Korea. When facing a legitimacy crisis, the Korean law enforcement system has typically responded with organizational restructuring. Strong myth-building patterns compensate for the lack of moral legitimacy of the police, particularly under authoritarian-military regimes that suppress democratization movements in Korea. Even after seemingly radical organizational changes aimed at placing the police under democratic control, highly institutionalized core structures of the police remain in place. Performance reform after the economic crisis, which was proceeded from reformers' shared belief in the market-driven solutions, diagnosed the Korean police as a big, inefficient,

*This chapter was previously published as Change and Continuity in Police Organizations: Institution, Legitimacy, and Democratization, in *The Korean Journal of Policy Studies*, Vol. 32, No. 1 (2017), pp. 149–174.

The Experience of Democracy and Bureaucracy in South Korea
Public Policy and Governance, 113–139
doi:10.1108/S2053-769720170000028005

*and self-serving bureaucracy, a diagnosis that eventually caused gradual
deterioration in the taken-for-grantedness of policing activities. The internet
and social media made the Korean police even more vulnerable to external
challenges and a questioning of its legitimacy.*

Keywords: Institution; legitimacy; policing; democratization; police

Police aim to control those behaviors by citizens that are dangerous to other
citizens, although its level of perceived legitimacy varies in context (Tyler &
Fagan, 2008). Developmental states try to induce societal changes, and therefore the legitimization of the police force is often the key to accomplishing
development goals (Hinton & Newburn, 2008; Im et al., 2011; Marenin,
1996), especially as law enforcement institutions play a critical role in the
democratic transformation of society (Bayley, 2006; Cheng, Haggard, &
Kang, 1998). Further, through their visibility, police forces can influence
the economic, social, and moral stability of a society (DiIulio, 1996), both
indirectly and directly, which is likewise related to democratic development
(Johnson, 1989, 2008; Cho et al., 2013; Im et al., 2013).

Studies about the role of the Korean police in Korea's democratic
development are often very normative and/or prescriptive (Kim, 2000)—
not many studies have explored the changes the police has experienced
in Korea and how these changes have affected democratic development.
A more balanced approach is required to evaluate how and why police
organizations in Korea have developed in the way they have and how the
democratization movement has affected and been affected by these changes.

This chapter approaches the phenomena from an institutional perspective, focusing on the concept of organizational legitimacy. The reason this
study focuses on the legitimacy concept is that it is central to understanding
the nature of institutional continuities and changes in the modern Korean
police. Institutionalist orientations contend that past outcomes are institutionalized in the organizational structure, and the fluctuating history of
Korea since the liberation of the country has encouraged such institutionalization. Further, the institutional perspective argues that the organization incorporates certain forms not necessarily because they are efficient
but because they are considered legitimate, which is relevant to explaining
changes in police organizations during the democratic transformation of
Korea.

THEORETICAL FRAMEWORK:
THE INSTITITIONAL PERSPECTIVE

Among variant theories of (neo)institutionalism, this study's perspective is closest to a sociological/organizational tradition in which organizations are viewed as being infused with expectations, values, and meanings from their external environment (Jay, 2013). This strand of institutionalism emphasizes legitimacy, routines, and schema (Meyer & Rowan, 1977).

Institutionalism, Persistence, and Change

Institutionalism provides an explanatory account of how organizations respond to institutional pressure (Seo & Creed, 2002). According to this view, organizational survival is dependent on whether the organization is able to meet institutional expectations, even if these expectations are not always technically related to what the organization does (DiMaggio & Powell, 1991), because what is expected of organizations is regularized by values, ideas, and beliefs that originate in the institutional context (Meyer, Scott, & Deal, 1983). This means that actors in the institutional context may unwillingly accept the prevailing template as the right way of doing things (Tolbert & Zucker, 1983; Olsen, 2009). Therefore, institutionalism emphasizes the stability of organizational arrangements (Farjoun, 2010) and even treats the unfolding of organizational change as one of constant reproduction of existing modes of thought (Greenwood & Hinings, 1996).

Institutional pressure is a powerful force against organizational change (Buckho, 1994; Ledford, Mohrman, Mohrman, & Lawler, 1989).[1] However, Oliver (1992) adopts the notion of "dissipation," which refers to a gradual deterioration in the acceptance of a particular institutionalized practice. In this conceptual framework, environmental factors contribute to deinstitutionalization—changing values, conflicting internal interests, and increasing social fragmentation result in institutionalized practices being replaced by new ones, which in turn leads to organizational change.[2] DiMaggio and Powell (1991) suggest that in the shift from the old to the new institutionalism, power becomes less important. This argument about the processes of changing legitimated templates has drawn scholarly attention to the role of intra-organizational dynamics in organizations' rejection of institutionalized practices.

On the other hand, a political model of organizational change suggests that power is paramount (Clegg, 1975). Fligstein (1991) argues that organizational change occurs when a new set of actors gains power or when those in power have an interest in altering the organization's goals. Greenwood and Hinings (1996) suggest that organizationally defined groups have differential power, meaning different abilities enable them to make organizational change. Social audiences listen more keenly to certain groups, and these groups have more power to enable or resist organizational changes—further, these powerful groups are able to constitute or recreate organizational structures according to their preferences (Ranson, Hinings, & Greenwood, 1980). The differential power that groups have is useful to understanding the operation of interests. Organizational studies on political power claim that organizational change is accomplished by appeals to the normative visions of the social audiences of organizations (Collins & Porras, 1991).

Isomorphic organizational change is another key institutionalist concept. Isomorphism incorporates elements that are externally legitimated, and organizations' dependence on externally fixed institutional practices stabilizes the environment within which they are operating (DiMaggio & Powell, 1991). Isomorphic changes are classified as coercive, mimetic, and normative (Mizruchi & Fein, 1999). Coercive isomorphism results from the legitimacy problem and political influence; mimetic isomorphism stems from standard responses to uncertainty; and normative isomorphism is caused by professionalization. We should note that mimetic, normative, and coercive mechanisms are parts of the institutional context and that the strength of these kinds of pressure is not equivalent.

Legitimacy: Social Audience, Value, and Myth Building

This study particularly focuses on the institutional legitimacy.[3] Legitimacy explains what an organization is doing and why (Jepperson, 1991). Legitimacy enhances organizational survival, stability, and continuity and protects organizations from institutional pressure (Ashforth & Gibbs, 1990; Meyer & Rowan, 1977; Suchman, 1995).[4] Legitimate organizations are able to choose their organizational structure and enjoy substantial freedom to pursue their affairs in the way they want (Brown, 1998; Deephouse, Bundy, Tost, & Suchman, 2016; Knoke, 1988).

Institutionalist researchers tend to conceptualize legitimacy as a set of institutionalized beliefs (DiMaggio & Powell, 1983, 1991; Meyer & Rowan, 1991; Meyer & Scott, 1983; Zucker, 1987).[5] Meyer and Scott (1983) take the view that organizational legitimacy refers to the degree of "cultural support" for an organization. This conceptualization highlights cognitive aspect of legitimacy, treating it as the array of established cultural accounts explaining an organization's existence—the emphasis on cultural conformity rather than on overt self-justification of an organization's right to exist is a noteworthy contribution of this conceptualization. According to this view, no question is raised about a completely legitimate organization—the absence of questioning is central to this concept.[6]

Suchman (1995) highlights that legitimacy is a generalized perception within a socially constructed system of norms, acknowledging the role of social audience in legitimization dynamics. Social audiences perceive legitimate organizations as more meaningful, not just as more worthy of existing. Social audiences of organizations supply resources to them, allowing them to persist (Parsons, 1960). External audiences can determine how the organization is built, how it is run, and how it is understood. Meyer and Rowan (1991) suggest that organizations build myths using institutionalized programs, and diffuse them via a relational network. Institutionalized activities of legitimate organizations are supported by the mobilization of myths embedded in the system (Suchman, 1995; Zucker, 1988).

Legitimacy is defined in the scholarly literature as having three dimensions: pragmatic, moral, and cognitive (Suchman, 1995). Pragmatic legitimacy is based on the self-interested calculations of social audiences whose well-being is affected by organizations' activities. Moral legitimacy, by contrast, is based on normative evaluations (Aldrich & Fiol, 1994; Palthe, 2014)—this is why the institutionalist tends to refer to moral legitimacy as normative legitimacy (Powell & DiMaggio, 1991). Moral legitimacy is not judged by the expected benefits of an organization's activity but by whether the activity is the right thing to do—therefore, social audiences' socially constructed value system is reflected in this judgment. Although the ascription of moral legitimacy is not completely interest free, social audiences' prosocial evaluation is different from purely self-interested consideration. Cognitive legitimacy is based on taken-for-grantedness. This taken-for-grantedness is the most powerful source of legitimacy, because it has the effect of making alternatives unthinkable and challenges nearly impossible (Zucker, 1983).

Institutionalism and Legitimacy in Police Studies

Police departments and law enforcement units are highly institutionalized organizations and therefore are well suited to being approached from an institutionalist perspective (Carter, 2016; Crank & Langworthy, 1992). Crank and Langworthy (1992) argue that an institutional orientation emerged in police studies as a reaction to the limitation of a normative focus on the traditional theory of police organization—that is, disappointment with the results of normative theories of reforms in police organizations in the United States led scholars to pay attention to the institutional environment. Police research in the normative mode links particular types of organizational structure to desired goals, but Langworthy (1986) suggests that the search for the best structure for police organizations in this traditional normative research fails to explain the role of institutional contexts that mediate between structure and effectiveness.

Crack and Langworthy (1992) emphasize the role of institutional environments and myth building in attaining police legitimacy—according to this view, survival of a police agency and its ability to secure resources to support its fundamental well-being are dependent on whether sovereigns accept the legitimacy of the police organization. Symbolic attributes such as police uniforms, ranks, insignia, and traditional titles are important sources of legitimacy (Crank & Langworthy, 1992).

The institutionalist perspective has been mainly used to explain community-policing movements in the United States. In 1960s, a drastic increase in crime and media-depicted police brutality against civil rights protesters significantly delegitimized existing myths about the police's professionalism and autonomy in the fight against crime. A relegitimization strategy was the community-policing movement grounded in the myth of community (Crank, 1994). Community policing was originally a means of overcoming the limitations of the professionally based policing model, but after a certain point, community policing itself came to be taken for granted as the right way to police. Zhao et al. (2001) explain why organizational priorities in American policing have remained unchanged even after the proliferation of community-policing programs in the United States. They argue that the community-policing paradigm has been used somewhat strategically by police organizations to buffer the undesired impact of challenges to the professional model of policing.

Police studies with an institutionalist orientation tend to emphasize the idea that organizational change is affected by external pressure—legitimatization by sovereigns is a key concept. High visibility and the investigative nature of policing require relatively higher levels of acceptance of legitimacy from sovereigns compared to the other government activities. On the other hand, it should be noted that core features of police organizations have been found to persist over time and that change is in fact more peripheral.

This study analyzes the modern history of Korean police organizations using the institutional perspective. We draw on institutionalist concepts such as sovereign, legitimacy, myth building, isomorphism, and ceremonial/ritual activities to explain how the Korean police has adopted certain practices and what features have persisted.

CONTINUITIES AND CHANGES IN THE KOREAN POLICE

In Korea, the police has traditionally been a national/federal organization—all provincial and city police are under the jurisdiction of the national police. The Korean police has maintained strong paramilitary characteristics, and its activities tend to be highly investigative. The national police system of Korea has been developed via institutional interaction with diverse actors such as domestic political leaders, civil society, the military, and other countries. Since its establishment in 1894, the modern Korean police has experienced dramatic events such as colonialization of the country, civil war, military coup, and subsequent political instability. Over the course of this turbulent history, the legitimacy of the Korean police has been challenged and re-established, a process that has been closely connected with the country's democratization process.

Colonial Police (1910–1945): Modernization of Brutality

Many authors agree that the traditional focus of the Korean police was law enforcement activities, and that this focus dates back to the history of Japanese occupation of Korea (Lee, 2007). The Japanese colonial regime annexed Korea in 1910 and controlled Korea for almost half a century. The Japanese deployed the colonial police to monitor Korean citizens while they pursued their exploitative goals and eventually to oversee law enforcement on the peninsula as a part of Japan's imperialist regime (Kim, 2012). Japanese officers were dispatched at all levels of the colonial police organization and supervised Korean law enforcement personnel from patrolmen to top-rank managers (Cho, 2015). Because of this close supervision at every level, colonial police organizations were a carbon copy of the Japanese police (Esselstrom, 2009; Hoffman, 1991), although the colonial police in Korea were much more brutal than the native police (Choi, 2008). Korean people came to have a deep-seated hatred of the police force during this period, which is evidenced in the series of events after the independence of the nation such as the killing of former colonial officers and the burning of their houses (Kim, 2012).

From the fourteenth century until the late nineteenth century, Korea's police unit was a part of the army (Lim, 2010). Crime control was a responsibility of this semi-military organization, and communities collaborated with it (Lee, 2007). In 1894, the Korean police was separated from the military when Japan intervened in Korea's internal affairs as part of its initial imperialistic move (Kim, 2012). The Japanese imported their centralized modern police organization into Korea as a means of controlling of the colonized (Esselstrom, 2009), and Japanese police officers were stationed in almost all major cities, where they took control of police organizations and investigated anti-Japanese movements (Pyo, 2001; Heo, 2005). In 1907, the Japanese intention to colonize Korea became more apparent, and police administration was restructured to allow Japanese police personnel to occupy every important position in the law enforcement system in Korea (Cho, 2015)—this granted the Japanese police authority to closely monitor publication, immigration, and residential registration in the colony.

By 1908, the number of Japanese police personnel in Korea had increased to more than 50% of the entire Korean police force (Kim, 2012; Myong, 1959). Japanese police were at the frontline of the colonization attempt (Steinberg, 1968), with the number of police being one for every 400 Korean citizens (Esselstrom, 2009; Hoffman, 1991).

In 1910, just after it secured full control over the Korean police force, the Japanese colonial regime formally annexed Korea as a part of its territory (Cho, 2015). Colonial police in Korea were under the direct supervision of the Japanese governor general, and brutal repression of the colonized people was the most prominent feature of policing in this period (Kim, 2012; Myong, 1959). Military-like colonial police stations were established in rural areas in Korea, and more than 12,000 colonial police officers were dispatched to these stations to control Korean citizens (Heo, 2005). The Japanese colonial regime dramatically increased the number of colonial police stations from 480 to 730 within the three years after the formal annexation of Korea, and Japanese police personnel in Korea held high-ranking positions (Hoffman, 1982; Myong, 1959).

Colonial police officers were granted very extensive authority over the populace, including the power to censor publications. The colonial police extended its control beyond what was legal; it frequently arrested Korean people without warrant and then kept them imprisoned for long periods without holding trials, denying them bail (Lee, 2015). There was no habeas corpus; indeed, those arrested were tortured instead (Chung, 1921).

The criminal court of this period served the colonial government, and almost all judges were Japanese, which meant there was no right to appeal a conviction (Lee, 2015). Colonial police also executed Korean citizens who supported exiled Koreans whose activities were directly or indirectly related to the independence movement (Esselstrom, 2009; Lee, 2007).

In the early 1920s, after massive nonviolent independence demonstrations in Korea, the Japanese colonial police began to turn over crime control and peace-keeping duties to civilian colonial officers (Kim, 2012; Myong, 1959). However, the real aim of this change was to use the civilian officers to monitor the daily activities of Korean citizens to prevent any anticolonial activity and to disseminate colonial ideology to the population in an attempt to secure support for the imperialist regime. The colonial civilian police force could still exercise almost unbounded discretion to treat the Korean populace violently.

Through coercive processes, the Japanese colonial regime produced a carbon copy of its centralized policing system in the Korean context. The brutality of policing in the colonial period instilled a hostility toward police that was passed on for decades between generations (Kim, 2012; Lee, 2007). A lack of moral legitimacy among police has been found to be a negative legacy of this period.

Postcolonial Police and Civil War (1945–1953): Response to Uncertainty

When Korea was liberated after the Second World War, the United States occupied the south of the peninsula while the Soviet Union occupied the north for a temporary peace-keeping purpose. The American occupation force, also called the U.S. military government of Korea, reorganized the police in postcolonial Korea to fill the administrative vacuum that remained after the Japanese retreated (Kim, 2008). In 1945, the U.S. military government established a police bureau as the national policing unit, putting the national defense director in charge of supervising it. In 1946, the national police department was designated to oversee the police, replacing the national defense director. This structural reform was based on U.S. advisors' recommendations. It was hoped that this reform would help the police force recruit more Koreans as police officers and procure advanced equipment and lead to the establishment of a modernized police school, the elimination of summary punishment, the creation of a national police board, and the enactment of civil right laws (Kim, 2006).

Unfortunately, despite some meaningful attempts to modernize the law enforcement system, the postcolonial regime governed by the U.S. military government did not succeed in shifting the orientation of police activity in Korea from a service-to-government one to a service-to-citizen one (Kim, 2009; Meade, 1951; Moon & Morash, 2004). This is at least partly because the reorganization of police in this period was heavily based on the Japanese model (Kim, 2008). For example, the U.S. military government decided to utilize former colonial police officers, who served the interests of the Japanese colonial regime, to deal with the shortage of police-trained manpower and to manage postcolonial social instability (Meade, 1951).[7] Out of 25,000 police officials in 1946, more than a half of the officers were former colonial officers. Due to the organizational and behavioral similarities between the colonial and postcolonial police, the populace's deep-seated hatred toward colonial police remained intact.

When the Korean War broke out in 1950, just two years after Korea was established as an independent modern nation, the police had to take on military-like responsibilities such as counterguerrilla activities, military traffic control, intelligence operations, and refugee control (Bark, 1966). During the war, more than 10,000 Korean police officers were killed in action, and many more were severely injured. The military-like operations during the Korean war were an extension of the types of activities carried out by the centralized and highly investigative police force before the war, and police involvement in full-scale war further institutionalized the military-style investigative tradition of Korean police.

After liberation, the political vacuum in postcolonial Korea generated much uncertainty, which led the new government to rely on pre-existed organizational forms and to even hire former colonial officers. Deep-seated hatred toward the former colonial policing system was the evident source of the legitimacy challenges that this colonial, bureaucracy-based police force faced. However, at the same time, the public's acceptance of the need for military-like operations and the urgency of the manpower shortage aided the isomorphic absorption of the colonial police force and its centralized paramilitary organizational templates.

The Postwar Police under Syngman Rhee (1953–1961): A Political Force

The Korean War ended in 1953, but the threat from North Korea persisted, which occasionally even attempted territorial incursions.[8] In order to manage the North Korean military threat and its intelligence activity, the political leadership in the Republic of Korea wanted to maintain a paramilitary police force (Seo, 1996). This highly centralized police organization did not just serve national defense purposes, however—it also served the political goals of President Syngman Rhee and his ruling political party (Heo, 2005; Kim, 2009). An excessive use of police force was unacceptable to the Korean people, who had experienced the brutality of the Japanese colonial police (Bark, 1966).

That a highly centralized and repressive law enforcement organization remained in place even after the Korean War had ended and the threat from North Korean incursion diminished can be attributed to fact that the police template from the colonial era was deeply institutionalized (Ha, 2002; Kim, 2008). Once this form of modernized and centralized policing was institutionalized, the populace accepted it as a taken-for-granted form of law enforcement.

After the anti-dictatorship movement got under way in Korea in 1950s, the Korean police was used by the authoritarian government to coerce the population to fall in line with the interests of top political leaders (Heo, 2005; Kim, 2000). For example, the Korean police was deeply involved in manipulating elections, most prominently the presidential elections of the 1960s, and it arrested and interrogated political rivals of ruling parties (Jung & Kim, 2014). There were various clashes between anti-authoritarianism movement leaders and the police due to the human rights violations committed by the Korean police. Resentment over the police's involvement in manipulating elections challenged the legitimacy of policing activities, although propaganda idolizing the cause of national defense was an effective strategy that buffered questioning against oppressive and punitive law enforcement.

In spite of the inertia preventing nonsuperficial reform in policing, there were certainly attempts to effect change. The political dissent against President Syngman Rhee gradually assumed a strength that led to his eviction from office in early 1960 (Hong, 1995). When it was revealed that the police was involved in manipulating the results of the presidential election in 1961, anger over the corrupt system, which was maintained by repressive law enforcement organizations, led a massive group of college students to demonstrate in the streets (Jung & Kim, 2014). Korean police confronted these protesters with a violent show of force that caused hundreds of deaths, which in turn resulted in uncontrollable outrage from the public (Kim, 2001).

Prime Minister Myun Jang tried to stabilize the political situation after the resignation of the president, and the newly established government under the Prime Minister attempted to restructure the police force and the law enforcement system (Ha, 2014). The public safety commissioners were given the authority to create police policy, and these commissioners had to be approved by the legislature. There was an initial attempt to ensure police neutrality and to reorient the organization toward more citizen-serving purposes. However, this attempt to reorient the police failed to be institutionalized because of the military coup in 1961.

Policing under Military Dictatorship (1961–1987): Myth Building

Attempts to para-militarize Korean policing patterns returned after the coup in 1961 mounted by the military officer Chung-hee Park (Kim, 2004), who reorganized the national police force in his authoritarian military government. At this stage, however, even a dictator could not fully overlook the public's democratic aspirations (Yi, 2006). In response to the democratic movement growing in the country, Park adopted so-called "managed democracy" (Wolin, 2010), responding to external pressure with superficial and peripheral changes in governing. This "fake" democracy, as a closely contested electoral race makes clear, was managed by propaganda issued by the police and the intelligence agency (Heo, 2005; Kim, 2004). The assertion of a national security crisis, whether substantial or exaggerated, was a powerful legitimization strategy (Kim, 2004).

Intelligence activity formerly carried out by the police was the responsibility of a newly established counterintelligence agency (Kim, 2004). This intelligence organization was empowered with authority to monitor and control Korean citizens as a means of counteracting the communist revolution in the south (Suh, 1976; Vreeland, 1975, p. 324), and policing was under the supervision of this agency as well. Ex-military officers were employed to fill high-ranking police positions, and they collected information about political dissent, labor activists, and antigovernment student movements (Heo, 2005; Holtman, 1982).

A national police affairs office was established in 1974. The director general of police was given very extensive policing power, and the political influence from the military government continued to increase (Heo, 2005). Military-like activities were still common even decades after the Korean War ended. The Korean counterintelligence agency likewise carried out such activities, arresting, investigating, interrogating, and detaining protestors against the dictatorship and political revolutionaries, who were subsequently punished by the court under the guise of eliminating the security threat from communist North Korea (Jun & Yoon, 1996; Vreeland, 1975). The democratic movement was suppressed even more after President Park declared martial law, recasting the constitution into a highly authoritarian document (Chung, 2006).

It was an irony that President Park was assassinated by the chief officer of his own intelligence agency in 1979 after having survived several previous assassination attempts by the North Korean government. President Park's assassination brought another military regime into power, headed up by Chun Doo-hwan, who dissolved the Korean national assembly and maintained an authoritarian military government in Korea until 1987. In the process of his military coup, Chun ordered special units to hunt down democratization activists in Gwang-ju city, which massacred more than 2000 civilians, including many innocent citizens (Kim, 2014). After Chun became a president with a rubber-stamp election in 1980, the authoritarian regime continued to suppress the democratization movement and the police was again at the frontline (Im, 2004).

During this period, Korean citizens were reluctant to actively ask for any changes in policing because to do so would be regarded as part and parcel of a communism-driven revolutionary plot (Jung & Kim, 2014). Further, foundation of civil society in Korea was very vulnerable partly due to the colonial legacy and in part owing to the public's resentment on betrayal of the business class in Korea, which was supposed to support the anti-government movement but which subserviently collaborated with the Japanese colonial regime and supported President Rhee's corrupt government (Bark, 1996; Cho, 2015; Heo, 2005).

During the authoritarian period, external pressure for democratic control of the police by the citizenry gradually intensified (Jung & Kim, 2014; Kim, 2000). Although the change was gradual, the police became more oriented toward peacekeeping and crime control. Some scholars argue that it was effective in crime control (Kim, 2005)—compared to other developing countries, Korea has maintained relatively higher level of safety in its streets, neighborhoods, and cities (Im & Park, 2010).

On the other hand, the national police did engage in public relations efforts in an attempt to retain a level of police legitimacy, promoting a citizen-friendly image (Korean National Police, 1981). The myth-building efforts under the guise of the North Korean communist threat served their purpose, as the peace lasted for decades without full-scale war. The British-American model of law enforcement and its citizen-oriented policing were first introduced in Korea in the late 1970s as methods of re-legitimizing the Korean police. For example, government publication materials emphasized citizen-friendly policing activities while only briefly mentioning the law enforcement function (Kim, 2006)—blending of professionalism and elitism with police image was another message sent via these police publications.

This was certainly a change, as the printed police materials before this period had emphasized only the urgent need to strike at and sweep away the so-called communist remnants from the south. However, the citizen-serving model was not truly adopted as an institutionalized organizational template of the police organization because no substantial restructuring took place. Changes were superficial, merely declared in printed materials and not carried out. The claim to have restructured can be understood as a myth-building strategy to defuse external pressure for democratic control over the police.

Democratic Control over the Police (1987–1998):
Accomplishments and Limitations

During the late 1980s, the later phase of the military dictatorship, the police was deployed to break up democratization movements. Violent clashes between police and demonstrators resulted in serious injuries and deaths, and the legitimacy of police activities under the authoritarian regime gradually deteriorated (Jung & Kim, 2014; Kim, 2004; Moon & Morash, 2009). The external pressure brought to bear for democracy was no longer negligible—it became too difficult for the political regime to insulate oppressive police activities by claiming they were necessary owing to the threat from North Korea.

To address the Korean police's political neutrality problem, several reforms were introduced in the early 1990s. Under the Police Act enacted in 1991, a national police agency was established, and in order to ensure its political autonomy and democratic control, it was not subject to the supervision of the Ministry of the Interior (Heo, 2005). This reform was focused on changing the structure of the interorganizational relationship that had long made the police subservient to the undemocratic political leadership (Kim, 2004; Moon & Morash, 2009).

Civilianizing the police was one of the major efforts undertaken to change the police bureaucracy, and for this purpose, the government appointed non-military and nonpolice civilians as head of the police and created civilian boards and committees in public safety policy decision making. For example, a national police board was created to increase democratic control over police administration (Kim, 2006). This civilian board took part in budgetary/financial management, personnel administration, and investigation of police's human rights abuses. The national police agency had to adopt, at least in appearance, very extensive operational reforms, such as restrictions in the use of tear gas in dealing with public protests. The image of brutality and lack of democratic control were major sources of the delegitimization of the police in this period, and therefore, it needed to seriously consider the shared value of democracy in the institutional environment.

President Kim Young-sam's regime (1993–1998) was considered a truly civilian government after decades of military dictatorship, and it implemented numerous administrative reforms, including breaking up the central police force into localized street-level police stations so that it would be able to react more effectively to crime in the communities (Moon & Morash, 2009). In Korea, decentralization was considered one of the pillars of democratization (Im & Cho, 2008; Kang et al., 2012) and so this change can be understood as part and parcel of the democratization effort. This organizational change also reflected the growing need for crime protection (Heo, 2005).

However, many authors have pointed out that the police act had serious limitations in bringing substantive organizational change to the Korean police (Moon & Morash, 2009; Yoon, 2001). The institutionalized core of the bureaucracy remained intact, and the police force continued to serve the interests of ruling government, violently dealing with many student protests (Jung & Kim, 2014). The civilian board did not (or could not) exercise any constraining influence on police behavior. The political autonomy of the police was not fully ensured by this structural change because the primary supervising office was still under the Ministry of the Interior, and furthermore there were numerous indirect ways to influence on police (Kim, 2006). The commissioner general and all high-rank police managers tended to be appointees of a patronage system, which served a strong control mechanism over the police.

Again, the change was superficial despite its "looking" very different. The democratization measures in the early 1990s restrained police activities only in part. In fact, these measures were utilized as a relegitimization strategy to address external pressure to allow democratic control of the police by the civilian populace and to deflect attention away from the fact that changes in the core structure were minimal.

Performance Reform in Policing (1998–Present):
Financial Pressure in the Digital Era

Starting in the late 1990s, Korean society faced drastic social changes generated by economic crisis and the growth of the internet. In 1997, a fall in foreign currency reserves, caused by a profound moral-hazard problem embedded in the economic structure, forced the country to seek a rescue loan from the International Monetary Fund. The International Monetary Fund required Korea to completely restructure its economy and government administration (Campbell & Cho, 2014; Kim & Cho, 2012). Major companies were bankrupted, and many workers lost their jobs. The financial burden for the Korean government was significant, and the public sector was one of the primary targets of the reform (Im et al., 2014; Kim & Cho, 2014). Newly elected president Dae-jung Kim declared that the economic crisis was the greatest national challenge the country had faced since the Korean war.

This economic crisis led to external pressure for the police to reorganize itself into more efficient and citizen-oriented institution (Yoon, 2001), and so in 1998, the Korean police created a task force to initiate and implement performance reform. The Korean government pushed the national police agency to develop a more market-, performance-, and customer-oriented structure (Yun & Cheong, 2010), which led reformers to look to the New Public Management (NPM) (Cho, 2013). Among the reformers, who emerged as important actors in the institutional environment of police, there was a strong shared belief that NPM measures could completely resolve the problems of the Korean police bureaucracy (Lee & Lee, 2009) and more the magic of NPM could create a "small, efficient, and better-serving" government. Besides the controversy regarding whether the NPM could actually turn the Korean police into a born-again organization, another notable aspect of this performance reform is that it depicted the Korean government as a big, inefficient, and self-serving bureaucracy, which seriously eroded its pragmatic legitimacy as well as that of the national police agency. It is interesting that reformers drew on this NPM-driven Western-style performance management not only as a way to question the legitimacy of the police but also a re-legitimatization strategy insofar as the accomplishments of the market-oriented solutions adopted by police organizations were held up for praise.

Studies have found that these results-oriented performance reforms did not much improve the efficiency of the police (Lee & Lee, 2009). Many of the changes were not well-institutionalized, especially in the street-level bureaucracy (Cho, 2013). Some studies even show that the performance reform measures have gradually been deinstitutionalized over the last several years (Lee & Lim, 2012). High-ranking members of the Korean police resisted many elements of the performance-driven restructuring (Cho, 2013).

Even if one acknowledges that the organizational structure changed quite extensively at least formally, such as in the creation of subunits and the merging of related departments in this period, the police remained in essence a highly institutionalized service-to-government entity, especially in the behavioral patterns of police officers (Lee & Lee, 2009). Police officers in the authoritarian era were socialized in an organization where investigative ways of policing were highly institutionalized, and so it is not surprising that the organizational culture lacks a citizen-serving spirit even after a series of customer-oriented reforms. Many police officers try to maintain the traditional police model, but they face very serious citizen resistance. Cho (2013) has shown that many Korean citizens do not accept even legitimate police discretion such as stop and frisk.

Another characteristic of the institutional environment in this period was the growth of the internet (Im et al., 2014; Porumbescu, 2016), which posed great challenges to the legitimacy of Korean law-enforcement organizations. Instances of discretionary use of power on the part of the police can be depicted as misconduct and easily exposed and spread via the internet through blogs, internet journals, and social media such as Facebook and Twitter (cf. Porumbescu, 2015). In this environment, citizens began to question the legitimacy of the police and revealed their deep-seated hatred toward the police. The discretionary authority of police officers is now often ignored, and one consequences of this is that the Korean police feels unauthorized to perform even its peace-keeping duties (Cho, 2013).

This lack of legitimacy is combined with historically rooted antagonism toward the Korean police. There have been cases in which citizens have attacked police stations and beat police officers, and street-level police officers are often punched, kicked, and struck by citizens. Thus, some Korean police officers have recently refused to actively become involved in crime control and remain as by-standers even when a crime is being committed in their presence (cf. Cho, 2013; Lee & Lee, 2009).

Most recently, the Korean police has emphasized community policing (Kim, 2002) as both a citizen-serving tool and a possible source of re-legitimation. This echoes to an extent how community policing in the United States operated. However, the myth of community and/or the mythology of the watchman does not figure in the Korean context, and therefore, it is questionable how well community policing can be institutionalized as a legitimization strategy.

DISCUSSION: INSTITUTION, LEGITIMACY, AND DEMOCRATIZATION

The results of the institutional analysis of this study are summarized in Table 1. We found that throughout all periods institutional pressures have encouraged

Table 1. Continuity and Change in Police Organizations in Korea.

Period	Institutional Environment	Challenges to Legitimacy	Myth-Building Strategies	Organizational Changes/Shifts	Continuity/Inertia
Colonial police [1910–1945]	Colonization (exploitation of the colonized)/ anti-imperialist movement	Lack of moral support for colonial regime	Emphasis on modernization of police force/ transplantation of colonial identity	Coercive semi-militarization/ co-optation of colonial officers/ institutionalization of unbounded discretion	Centralized bureaucracy/ paramilitary structure
Postcolonial and wartime police [1945–1953]	Social uncertainty/ administrative incompetency/ full-scale warfare	Deep-seated hatred toward former (colonial) policing system/resistance to foreign (external) influence	Emphasis on need for military-like missions/ emphasizing urgency of manpower shortage	Isomorphic absorption of colonial police force/establishment of a police bureau	Focus on investigative policing activities/ centralized control over police bureaucracy
Postwar police [1953–1961]	Political chaos/ continuing security threat/ territorial incursions	Resentment over police's involvement in manipulation of elections/antagonistic confrontation with civil society	Propaganda management (idolizing the cause of national defense)/ highlighting of postwar stabilization	Efforts to institutionalize legislative approval requirement for public safety commissioners (failed owing to coup)	Service-to-government orientation/ oppressive and punitive law enforcement/control orientation
Military dictatorship [1961–1987]	Nation-wide democratization movement/ rising crime caused by drastic urbanization	Intensifying protests against dictatorship/ citizen's questioning of police neutrality/ growing hostility toward police as a result of its abuse of power	Accentuation of urgent need to counteract communist revolution/ blending of police professionalism and elitism/introducing citizen-friendly policing	Publications promoting citizen-friendly and professional image (published in greater numbers)/ empowerment of counterintelligence function of police	Reliance on investigative tradition/ authoritarian control by police forces/military-like organizational culture

Democratic control [1987–1998]	Establishment of civilian (nonmilitary) regime/ intensification of populace's desire for democracy/ lower security threat	Citizens' dissent against continued oppressiveness of policing activities/ strong social demands for anticorruption measures	Civilianizing of police (e.g., appointment of nonmilitary and nonpolice civilian as the head of police)/creation of civilian boards and committees (e.g., the national police board) for public safety policy making	Establishment of a national police agency (1991 police act)/ assurance of *de jure* independence of police from Ministry of Interior/breakup of central police force into local street-level stations (decentralization)	*De facto* control by Ministry of Interior (indirect and informal)/inability of civilian board to exercise substantial influence on decision making
Performance reform in policing [1998–present]	National economic crisis/external monitoring and advising on admin reforms/diffusion of Internet and social media (high visibility)	Reformers' prescription for a small, efficient and better-serving police force (external pressure/citizens' disapproval of police's discretionary authority/viral social media reports on police misconduct	Adoption of NPM-driven measures (idolization of market-oriented solutions/marketing of customer-oriented policing policies/ introduction of community-policing paradigm	Creation of a police reform task force/ implementation of Western-style performance management/use of citizen satisfaction as performance indicator	Professionalism-based model of policing/lack of citizen-serving organizational culture

both continuity and change in the Korean police. A typical response to legitimacy crises faced by the police has been to restructure the Korean law enforcement system. Myth-building strategies have been formulated to compensate for the questioning of the legitimacy of the police by social audiences. But even in the wake of seemingly radical organizational changes, highly institutionalized core structures of the police remain intact.

Repressive policing was institutionalized in Korea during the Japanese colonial period, and this institutionalized style of policing has persisted, although it has been modified. The government's decision to absorb the colonial police force into the newly established independent Republic of Korea deprived the new police force of moral legitimacy. This in turn led to a series of myth-building efforts by the authoritarian regime. A lack of moral legitimacy constitutes an important institutional "previous-ness" for the Korean police force and remains one of the key characteristics of Korean law enforcement institutions even today. This has served as a driver, pushing the police to constantly seek ways to compensate with other types of legitimacy, such as pragmatic legitimacy, and with myth building centered around symbols and ceremonies.

The Korean War and the security threat from North Korea created an institutional environment that led Korean citizens to be more accepting of the pragmatic legitimacy of repressive policing (Kutnjak, Ivkovic & Kang, 2012). However, during the democratization of Korea, decision makers had to deal with the strong desire of the public to wield democratic control over the police force. As a result, in 1991, the Korean police was drastically reorganized and were now expected to be politically neutral. Even with these dramatic changes, however, a number of core policing functions have persisted, because in this different institutional environment, the police sought legitimization by changing lower and less fundamental layers of their organization.

The Korean police and its legitimacy have been greatly challenged in years between the economic crisis and the present. The economic crisis of Korea required the government to adopt reforms that would introduce efficient and cost-saving operations. In this performance-reform process, the pragmatic legitimacy of the police bureaucracy seriously deteriorated, while the lack of moral legitimacy and deep-seated hatred remained. This deterioration led Korean citizens to resist police actions that until then had been largely taken for granted as acceptable. The growth of the internet, which had made it possible to report the misconduct of police officers on a real-time basis via social media, reinforced this deterioration, leaving the legitimacy of the police vulnerable to citizens' questioning, for example. That is, the development of the internet and information technology has put rise new and very different pressures on the police.

CONCLUSION

This chapter shows how the Korean police organization has both changed over time and retained certain characteristics of its highly institutionalized core structure. When it faced a legitimacy crisis, it attempted an organizational restructuring. However, there was continuity even in the wake of this seemingly radical organizational change, and the behavior of Korean police officers has been affected by these stable elements. The analysis in this study has demonstrated that the Korean police has resisted changes that conflict with the values shared by the public and has only undertaken changes that conform with those values.

As we have shown in this chapter, contemporary policing issues and problems in Korea are best understood in the broader institutional context. This institutional understanding of Korean police organizations is necessary in order to change them so that they end up meeting the needs of citizens they serve. Further investigation into the cultural dimensions of the institutional context is required to formulate practical strategies for solving public safety issues in Korea. The findings of this research should also contribute to the growing literature on governance legitimacy (Christensen et al., 2016; Yang, 2016). Regarding the contemporary challenges of public cynicism that the Korean police faces, better communication with citizens and online engagement that keeps them better informed about what is going on in public safety issues might be helpful (see Ho & Cho, 2017).

NOTES

1. March and Olsen (1983, 1996) have identified internal factors that produce resistance to organizational changes, while Meyer and Rowan (1991) have identified external factors that force organizations to embark on change. A two-stage dissemination model of change is suggested by Tolbert and Zucker (1983)—in this model, institutional pressures become more important in the later stage of the development of an organizational field, whereas technical performance requirements are more salient in the earlier stages of the development of the field. Institutionalists have subsequently proposed mechanisms of imitation, focusing on interlocking directorates (Davis & Powell, 1992; Palmer, Jennings, & Zhou, 1993).

2. Greenwood and Hinings (1996) suggest that organizational change is instigated by dissatisfaction with the way that interests are accommodated within an organization, proposing that interest dissatisfaction leads to radical change only if it is associated with a competitive pattern of value commitments—this means that interest dissatisfaction otherwise precipitates convergent change.

3. Suchman (1995) states that institutionalization and legitimacy are almost synonymous.

4. There are three different sources of legitimacy (Meyer & Rowan, 1977)—rational effectiveness, legal mandate, and collectively valued purpose—dimensions that have been renamed in more recent literature as pragmatic legitimacy, regulatory/sociopolitical legitimacy, and normative/moral legitimacy, respectively.

5. Early institutionalist literature embraced Weber's analysis of legitimacy and regarded legitimacy as the congruence of an organization with social norms and values (Parsons, 1960; Dowling & Pfeffer, 1975).

6. Hirsch and Andrew (1986) identify two different ways of organizations that are not perceived as wholly legitimate are questioned, namely by probing how well agreed-on goals are met (performance challenge) and by inquiring about an organization's mission (value challenge).

7. Given the absence of proper background checks and a failure to establish criteria for hiring, many unqualified personnel, some even with criminal records, were recruited.

8. Officially, it was a ceasefire that was secured via a truce agreement.

ACKNOWLEDGMENT

This research is supported by National Research Foundation of Korea (NRF 2014S1A3A2044898).

REFERENCES

Aldrich, H. E., & Fiol, C. M. (1994). Fools rush in? The institutional context of industry creation. *Academy of Management Review, 19*(4), 645–670.

Ashforth, B. E., & Gibbs, B. W. (1990). The double-edge of organizational legitimation. *Organization Science, 1*(2), 177–194.

Bark, D. S. (1966). The history of Korean police administration, 1945–64. *Korean Journal of Public Administration, 4*(2), 49–94.

Bayley, D. H. (2006). *Changing the guard: Developing democratic police abroad.* Oxford: Oxford University Press.

Brown, A. D. (1998). Narrative, politics, and legitimacy in an IT implementation. *Journal of Management Studies, 35*(1), 35–58.

Buchko, A. A. (1994). Conceptualization and measurement of environmental uncertainty: An assessment of the Miles and Snow perceived environmental uncertainty scale. *Academy of Management Journal, 37*(2), 410–425.

Campbell, J. W., & Cho, W. (2014). Two faces of government-business relations during South Korea's developmental period. *Korean Comparative Government Review*, *18*(1), 47–66.

Carter, J. G. (2016). Institutional pressures and isomorphism: The impact on intelligence-led policing adoption. *Police Quarterly*, *19*(4), 435–560.

Cheng, T. J., Haggard, S., & Kang, D. (1998). Institutions and growth in Korea and Taiwan: The bureaucracy. *Journal of Development Studies*, *34*(6), 87–111.

Cho, S. T. (2015). Review of the police's role during the Japanese colonial era. *Korean Public Administration History Review*, *37*, 79–102.

Cho, W. (2013). Discretionary behavior of public employees in police organizations: Grounded theory approach to public management in Korea. *Korean Public Administration Review*, *47*(3), 389–423.

Cho, W., Im, T., Cha, S., Jeong, J., & Lee, M. (2013). A cross-county comparison of government competitiveness: Measures and evaluations. *Korean Comparative Government Review*, *17*(2), 95–124

Choi, S. (2008). *A study of the Korean police in the disappointed era of the Korean empire.* Seoul: National Research Foundation of Korea.

Christensen, T., Laegreid, P., & Rykkja, L. H. (2016). Organizing for crisis management: Building governance capacity and legitimacy. *Public Administration Review*, *76*(6), 887–897.

Chung, I. J. (2006). Antinomy of the Yushin system and ROK-US conflicts: National security without democracy. *Society and Theory*, *70*, 149–178.

Clegg, S. (1975). *Power, rule, and domination: A critical and empirical understanding of power in sociological theory and everyday life.* London: Routledge and Kegan Paul.

Collins, J. C., & Porras, J. I. (1991). Organizational vision and visionary organizations. *California Management Review*, *34*(1), 30–52.

Crank, J. P. (1994). Watchman and community: Myth and institutionalization in policing. *Law and Society Review*, *28*(2), 325–351.

Crank, J. P. (2003). Institutional theory of police: A review of the state of the art. *Policing: An International Journal of Police Strategies and Management*, *26*(2), 186–207.

Crank, J. P., & Langworthy, R. (1992). An institutional perspective of policing. *Journal of Criminal Law and Criminology*, *83*(2), 338–363.

Crank, J., & Langworthy, R. (1996). Fragmented centralization and the organization of the police. *Policing and Society: An International Journal*, *6*(3), 213–229.

Davis, G. F., & Powell, W. W. (1992). Organization-environment relations. *Handbook of Industrial and Organizational Psychology*, *3*, 315–375.

Deephouse, D. L. & Suchman, M. (2008). *Legitimacy in organizational institutionalism.* Thousand Oaks, CA: Sage.

Deephouse, D. L., Bundy, J., Tost, L. P., & Suchman, M. C. (2016). Organizational legitimacy: Six key questions.

DiIulio, J. J. (1996). Help wanted: Economists, crime and public policy. *Journal of Economic Perspectives*, *10*(1), 3–24.

DiMaggio, P., & Powell, W. W. (1983). The iron cage revisited: Collective rationality and institutional isomorphism in organizational fields. *American Sociological Review*, *48*(2), 147–160.

DiMaggio, P. J., & Powell, W. W. (Eds.). (1991). *The new institutionalism in organizational analysis.* Chicago: University of Chicago Press.

Dowling, J., & Pfeffer, J. (1975). Organizational legitimacy: Social values and organizational behavior. *Pacific Sociological Review*, *18*(1), 122–136.

Esselstrom, E. (2009). *Crossing empire's edge: Foreign ministry police and Japanese expansionism in Northeast Asia.* Honolulu: University of Hawaii Press.

Farjoun, M. (2010). Beyond dualism: Stability and change as a duality. *Academy of Management Review, 35*(2), 202–225.

Fligstein, N. (1991). The structural transformation of American industry: An institutional account of the causes of diversification in the largest firms, 1919–1979. In W. W. Powell and P. J. DiMaggio (Eds.), *The new institutionalism in organizational analysis.* Chicago: University of Chicago Press.

Greenwood, R., & Hinings, C. R. (1996). Understanding radical organizational change: Bringing together the old and the new institutionalism. *Academy of Management Review, 21*(4), 1022–1054.

Ha, T. (2002). Institution transfer, indigenization, and new institutionalism. *Korean Journal of Public Administration, 40*(1), 45–69.

Ha, T. (2014. Central government organizational revamp at the launch of the 2nd republic. *Social Science Studies, 25*(1), 25–54.

Heo, N. (2005). *History of the Korean police system.* Seoul: Jigu.

Hinton, M. S., & Newburn, T. (2008). *Policing developing democracies.* New York: Routledge.

Hirsch, P. M., & Andrews, J. (1986). Administrators' response to performance and value challenges: Stance, symbols, and behavior'. In *Leadership and organizational culture: New perspectives on administrative theory and practice* (pp. 170–185). Urbana: University of Illinois Press.

Ho, A. T.-K., & Cho, W. (2017). Government communication effectiveness and satisfaction with police performance: A large-scale survey study. *Public Administration Review, 77*(2), 228–239.

Hoffman, V. J. (1982). The development of modern police agencies in the Republic of Korea and Japan: A paradox. *Police Studies, 5*(3), 3–16.

Hoffman, V. J. (1993). Role of police in the process of societal change: Korean and American examples. *Police Studies, 16*(3), 84–89.

Hong, Y. P. (1995). *State security and regime security: The security policy of South Korea under the Syngman Rhee government, 1953–1960.* University of Oxford.

Im, H. B. (2004). Faltering democratic consolidation in South Korea: Democracy at the end of the "three Kims" era. *Democratization, 11*(5), 179–198.

Im, T., & Cho, W. (2008). Decentralization and economic growth in Korea. *Korean Journal of Policy Studies, 23*(1), 49–71.

Im, T., & Park, J. (2010). Korea's experiences with development: Revisiting MDGs from a time perspective. *Korean Journal of Policy Studies, 25*(3), 125–145.

Im, T., Cho, W., & Porumbescu, G., (2011). An empirical analysis of the relation between social spending and economic growth in developing countries and OECD members. *Asia Pacific Journal of Public Administration, 33*(1), 37–55.

Im, T., Cho, W., Cha, S., Jeong, J., & Lee, M. (2013). A cross-county comparison of government competitiveness: Measures and evaluations. *Korean Comparative Government Review, 17*(2), 95–124.

Im, T., Cho, W., Porumbescu, G., & Park, J. (2014). Internet, trust in government, and citizen compliance. *Journal of Public Administration Research and Theory, 24*(3), 741–763.

Im, T., Lee, H., Cho, W. and Campbell, J.W., (2014). Citizen preference and resource allocation: The case for participatory budgeting in Seoul. *Local Government Studies, 40*(1), 102–120.

Jay, J. (2013). Navigating paradox as a mechanism of change and innovation in hybrid organizations. *Academy of Management Journal, 56*(1), 137–159.

Jepperson, R. L. (1991). Institutions, institutional effects, and institutionalism. In W. W. Powell and P. J. DiMaggio (Eds.), *The new institutionalism in organizational analysis* (pp. 143–163). Chicago: University of Chicago Press.

Johnson, C. (1989). South Korean democratization: The role of economic development. *Pacific Review*, *2*(1), 1–10.

Johnston, M. (2008). Japan, Korea, the Philippines, China: Four syndromes of corruption. *Crime, Law, and Social Change*, *49*(3), 205–223.

Jun, J. S. & Yoon, J. P. (1996). Korean public administration at a crossroads: Culture, development, and change. In A. S. Huque (Ed.), *Public administration in the NICs* (pp. 90–113). Basingstoke, UK: Palgrave Macmillan.

Jung, W., & Kim, J. (2014). A study on the historical evolution and characteristic of assembly and demonstrations culture. *Korean Public Administration History Review*, *35*, 257–284.

Kang, Y., Cho, W., & Jung, K. (2012). Does decentralization matter in health outcomes? *International Review of Public Administration*, *17*(1), 1–32.

Kim, B. (2006). Paradigm Changes in the Korean Police and Critical Issues in the Historic Record, *Korean Association of Police Science Review*, *11*(3), 3–24.

Kim, C. Y. (2008). A study of police policy in Korea during the American military occupation. *Korean Academy of Public Safety and Criminal Justice*, *17*(4), 13–56.

Kim, H. (2014). *The establishment of Chun Doo Hwan's regime in the 1980s, with a focus on the Special Committee for National Security and the Legislative Assembly Secretariat for National Security*. Seoul: National Research Foundation of Korea.

Kim, J. (2000). Analysis of change in the Korean police force. *Korea Police Journal*, *2*, 45–66.

Kim, J. (2004). The Korean police: Its development and future courses. *Korean Association of Police Science Review*, *7*, 63–84.

Kim, J. (2005). A study of the characteristics of the Korean police. *Law Review*, *20*, 245–262.

Kim, J. (2009). The role of the Korean national police in South Korean politics, 1946–1948, *Daegu Historical Review*, *97*, 77–108.

Kim, N., & Cho, W. (2012). Expertise of public employees in the Board of Audit and Inspection in Korea. *Korean Public Personnel Administration Review*, *11*(2), 165–194.

Kim, N., & Cho, W. (2014). Agencification and performance: The impact of autonomy and result-control on the performance of executive agencies in Korea. *Public Performance and Management Review*, *38*(2), 214–233.

Kim, S. (2002). *Redesigning the function of the Korean police: Community policing and fear of crime*. Seoul: Korean Institute of Criminology.

Kim, S. J. (2001). *Master of manipulation: Syngman Rhee and the Seoul-Washington alliance, 1953–1960*. Seoul: Yonsei University Press.

Kim, Y. (2012). A study of the history and significance of the investigative authority of judicial police and prosecutors, with a focus on the end of the Chosun dynasty, the Japanese colonial era, and the period r of the U.S. Military government in Korea. *Journal of Police and Law*, *10*(2), 259–288.

Knoke, D. (1988). Incentives in collective action organizations. *American Sociological Review*, *53*(3), 311–329.

Kutnjak Ivkovic, S., & Kang, W. (2012). Police integrity in South Korea. *Policing: An International Journal of Police Strategies and Management*, *35*(1), 76–103.

Langworthy, R. H. (1986). *The structure of police organizations*. New York: Praeger.

Ledford, G. E., Mohrman, S. A., Mohrman, A. M., & Lawler, E. E. (1989). *Large-scale organizational change*. New York: Wiley.

Lee, D. H. (2015). Abuse of judicial disposition as a means of suppression of activists for independence during the era of Japanese colonialism. *Oriental Studies*, *58*, 135–150.

Lee, H., & Lee, Y. (2009). The effects of performance-oriented culture on organizational performance, with a focus on police officials' perceptions. *Social Science Studies*, *35*(2), 81–108.

Lee, S., & Lim, H. Study of factors affecting police performance. *Korean Public Administration Review*, *46*(3), 357–378.

Lee, S. (2007). A historical review of the Korean police during the Japanese occupation of the Korean Peninsula. *Korean Public Administration History Review*, *20*, 77–96.

Lim, J. T. (2010). A study of the brief history of Korean modern policing. *Korean Academy of Public Safety and Criminal Justice*, *19*(4), 375–414.

March, J. G., & Olsen, J. P. (1983). The new institutionalism: Organizational factors in political life. *American Political Science Review*, *78*(03), 734–749.

March, J. G., & Olsen, J. P. (1996). Institutional perspectives on political institutions. *Governance*, *9*(3), 247–264.

Marenin, O. (1996). *Policing change, changing police: International perspectives*. New York: Taylor & Francis.

Meade, E. G. (1951). *American military government in Korea*. New York: King's Crown Press.

Meyer, J. W., & Rowan, B. (1977). Institutionalized organizations: Formal structure as myth and ceremony. *American Journal of Sociology*, *83*(2), 340–363.

Meyer, J. W., & Scott, W. R. (1983). *Organizational environments: Ritual and rationality*. Thousand Oaks, CA: Sage.

Mizruchi, M. S., & Fein, L. C. (1999). The social construction of organizational knowledge: A study of the uses of coercive, mimetic, and normative isomorphism. *Administrative Science Quarterly*, *44*(4), 653–683.

Moon, B., & Morash, M. (2009). Policing in South Korea: Struggle, challenge, and reform. In M. S. Hinton (Ed.), *Policing developing democracies*. New York: Routledge.

Myong, C.S. (1959). The police system in the Republic of Korea. Unpublished paper, Michigan State University.

Nahm, A. (1988). *Korea: Tradition and transformation*. Elizabeth, NJ: Hollym International Corporation.

Oliver, C. (1991). Strategic responses to institutional processes. *Academy of Management Review*, *16*(1), 145–179.

Olsen, J. P. (2009). Change and continuity: An institutional approach to institutions of democratic government. *European Political Science Review*, *1*(1), 3–32.

Palmer, D. A., Jennings, P. D., & Zhou, X. (1993). Late adoption of the multidivisional form by large US corporations: Institutional, political, and economic accounts. *Administrative Science Quarterly*, *38*(1), 100–131.

Palthe, J. (2014). Regulative, normative, and cognitive elements of organizations: Implications for managing change. *Management and Organizational Studies*, *1*(2), 59–66.

Parsons, T. (1960). *Structure and process in modern societies*. New York: Free Press.

Porumbescu, G. A. (2015). Comparing the effects of e-government and social media use on trust in government: Evidence from Seoul, South Korea. *Public Management Review*, *18*(9), 1–27.

Porumbescu, G. A. (2016). Linking public sector social media and e-government website use to trust in government. *Government Information Quarterly*, *33*(2), 291–304.

Pyo, C. (2001). Policing: The present and future. *Crime and Justice International*, *17*(51), 7–8, 27.

Ranson, S., Hinings, B., & Greenwood, R. (1980). The structuring of organizational structures. *Administrative Science Quarterly*, *25*(1), 1–17.

Ritti, R. R., & Mastrofski, S. D. (2002). *The institutionalization of community policing: A study of the presentation of the concept in two law enforcement journals: Final report to the National Institute of Justice*. Manassas, VA: George Mason University.

Seo, J. S. (1996). The formation of the modern Korean state: The state apparatus of the first republic and the legacy of the Korean war. Ph.D. Dissertation, Seoul National University.

Seo, M. G., & Creed, W. D. (2002). Institutional contradictions, praxis, and institutional change: A dialectical perspective. *Academy of Management Review, 27*(2), 222–247.

Steinberg, D. T. (1968). *Korea: Nexus of East Asia.* New York: American-Asian Educational Exchange.

Suchman, M. C. (1995). Managing legitimacy: Strategic and institutional approaches. *Academy of Management Review, 20*(3), 571–610.

Suh, K. (1976). *History of the Korean police.* Seoul: Soo Eun.

Tolbert, P. S., & Zucker, L. G. (1983). Institutional sources of change in the formal structure of organizations: The diffusion of civil service reform, 1880–1935. *Administrative Science Quarterly, 28*(1), 22–39.

Tyler, T. R., & Fagan, J. (2008). Legitimacy and cooperation: Why do people help the police fight crime in their communities? *Ohio State Journal of Criminal Law, 6,* 231.

Vreeland, N., Just, P., Martindale, K., Moeller, P., & Shinn, R. (1975). *Area handbook for South Korea.* Washington, DC: Foreign Area Studies.

Wolin, S. S. (2010). *Democracy incorporated: Managed democracy and the specter of inverted totalitarianism.* Princeton, NJ: Princeton University Press.

Yang, K. (2016). Creating public value and institutional innovations across boundaries: An integrative process of participation, legitimation, and implementation. *Public Administration Review, 76*(6), 873–885.

Yi, P.-C. (2006). *Developmental dictatorship and the Park Chung-Hee Era: The shaping of modernity in the Republic of Korea.* Paramus, NJ: Homa and Sekey Books.

Yoon, H. (2001). Analysis of the evolution of the police bureaucracy approached from a Path-Dependency Perspective with a focus on the national police agency from 1991 to 2010. *Korean Academy of Public Safety and Criminal Justice, 20*(1), 188–217.

Yun, I. H., & Cheong, J. S. (2010). Introduction to the performance-based management system of the Korean Police and its policy implications. *Korean Academy of Public Safety and Criminal Justice, 19*(3), 191–218.

Zhao, J., Lovrich, N., & Robinson, H. (2001). Community policing: Is it changing the basic functions of policing? *Journal of Criminal Justice, 29*(5), 365–377.

Zucker, L. G. (1988). Where do institutional patterns come from? Organizations as actors in social systems. In L. G. Zucker (Ed.), *Institutional patterns and organizations: Culture and environment* (pp. 23–49). Cambridge, MA: Ballinger.

CHAPTER 6

SUPREME AUDIT INSTITUTION AND DEMOCRACY: THE FUNCTION OF THE BOARD OF AUDIT AND INSPECTION (BAI) OF KOREA FOR DEMOCRATIZATION

Nanyoung Kim

ABSTRACT

This chapter explores the relationship between bureaucracy and the democratization of the Republic of Korea by analyzing the roles and responsibilities of the Board of Audit and Inspection of Korea (BAI) and how Korea's unique type of supreme audit institution (SAI) have been involved throughout the democratization process of Korea over the last two decades. Unlike western supreme audit institutions which mainly functioned for financial and performance auditing, Korea's SAI, BAI bureaucracy, has functioned to reduce corruption, in cooperation with citizen's participation which gives unique cases for the context of developing countries. The most important finding of this study is that bureaucracy can be an effective vehicle in a country's political trajectory towards

The Experience of Democracy and Bureaucracy in South Korea
Public Policy and Governance, 141–157
Copyright © 2017 by Emerald Publishing Limited
All rights of reproduction in any form reserved
doi:10.1108/S2053-769720170000028006

*democratization given that the public institutions and agencies have spe-
cific traits such as having clear and comprehensive mandates, retaining
high sensitivity to external needs, and maintaining well-qualified staff
with active utilization of Information Technology. The main targets of
the analysis are the conditions under which BAI bureaucracy could effectively exert its mandates and successfully fulfill its duties; also the question of how the BAI bureaucracy has facilitated democratization as being
the locus of participatory democracy will be addressed.*

Keywords: Bureaucracy; democracy; Supreme Audit Institution; citizen
engagement; Board of Audit and Inspection of Korea

ARGUES WITH THIN EVIDENCE

The terms "bureaucracy" and "democracy" are often understood, both in
academic and nonacademic literatures, as antithetical approaches to providing governance for a society (Etzioni-Halevi, 1983; Peters, 2010:1).
There exists a rich and robust literature on bureaucracy which has
argued that government institutions and agencies are a major source of
problems as they tend to limit the capacity of democratic political systems in effectively responding to their citizens (Peters & Pierre, 2006).
For example, while Neo-Marxist perspectives take a negative stance regarding bureaucracy by pointing out its lack of autonomy, a number of political science theories contend that bureaucracy tends to remain as a parasitic
apparatus under authoritarian regimes as a mere instrument of the ruling
class. Yet, it is noteworthy that empirical research or studies that corroborate
such theories are rarely found in academia.

In contrast, Peters (2010) argues that public bureaucracies have
been typically conceptualized as a necessary ingredient for a regime
in maintaining effective administration of public programs which may
be important for upholding a well-functioning democracy. In a similar way, a number of public administration researches focus on how to
make bureaucracy more effective for the better achievement of policy
outcomes (Boyne, 2004; Kim, N. & Cho, W. 2015). Furthermore, Peters
(2010), Peters and Pierre (2006) argue that the public sector is increasingly becoming an important "locus" for democratic participation and
responsiveness in the contemporary era.

Therefore, the issue of whether bureaucracy is an obstacle or a facilitator to the process of democratization is a critical research theme in both practical and theoretical viewpoints. In analyzing the relationship between these two terms, institutional-context perspective needs to be applied as the relational dynamics between "democracy" and "public bureaucracy" could differ on a case-by-case basis depending on the sociopolitical environment of each individual country. While the roles of the bureaucracy for economic development and democratization are important in both developing and developed countries, this chapter claims that bureaucracy seems to be more important in the former than in the latter.

This is because developing countries tend to show common weaknesses in their investments, performances, and returns on social infrastructure (e.g., human resources, systems, and institutions), which highlight fundamental ineptitude of their civil society for promoting democracy. In contrast, bureaucracies in developing nations tend to reveal comparatively high levels of human resources, operational know-how in system management, and other organizational capabilities, which can be eventually utilized as momentum for democratic transition.

Despite all these discussions, the aforementioned relationship lacks empirical clarity. Therefore, in this sense, examining how a bureaucracy facilitates democratization in a country and what characteristics of its bureaucratic apparatus are specifically favorable for leading the democratization process are important research themes.

The Republic of Korea is a country that has reached economic development and democratization in a short, condensed time period. The rapid postwar development of South Korea is one of the most remarkable economic stories of the twentieth century: Korea's place in the world during the 1960s as a small Asian nation ridden with poverty and despair with a gross domestic product roughly equal to that of Ghana, was transformed into the world's twelfth largest, and Asia's fourth largest economy by 1995 (Campbell, 2012). Therefore, how Korea was able to accomplish this remarkable transition is a matter of interesting research in both descriptive and prescriptive ways. Some studies have argued that the key factors of economic development in South Korea were centralized government planning through its bureaucracy (which had comparatively high levels of human and material resources and systems in one of the world's poorest countries). However, the role of bureaucracy in the phenomenal political democratization over the last two decades in South Korea is little known. Furthermore, little progress has been made on delineating the relationship between Korea's successful democratization and the role of SAI bureaucracy which has retained the duty of audit and inspection to oversee the government through which unlawful public officials were held accountable.

This study aims at empirically elucidating the relationship between bureaucracy and the respective nation's democratic trajectory by analyzing the roles and responsibilities of the Board of Audit and Inspection of Korea (hereinafter referred to as BAI) in democratization process of South Korea over the last two decades.

BAI'S FUNCTIONING FOR DEMOCRATIZATION

Detecting Corruption based on the law

Diamond (2004) conceptualized democracy as a system of government with four key elements : active citizen participation, protecting human rights of citizens, a rule of law, and a political system for choosing and replacing the government. In many countries under this democratic transition, one of the common features is that the authority and power of the legislative branch is significantly weaker than its executive counterpart, while their political decision-making processes lack democratic components of citizen participation. In Korea, such a phenomenon has confirmed, through a series of interviews with public servants, civil society leaders, and senior auditors who worked for BAI more than 20 years, that the nation's bureaucratic apparatus has functioned as an indirect and alternative channel for alleviating people's grievances and promoting their general interest. This was made even more palpable as Korea's National Assembly largely remained as a "rubber stamp" during the authoritarian era; in contrast, the nation's administrative bodies—though they did not engage citizens directly in policy making—strove for defining and advocating public interest at a relatively more impartial position than the legislative branch. For instance, Korea's social welfare system was first introduced by the bureaucrats' initiatives on mitigating the fallouts and side effects of the nation's rapid drive for industrialization.

The function of the Supreme Audit Insitution in western countries focuses on the performance of bureaucrats. However, the uniqueness of Korean Superme audit insitution is that BAI is more focused to reduce corruption of bureaucracy.

BAI'S TRAITS FOR FUNCTIONING

The World Bank (2001) suggested that in order to measure the capability of Supreme Audit Institutions, the following features are necessary: clear mandates, independence, comprehensive mandates, adequate funding, facilities and staff, and sharing of knowledge and experiences. However, these are necessary conditions for SAIs to function as democratic facilitators as well. Korea's SAI: BAI have continuously developed those conditions.

1. Clear and Comprehensive Mandates
The BAI is a constitutional agency whose functions, status and organization are stipulated in Articles 97 to 100 of the Constitution. The Constitution stipulates explicitly regarding BAI to guarantee, by laying the foundation for the independence and neutrality of BAI, that the mandate and work scope of BAI are not changed by statutes unscrupulously.

The BAI shall be established to inspect and examine the settlement of the revenues and expenditures of the State, the accounts of the State and other organizations specified by Act and the job performances of executive agencies and public officials (see Article 97 of the Constitution). The BAI shall inspect the closing of accounts of revenues and expenditures each year, and report the results to the President and the National Assembly in the following year (see Article 99 of the Constitution states).

Though Article 97 of the Constitution states that "BAI shall be established under the direct jurisdiction of the President," the BAI enjoys its complete independence in function by deciding what to audit as well as how to audit with its own authority (Kim, S. 2015:2). As BAI's functions, status, and organization are explicitly stipulated by the Constitution, its independence and political neutrality have a strong foundation. Its independence in operations is also spelled out in its organic law, the Board of Audit and Inspection Act of 1963.

The BAI has comprehensive audit mandates over both function and audited and inspected objects. Kim (2015) points out that these comprehensive audit mandates and supporting access rights enable the BAI to respond to citizens' demands in a direct and timely manner.

In the aspect of function, unlike most SAIs, the BAI is mandated to inspect the performance of public institutions and their employees, in addition to auditing government accounts (Kim, 2015).[1]

Therefore, the BAI's key functions are to verify the final accounts of the state, to carry out financial and performance audits, and inspect the performance of public sector employees. First, BAI examines the final accounts of the state and verifies that the nation's resources have been spent wisely to benefit the public (Article 99 of the Constitution; Article 21 of the BAI Act). Second, BAI audits the central government, local autonomies and public institutions to ensure that the budget which comes from taxpayer money is being used properly for the nation and its citizens (Articles 22 & 23 of the BAI Act). Apart from audit, BAI carries out inspections to ensure that the work of government agencies, local autonomies and public institutions and the performance of their employees are being carried out according to the law and principles (Article 24 of the BAI Act). Just as financial audit is the examination of an auditees' finance, inspection is examination of public employees' performance to ensure that they are doing their work properly. Also BAI has assessed and supervised the performance of public sector internal audit units since 2009.

The BAI Act defines those entities subject to mandatory audit: central government, provincial and local government, local autonomous bodies, and the Bank of Korea. Those entities that have received—directly or indirectly—grants or financial assistance from any of the mandatory audit entities are also subject to the BAI's discretionary audit. As of December 2013, over 60 thousand entities are subject to the BAI audits.

Along with its basic duties, BAI acts on the people's requests. That is, BAI has a system by which an ordinary citizen can file a civil request for an audit. Currently, BAI receives audit requests from three channels: from the National Assembly, from citizens, and public entities.

2. High Independence

To ensure the independence of BAI, the Chairman of BAI, like the Chief Justice and the Prime Minister, is appointed by the President with the consent of the National Assembly. The term of office of the Chairman shall be four years with only one-time reappointment possible.

The BAI is an organization with a council system for decision-making in which the work is processed by the Council of Commissioners. This means that greater emphasis is placed on fairness instead of efficiency and expediency in BAI system.

3. High Sensitivity to External Needs

BAI's vision has evolved in meeting national, economic and social needs since its establishment. During the dictatorship, the visions of BAI were not toward citizens: establishing BAI system in 1963 through 1971; supporting national reform of political and bureaucratic abuse and establishing its own discipline 1971 through 1980; improving efficiency and globalization of audit work 1980 through 1988.

After the dictatorship, the vision of BAI has been toward citizens: promoting citizen convenience and setting up its status 1988 through 1998; advancing audit quality and disclosing audit work to citizen 1998 through 2008; trust from citizen through 2008 (Board of Audit and Inspection of Korea, 2008; 2012; 2013; 2014; 2015a).

4. Improving Responsiveness and Efficiency by Using IT

South Korea has actively introduced IT (Information technologies) across all areas in both the public sector and the private sector over the past 20 years, which has contributed to economic development (Campbell, 2012).[2] In particular, national informatization and applying IT to the public administrative services of Korean government did much for administrative efficiency and public benefit.[3]

In accordance with national informatization, applying IT to public administrative services of government in 1990's (BAI, 2008:371), BAI has been active in introducing IT to improve audit performance and managerial efficiency and to strengthen the communication with stakeholders such as citizens. The contribution of IT technology to democratization can be indirectly found through a change in the way the Civil Petition is submitted over the last 10 years. As Table 1 shows the number of submissions of the Civil Petition has increased and the submissions by internet among them have increased and the rate has been over 50% since 2006.

Already from 1970's, BAI has promoted the computerization of audit work to improve its efficiency and performance corresponding to sharply increasing audit requests. In 1971, BAI embarked on the computerization of audit work including the development of the "Computerization program of contrast work of certified documents of calculation".

In 1982, BAI introduced "an independent computerized system" to make the information production system active and to expand the work processed by computer. BAI established "an audit comprehensive information system" in 1985 and computer supervisor in 1986. Also, BAI has established the "computerized business development four-year plan" which aims to build the infrastructure for computerized audit corresponding to the national trend of administrative computerization. Also BAI established the "Computer Training Plan 4 steps" and strengthened computer education to cultivate understanding of computer and the ability to use computers, to improve efficiency of work process and capabilities of audit, using computers. Office automation has been strengthened in ways such as replacing a manual typewriter with a word processor since 1986 (Board of Audit and Inspection of Korea, 2011: 525–31).

Table1. The ways a Civil Petition is submitted (by year).

	internet		mail		interview		fax		telephone		transmitted		total	
	number	%	number	%	number	%	number	%	number	%	number	%	number	%
2000	1,003	13.6	4,840	65.8	325	4.4	360	4.9	698	28.5	125	5.1	7,351	100
2001	1,809	25.1	3,707	51.5	536	7.4	297	4.1	749	31.2	107	4.5	7,205	100
2002	1,890	29.5	3,267	51.1	442	6.9	196	3.1	477	22.4	127	6.0	6,399	100
2003	2,933	40.2	3,199	43.9	433	5.9	232	3.2	331	13.6	165	6.8	7,293	100
2004	3,147	43.0	3,371	46.1	356	4.9	192	2.6	78	3.2	168	6.9	7,312	100
2005	3,378	46.5	2,968	40.8	464	6.4	187	2.6	24	1.0	246	10.2	7,267	100
2006	3,884	52.6	2,524	34.2	468	6.3	246	3.3	146	5.9	113	4.6	7,381	100
2007	3,691	51.8	2,452	34.4	504	7.1	247	3.5	124	5.2	103	4.3	7,121	100
2008	8,922	69.8	2,647	20.7	531	4.2	330	2.6	172	4.0	182	4.3	12,784	100
2009	5,607	56.8	2,719	27.5	795	8.0	339	3.4	287	8.7	131	4.0	9,878	100
2010	4,964	55.0	2,686	29.8	604	6.7	415	4.6	214	7.1	145	4.8	9,028	100
2011	5,233	50.6	3,543	34.3	657	6.4	490	4.7	338	9.8	75	2.2	10,336	100
2012	5,751	54.8	3,057	29.1	801	7.6	573	5.5	288	8.2	24	0.7	10,494	100

Source: BAI (2013a). Annual Report; BAI (2013b). White paper on audit request).

In 1994 BAI developed an "automatic calculation program for travel expenses, management program of external information". Also BAI made the "National Audit Activity Information System (NAIS)" to connect 43 institutions including 17 central ministries, 15 local governments, 10 cities with a computer network to reduce audit duplication among BAI and internal audit agencies (Board of Audit and Inspection of Korea, 2011: 694-9). In 1999 BAI promoted a "National Financial Informatization" project in cooperation with the Ministry of Finance. Calculation papers began to be submitted to BAI on-line and BAI began to operate the accounting information system by the submission of the financial data such as budgets, funding, expenditure, etc.

In 2004, BAI established an "Information Strategic Plan (ISP)" and set out the development of "The E-Audit System". "The E-Audit System" is composed of a portal processing electronically whole phases of audit work and all other corporate supporting business, and such sub-systems of knowledge and activity audit and inspection, data support, audit and inspection training, and audit and inspection research, etc.

The E-Audit System is composed of 5 parts. First, by the monitoring and audit work management system, all audit work processes including pre-audit monitoring, audit planning, implementation, result, and follow-up are integrated. Second, by the Requests of Action and Follow-up system, after audit work, audit reports and statistics on requests for action are inputted, and follow-up functions are performed. Third, by the Audit Knowledge Management System, all knowledge related to audit including data on audit work, audit techniques, publications for search and use are comprehensively managed. Fourth, under Fiscal Data Analysis System, a DB for the analysis of fiscal data such as government budget, receipts, expenditures, national properties, national contracts, bonds, debts, etc. is constructed by linking the digital budget and accounting system of the Ministry of Strategy and Finance. Lastly, under the public Audit Information System, public audit information is constructed to share knowledge and experience between the BAI and more than 260 internal audit units, and to promote the efficiency of the internal audit system which is based on the Act on Public Sector Audits (Park, 2014). Now the BAI has been developing the next-generation e-Audit System since 2012 to simplify complex functions to promote user convenience from information provision, search, management, and security of fiscal analysis.

Furthermore, the audited agencies shall report their implementation of BAI's decisions such as requests for disciplinary action, requests for correction, requests for improvement, and so on electronically and BAI shall follow up how the decisions are implemented in the audited agencies electronically since 2016.

Table 2.   Number of holders of professional certificates of total staff.

Year	Total	lawyer	account-ant	doctor	Tax accountant	Professional Engineers	Others
2000	85(9.5%)	10	32	22	7	13	1
2010	185(17.9%)	35	79	45	6	16	4

Source: BAI Human Resources Management Strategy (2011).

In addition, all BAI works and auditors' activities have been managed electronically since 2017.

5. Well Qualified Staffs

Human resources have been considered one of the key factors of Korean economic development in many researches. Korean bureaucracy had comparatively higher level of human resources and systems than any other organization in South Korea during democratization. BAI recruited talented persons by giving them comparatively higher ranks. That is, while other central departments recruited staff mostly in the ranks of ninth or seventh rank, BAI recruited auditors mostly in the ranks of seventh or fifth rank. Also a high level of integrity was required by the auditors. To support this, the remuneration of BAI auditors is higher than those of central government employees by 20%.

Since 1990, BAI has expanded, recruiting holders of professional certificates such as lawyer, accountant, doctor in the field of engineering, economics, and so on. The rate of the holders of the professional certificate of total staffs increased from the ratio of 9.5% in 2000 to 17.9% in 2010. BAI has devoted a lot of effort to training auditors. It established the Audit and Inspection Training Department in 1985 and opened the Audit and Inspection Training Institute in 1995.

AUDITING AND INSPECTION THROUGH CITIZEN PARTICIPATION

Participatory Auditing

Participatory auditing is designed to facilitate citizen participation throughout its audit process that includes planning, execution, reporting, and after-action feedback. It was widely expected that through widening citizens' participation in the audit process, major contributions could be made toward democratic consolidation as overall civic engagement and participation in governance, protection of human rights, the rule of law as well as grass-roots level trust in government and BAI can be achieved. In Korea, various practices for participatory auditing are found, and it is known that participatory auditing entails numerous formats and types of processes. This illustrates that Korea's practices in national auditing are in a constant stage of evolution and modification.

The BAI has gradually expanded its dimensions in the cooperative relationship with the citizenry since its establishment in 1963.[4] In this sense, BAI has contributed to the active participation of the people, protection of the human rights of all citizens, and a rule of law through actively strengthening citizen engagement.

In the beginning, citizens' involvement was confined to gathering information on fraud, misconduct, or abuse of power through citizens' complaints and petitions. As the number of citizens' complaints increased rapidly, the BAI decided to set up the Civil Petition & Complaint Reception Center in 1971 in order to handle citizens' complaints more efficiently.

In 1993, a "fraud hotline" was established which was intended to provide citizens with more convenient means to provide appropriate information— concerning abuse of public funds or complaints on certain administrative actions—to the BAI. The hotline served as a model for similar operations throughout the government in Korea. As the internet became a popular mode of communication in Korea, the BAI concurrently expanded its pre-existing 188 hotline to an internet-based fraud net. In February 2004, the BAI opened itself to receiving and resolving complaints from the business sector on the administration's inappropriate delays or refusals in handling permit and licensing applications.

With active participation and support from the academic and research community, some leading civil society organizations (CSOs) in Korea are well equipped with professional expertise in various areas. During the same timeframe, the 1988 reform of the Local Autonomy Act and the Local Finance Act triggered a tidal wave of decentralization, shifting responsibilities toward local government from central government, which was followed by direct election of local councils in 1991 and the popular election of governors and mayors in 1995 (Kim, S. 2015:7–9). Other government reform measures gave more managerial freedom and discretion to public service delivery organizations. However, coupled with weak internal audit functions in the public sector, these changes toward decentralization raised serious concerns over mismanagement and potential abuse of newly acquired authorities in the public entities that are in charge of service delivery (Kim, S. 2015:4). Against this backdrop, the BAI introduced the ARPI in 1996. The BAI laid down a legal foundation through its internal regulations, under which CSOs whose membership exceeds 300 or a group of citizens over 300 can make a request to the BAI to conduct an audit on specific issues for the sake of the public interest (Kim, S. 2015:4). In 2002, the Anti-Corruption Act was enacted for the first time in which another citizen engagement channel with the title of CAR was introduced (Kim, S. 2015:6).

In addition, from 2003, the National Assembly can request BAI to conduct a particular audit. Per the National Assembly Act, BAI must conduct the audit if the National Assembly requests, and must report the results back to the legislature within three months.

Lastly, BAI has made all audit reports public through its website (http://english.bai.go.kr/bai_eng/cop/bbs/listBoardArticles.do?mdex=bai_eng14&bbs Id=BBSMSTR_200000000002) since 2003, which is an unprecedented audacious move even when compared with SAIs in developed countries of the West.

Audit Request for Public Interest and Citizen Audit Request

An audit could be requested for public interest if one of the following conditions is fulfilled: should a public institution waste the national budget while carrying out major policies or projects; should policies or projects be delayed because of institutional or administrative self-interest; should measures and systems need to be improved because they are irrational; should public institutions break the law while conducting their work or use unfair practices thereby causing undue harm to the public good; and when a petition signed by at least 300 persons over the age of 19 is filed. Civic groups, the heads of institutions audited by BAI or local councils can all request this type of practices audit (BAI, 2015b).

Also, citizens can request BAI to conduct an audit if a public institution breaks a law or is engaged in corrupt activities that cause considerable harm to the public good. For this, at least 300 persons over the age of 19 must sign the petition. However, this type of audit cannot be carried out regarding the work of local autonomies.

Table 3 shows a rapidly increasing trend of audit requests over the period 1996–2012. From the introduction of the ARPI in 1996, the average number of annual audit requests remained around 20 until 2001, but it has increased eight-fold since then, and for the last three years, it jumped to about

Table 3. Number of Audit Request to BAI by citizen (1996–2012).

	1996	1997	1998	1999	2000	2001	2002	2003	2004	2005	2006	2008	2009	2010	2011	2012
ARPI	16	25	13	22	21	10	40	79	104	126	110	138	148	108	169	180
CAR							32	45	38	37	33	43	35	29	13	10
total							72	124	142	163	143	181	183	137	182	190

Source: BAI Annual Report (2013a); BAI White paper on audit request (2013b).

180 cases per year, which can be explained by the long-awaited enactment of Anti-Corruption Act of 2002. The increase in the number of audit requests reflects the fact that citizens and the CSOs consider the participatory audit as an important vehicle to improve transparency and accountability in the public sector, which in turn contributes to maturing participatory democracy. While ARPI sharply increase, CAR sharply decreases. This is because ARPI is much broader than CAR in terms of eligibility of requesters, audit scope, and time limit for reporting audit results.

Table 4 shows that citizens are the most active requesters, accounting for 57.8% of total audit requests. The rate of audit requests by citizens among the total ARPI increased sharply, to over 70% after 2008.

Civil Petition

BAI has made its utmost effort to ensure speedy and fair handling of Civil Petitions regarding irrational or cumbersome administrative practices to protect citizens' rights. The procedures of handling a Civil Petition are the following. In advance, those whose rights or interests have been infringed upon because of illegal or unjust administrative actions taken by agencies subject to BAI's audit, may file a civil petition to the Reception Center for Complaints of BAI about this case. And then BAI will examine the case, communicate the results of its examination to the individual who has made the claim and the head of the relevant agency. Lastly, the head of the relevant agency must take measures according to the BAI's decision. The individual can file an administrative litigation against the relevant agency by reason of his dissatisfaction with the agency's measures.

DISCUSSION

This research examines the relationship between a country's bureaucracy and its democratization process, and analyzes BAI's role in the Republic of

Table 4. Audit Requester Type through Audit Request for Public
Interests (ARPI) (1996–2012).

	Parliament		Local Council		Public Entities		CSO		Citizen		Total	
	Number	%	Number	%	Number	%	Number	%	Number	%	Number	%
1996	1	6.25	3	18.8	0	0.0	6	37.5	6	37.5	16	100.0
1997	0	0	4	16.0	2	8.0	13	52.0	6	24.0	25	100.0
1998	0	0	1	7.7	1	7.7	11	84.6	0	0.0	13	100.0
1999	0	0	2	9.1	1	4.5	18	81.8	1	4.5	22	100.0
2000	0	0	1	4.8	2	9.5	16	76.2	2	9.5	21	100.0
2001	0	0	1	10.0	0	0.0	9	90.0	0	0.0	10	100.0
2002	0	0	3	7.5	0	0.0	35	87.5	2	5.0	40	100.0
2003	0	0	1	1.3	1	1.3	46	58.2	31	39.2	79	100.0
2004	0	0	2	1.9	1	1.0	55	52.9	46	44.2	104	100.0
2005	0	0	4	3.2	9	7.1	54	42.9	59	46.8	126	100.0
2006	0	0	2	1.8	5	4.5	44	40.0	59	53.6	110	100.0
2007	0	0	3	2.5	2	1.7	38	32.2	75	63.6	118	100.0
2008	0	0	5	3.6	4	2.9	32	23.2	97	70.3	138	100.0
2009	0	0	13	8.8	3	2.0	26	17.6	106	71.6	148	100.0
2010	0	0	5	4.6	8	7.4	17	15.7	78	72.2	108	100.0
2011	0	0	5	3.0	9	5.3	34	20.1	121	71.6	169	100.0
2012	0	0	9	5.0	3	1.7	32	17.8	136	75.6	180	100.0

Source: BAI (2013a). Annual Report; BAI (2013b). White paper on audit request.

Korea's democratization process over the last two decades. The findings show
that bureaucracy, as a locus for democratization, could facilitate a nation's
political transition away from authoritarianism. BAI of the Republic of
Korea, through its citizen participation and involvement in auditing efforts
such as ARPI, CAR, petition, was able to meet the citizens' needs. By conducting its function, BAI was able to redress citizens' grievances, thereby
enhancing the nation's democratization over the past 20 years. The findings
are consistent with the opinion of many experts concerning the contribution
of BAI's participatory auditing toward democratization. The following is one
of the opinions.

> While citizens could file their complaints to various national authorities in the level of
> central government, local government level, extended government agencies, and so on,
> BAI's participatory auditing is special in a way that citizens can directly submit audit
> request to BAI – the main agency which claims auditing authority over the all work and
> agencies in the entire public sector. I believe citizens filing audit request to BAI is one of
> natural rights in democratic society.
>   Yun D.G. Professor and Chairman of Audit Request Review Committee, 2012.12.

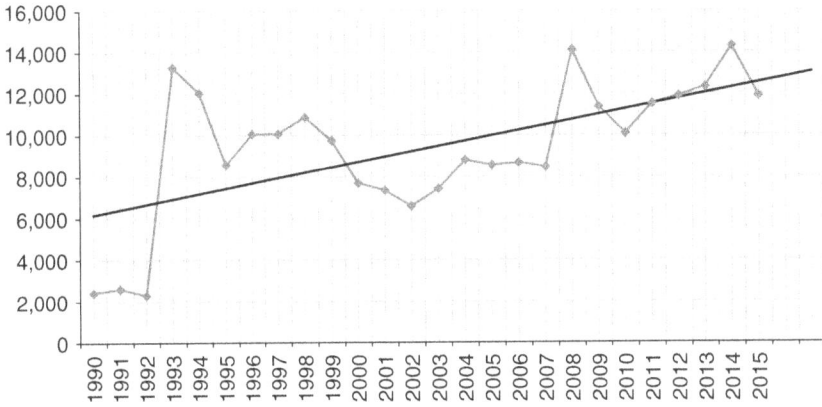

Fig. 1. Submission Number of Civil Petitions (1990–2012).
Source: BAI (2013a). Annual report; BAI (2013b). White paper on audit request.

Therefore, this chapter concludes that although BAI bureaucracy does not seem to be naturally associated with introducing an open political system for choosing and replacing the government through free and fair elections, the body has actually contributed to three key elements of democratization which Diamond suggests: (1) active citizen participation, (2) protecting human rights of citizens, and (3) strengthening a rule of law.

Also, this research confirms that bureaucracy can serve in democratizing a former authoritarian country, a process that can be made possible under certain conditions on which the bureaucracy could exert its mandates effectively and successfully fulfill its duties. Specifics of such preconditions could differ among individual organizations or institutions. For SAI, a few of the many preconditions are as follows: ensuring its clear mandate and independence, augmenting its functions with comprehensive mandates, fulfilling its high sensitivity to external needs, well-qualified staff, and actively utilizing various information technologies.

Lastly, while citizen participation in auditing has been useful for facilitating the BAI to better perform its oversight role—thereby improving the overall performance and accountability of the government—Kim (2005)'s comments on the factors associated with risk management also deserve a point of emphasis as citizen engagement or cross-sectorial collaboration often entails potential risks such as hampering independence and political neutrality of SAI, limited audit resources, and many other fallouts.

NOTES

1. The audit and inspection system of Korea has a history of more than 1,300 years (Board of Audit and Inspection of Korea, 2008). After the establishment of the Republic of Korea government, the Board of Audit was founded under the President as the supreme audit institution pursuant to the provisions of the Constitution of 1948. The Board of Audit carried out audits on the central government, local governments, government-invested organizations, and other organizations prescribed by laws. The Commission of Inspection was established under the President in accordance with the provisions of the Government Organization Act of 1948 to supervise and inspect the duties of the employees of central and local governments, government-invested organizations, and other organizations prescribed by law. The name of the Commission was changed to the Commission of Supervision and Control during the period 1955 to 1960. Then it was reorganized under the Prime Minister with its original name, the Commission of Inspection, in accordance with the Commission of Inspection Act of 1961. Audits by the Board of Audit and the inspections by the Commission of Inspection were in many cases so closely related and a line of the two could not be clearly drawn. Taking this into account, these two organizations were merged into the current BAI, which was established on March 20, 1963 under the revised Constitution of 1962 and the Board of Audit and Inspection Act of 1963.

2. Over the past seventeen years, Korea has become one of the leading IT nations (Campbell, 2012: 4). It has ranked number one among over 150 countries on the ICT Development Index followed by the Scandinavian countries of Sweden, Iceland, Denmark and Finland in 2011, 2012, 2013, and 2015. The ICT Development Index (IDI) is an index published by the United Nations International Telecommunication Union based on internationally agreed information and communication technologies (ICT) indicators.

3. South Korea ranked top in the UN E-Government assessment in 2010, 2012, 2014 and the number of internet users surpassed 40 million people in 2014.

4. Kim (2005) evaluates that BAI's participatory audit has gone through the information and consultation stages and has now reached the stage of partnership for decision making with citizens.

REFERENCES

Board of Audit and Inspection of Korea (BAI). (2008). *BAI 60 years history (in Korean)*. Seoul: Board of Audit and Inspection of Korea.

Board of Audit and Inspection of Korea (BAI). (2011). *Annual report (in Korean)*. Seoul: Board of Audit and Inspection of Korea.

Board of Audit and Inspection of Korea (BAI). (2012). *Annual report (in Korean)*. Seoul: Board of Audit and Inspection of Korea.

Board of Audit and Inspection of Korea (BAI). (2013a). *Annual report (in Korean)*. Seoul: Board of Audit and Inspection of Korea.

Board of Audit and Inspection of Korea (BAI). (2013b). *White paper on audit request (in Korean)*. Seoul: Board of Audit and Inspection of Korea.

Board of Audit and Inspection of Korea (BAI). (2014). *Annual report (in Korean)*. Seoul: Board of Audit and Inspection of Korea.

Board of Audit and Inspection of Korea (BAI). (2015a). *Annual report (in Korean)*. Seoul: Board of Audit and Inspection of Korea.

Board of Audit and Inspection of Korea (BAI). (2015b). *Fair audit, fair society BAY*. Seoul: Board of Audit and Inspection of Korea.

Boyne, G. A. (2004). Explaining public service performance: Does management matter? *Public Policy and Administration, 19*(4), 100–117.

Etzioni-Halevy, E. (1983). *Bureaucracy and democracy: A political dilemma*. London: Routledge & K. Paul.

Kim, N., & Cho, W. (2014). Agencification and performance: The impact of autonomy and result-control on the performance of executive agencies in Korea. *Public Performance & Management Review, 38*(2), 214–233.

Park, J. (2014). Building audit management system (e-audit system) and its operation, Lectures at BAI-KOICA capacity building program of GIV and SAV Employees.

Peters, B. G. (2010). Bureaucracy and democracy. *Public Organization Review, 10*(3), 209–222.

Peters, B. G. & Pierre, J. (2006). Bureaucracy and democracy. In International Political Science Association World Congress in Fukuoca, Japan, July 9–13, 2006.

CHAPTER 7

PUBLIC PROCUREMENT POLICY IN SOUTH KOREA: APPROACHES TO SUSTAINABLE DEVELOPMENT AND ANTI-CORRUPTION

Jesse W. Campbell

ABSTRACT

Due to the scope of procurement in the public sector, public procurement policy has the potential to shape the behavior of market actors and promote the growth of businesses with socially relevant characteristics. This chapter looks at the public procurement process in South Korea as well as the implementation of the country's e-procurement system. Public procurement is vulnerable to corruption in various ways, and Korea's KONEPS e-procurement system has reduced corruption in the procurement process by increasing transparency, the persistence of data, and the probability of detecting irregularities. Second, this chapter explores how Korea has increasingly incorporated sustainable procurement principles into procurement policy, attempting to foster innovative and environmentally friendly companies, as well as those led by individuals belonging to socially disadvantaged groups. The chapter concludes with a discussion of some of the historical and organizational factors underlying Korea's successes in public procurement in order

The Experience of Democracy and Bureaucracy in South Korea
Public Policy and Governance, 159–179
Copyright © 2017 by Emerald Publishing Limited
doi:10.1108/S2053-769720170000028007

to better understand the extent to which currently developing countries can draw upon the Korean case to improve their own procurement policies.

Keywords: Public procurement; e-government; KONEPS e-procurement system

Government organizations need to purchase goods and services from private sector firms to pursue their goals. Public procurement refers to this process and captures the entirety of the procurement process from tendering to contract fulfillment (Lee, 2010). Whereas in the private sector, procurement is viewed primarily through the lens of profit maximization, the evaluative criteria of the public-sector procurement process, like most government processes, are not limited to efficiency (Erridge, 2007). Government generally has a broad mandate to pursue socially beneficial outcomes and is additionally subject to high standards for transparency and accountability. Given that, additionally, the scope of public procurement is vast, averaging, for instance, around 12% of GDP for the 35 member countries of the Organization for Economic Cooperation and Development (OECD) (OECD, 2015), procurement is increasingly seen as a potentially powerful tool with which to incentivize socially responsible behavior among private suppliers and facilitate market conditions that favor entrepreneurs and businesses with socially relevant characteristics (Choi, 2010).

At the same time, because of its complexity and scope, there are many vulnerable points in the procurement process that can be hijacked by politicians or government officials hoping to extract individual benefits at the expense of the public good (Neupane et al., 2012; OECD, 2016). Such behaviors not only distort market prices and waste government resources, but also undermine trust and confidence in government over the longer term. In developing countries, there is often a significant amount of collusion between government officials and private sector firms in the awarding of public contracts. And while developing countries may make use of public procurement for developmental goals (Kattel & Lember, 2010), nevertheless, opportunities for corruption in the procurement process are multiplied in contexts that lack strong market-based mechanisms by which public resources can be efficiently allocated to development projects. Accordingly, due to its centrality among government functions as well as its susceptibility to corruption, the OECD has made improving procurement practices one of its key recommendations to countries in the developing world (OECD, 2016).

Case studies of successful procurement reform can be a source of practical insight for developing countries. This chapter examines key features of South

Korea's public procurement process. Korea's rapid economic development as well as its democratic transformation are well studied phenomena (Chibber, 1999; Im, Campbell, & Cha, 2013; Kim, 2000). In the process of development, however, Korea had to overcome many of the same challenges that face developing countries today. For instance, during Korea's development, significant levels of corruption between the public and private sector concentrated economic influence among a relatively small set of companies, and the close relationship between the state and the private sector, and particularly its largest firms, meant that the public procurement process lacked transparency and fairness. Today, such processes have been massively reformed, with Korea now taking a leading role in the development and diffusion of best practices for public procurement. Understanding this transition as well as how Korea's contemporary procurement process is being used to address the market and social distortions produced during its rapid development can help highlight strategies of public procurement reform for developing countries.

This chapter looks at the bureaucratic and technical approach to improving the fairness, effectiveness, and efficiency of public procurement in South Korea. To orient the discussion, I first provide an overview of the general characteristics of public procurement and its differences from procurement in the private sector. Next, I discuss the ways in which the public procurement process is generally vulnerable to corrupt practices. The next two sections focus on how Korea's e-procurement system works to combat corruption, as well as some of the broader ways that the Korean government has leveraged the procurement processes to benefit various groups that possess socially relevant characteristics. The final section summarizes these points and comments on the possibility of replicating these successes in alternative contexts.

PROCUREMENT IN THE PUBLIC SECTOR

Effectively procuring resources from external organizations is key to organizational survival and performance in both the private and public sector. However, there are several characteristics of public procurement that distinguish it from procurement by private businesses, and before turning to an evaluation and discussion of the South Korean government's procurement processes, it is helpful to first discuss the nature of procurement in the public sector. In this section, the three dimensions of public procurement proposed by Erridge and colleagues (Erridge, 2007; Erridge & McIlroy, 2002) are used to frame a discussion of Korea's procurement practices. The concept of sustainable procurement is also introduced.

Evaluative Criteria for Public Procurement

Erridge and McIlroy (2002) distinguished between three dimensions of the procurement process in the public sector. These factors differentiate public from private procurement and provide criteria by which various public procurement regimes in democratic countries may be evaluated. The first of these, which is common to both public and private sector procurement, is the commercial dimension. Procuring the resources necessary to pursue organizational goals is a key and core component of any organizational endeavor, and organizations in both the private and public sectors rely on external suppliers to furnish them with materials and services which they do not or cannot produce themselves. There are many similarities in the procurement process across sectors, including the necessities of determining the set of potential partners, evaluating the suitability of partners for a given contract, selecting a partner, formalizing the relationship, and so on. While, as we shall see, there are other values at play in public procurement, both public and private organizations must consider the economic efficiency of a given procurement contract, and the commercial dimension of public procurement emphasizes extracting the greatest value for money from the procurement process. Procurement effectiveness from this perspective involves whether the buyer can secure the necessary goods and services that are required in sufficient quantity and quality at the lowest possible price. Like in the private sector, the primary mechanism by which government purchasers seek to achieve efficient transactions is competition between potential suppliers. Because of this, the commercial dimension of procurement in the public sector is primarily market based.

While the commercial dimension of public procurement is shared with procurement practice in the private sector, public procurement is distinguished in several other ways. In the private sector, business activities, including procurement, are funded based on the revenue and profit of the venture. In contrast, the operations of government bureaucracy are funded largely by public funds. Public funding is a key dimension of "publicness," and has an impact on efficiency and effectiveness in the public sector (Andrews, Boyne, & Walker, 2011). Specifically, in the case of procurement, because public funds are used in the purchase of goods and services, and therefore, at least in democratic countries, there is a much stronger need for transparency and accountability in the procurement process. Consequently, while private organizations may conduct procurement operations in secret, and, indeed, in the private sector, a successful procurement strategy may be a key competitive advantage, in the public sector, ideally, all purchases and contracts should be open to the public, with the reasoning behind the selection open to scrutiny. As such, a second dimension of the public procurement process, and one that distinguishes public procurement from procurement in the private sector, is its strong regulatory character. In the public sector, procurement should often follow a strict and standardized rule-based format, where each step of the process is shaped by regulation and scrupulously recorded. Because the goods and services that are purchased by government are purchased using public funds, the regulatory aspect of public procurement ensures that competition for public contracts is fair, the criteria by which bids are judged are well known, and the final selection available as public knowledge. As such, although both public and private procurement are concerned with extracting maximum value for money in any given procurement contract, public procurement is distinguished by its legal-rational character and the imperative of transparency. From this perspective, the emphasis is placed on compliance such that both the government entity and its supplier must follow strict procedural rules or risk sanctions. In seeking to understand public sector procurement, therefore, it is always necessary to consider the legal framework within which all public purchases are made.

The third and most distinctive characteristic of procurement in the public sector is the imperative that public procurement be consistent with the broader policy goals of the government, which cannot be reduced to economic efficiency. Procurement in the public sector is also distinguished by the sheer scale of the enterprise, and estimates for the scale of public procurement in OECD countries, for instance, range from 8% to 25% of gross domestic product. As such, even the purchasing agendas of the largest private organizations are many times smaller than that of the government. Additionally, and closely related to this issue of size, is the much greater diversity of goals that the government pursues (Erridge, 2005). While even large and complex enterprises sometimes have only a relatively streamlined set of products or services on offer, the government is involved in everything from infrastructure to education to defense. Consequently, both the variety and number of goods and services procured by government far outstrips those procured by any given private sector organization. This greater scale and scope have several consequences, including that government procurement activities have a nontrivial impact on the national economy. Due to this influence, there is an imperative that government make central considerations about a range of values beyond economic efficiency in procurement decisions.

Due to the scale and scope of its procurement activities, government can shape the economic incentives and thereby behavior of the pool of potential private sector suppliers. In the private sector, were a given organization large enough to have a similar impact, there would be little obligation to produce socially valued outcomes through procurement, but rather only to produce stockholder value. In contrast, government has the mandate to pursue socially beneficial outcomes and public procurement activities can be an instrument by which to pursue them. The list of noneconomic concerns of government is long and countries can use the procurement process to focus on ways in which public procurement may, for instance, increase employment, promote equality, enable minority labor market participation, or support environmental sustainability. Additionally, and relatedly, unlike private organizations, where the ratio of profits to costs may serve as a metric of performance (in practice, of course, the situation is more complex), the public sector has a multiplicity of values beyond simple efficiency to which it must attend (Rainey, 2014, pp. 64–69). Again, while value multiplicity is a potentially defining characteristic of public organizations and has several significant consequences for their operation, values such as equity, effectiveness, and sustainability cannot be ignored in public procurement decisions. A distinguishing feature of public procurement, therefore, lies in the inclusion of noneconomic value criteria among purchasing criteria.

An extension of this value-based approach to procurement in the public sector is the concept of sustainable procurement. Walker and Brammer (2012, p. 257) define sustainable procurement as "the pursuit of sustainable development objectives through the purchasing and supply process, incorporating social [and] environmental aspects." The concept of sustainable procurement originated in the private sector supply chain management literature and initially focused on the idea of minimizing the impact of procurement on the environment. Sustainable procurement in the public sector, however, is a broader concept and refers to the potential of public procurement, through a range of purchasing policy and competition regulation, to incentivize socially desirable behavior on the part of private sector firms. Again, due to the scale and scope of procurement in the public sector, through shaping the competitive landscape government is in a unique position to encourage private firms to act in ways that enhance economic or operational sustainability and serve public ends (Linton, Klassen, & Jayaraman, 2007). The government can also adopt market-shaping procurement policy tools to favor any group of suppliers whose involvement in public procurement is thought to have socially beneficial effects beyond the bare extraction of economic utility. Again, this goal is pursued through the formal incorporation of noncommercial criteria into procurement decisions. This being said, socially oriented procurement goals still need to be balanced against the need for economic efficiency, which can lead to goal conflict in the procurement process, and these competing values can be found in the regulatory framework supporting much public procurement practice (Erridge, 2007).

Corruption in the Public Procurement Process

Corruption in public procurement affects all countries and all levels of government to various degrees. The negative effects of corruption in public procurement include the erosion of public confidence, inflation of operational and project costs, the undermining of trust in government, and a distortion of overall expenditure that in turn requires trade-offs that result in the underfunding of key programs and services necessary for development (Neupane et al., 2012). However, while corruption in the public procurement process is a problem everywhere, when individuals, either government officials or representatives of private companies, subvert public procurement processes for private gain, the consequences are significantly worse for developing countries, which are already resource and capacity constrained. Reducing corruption in the procurement process is therefore viewed as a critical imperative, with the OECD singling out the improvement of financial management and procurement as a key strategy for development (OECD, 2016).

At the same time, while corruption in the procurement process has significant negative consequences, preventing it is difficult, as procurement processes consist of different stages that each have unique vulnerabilities to corruption. For instance, in the project planning phase, a government official may request an unnecessary project from which they can personally gain, or, in the project design phase, project details may be specified that favor a particular supplier. The bidding process itself can be made unnecessarily complicated, presenting barriers to entry for many firms. At the tendering and contract awarding phase, there are several opportunities for abuse of power, including the most powerful contractors using coercive means by which to secure contracts (Neupane et al., 2012; OECD, 2016). Because these opportunities are so various, a comprehensive approach is needed to reduce corruption in the procurement process (OECD, 2009).

The public procurement process is susceptible to corruption for several reasons, many of which are inherently related to the structure of the procurement context itself. Agency theory provides a framework that captures the structural elements and the incentives that can work to undermine the procurement process. Agency theory describes a situation in which one individual or group, the principal, contracts a second party, the agent, to perform a service on their behalf (Eisenhardt, 1989; Jensen & Meckling, 1976). This relationship has two key characteristics, which together form the basis of the so-called principal-agent problem. First, as the agent is hired because of the relative expertise that they possess about the service which they are contracted to perform, it can be assumed that they have superior access to information about this service. Information is thus asymmetrically distributed between the two parties. The second assumption is that the interests of the principal and the agent are not perfectly aligned. For instance, while the agent generally wants the service they have contracted to be delivered at the highest possible quality for the lowest possible price and in the shortest possible time, in certain conditions the agent may have an interest in producing an expensive, inferior quality service over a drawn-out period. The principle-agent problem arises because the informational advantage possessed by the agent furnishes them with opportunities to further their own interests at the expense of the agent. While the assumptions of agency theory, especially the assumption of individual self-interest as the sole or main motivating factor of public servants, are often questioned or even contradicted by public administration scholars (Kim & Vandenabeele, 2010; Waterman & Meier, 1998), the theory nevertheless provides a useful set of assumptions as an initial point from which to examine inefficiencies and corruption in the public procurement process.

Agency theory sheds light on the procurement process in several ways. First, when potential service providers have more information than buyers (i.e., government purchasers) about the true cost of the service, this informational advantage may be leveraged to secure contracts above market rate. While this behavior may not strictly be defined as corruption, nevertheless it is highly inefficient from the point of view of the government. The principal instrument used to address this problem is the introduction of competition to the procurement process. In theory, competition provides a mechanism by which the lowest possible price for a given service or resource may be revealed without the necessity of the buyer having expert information about the production of the object of purchase. However, particularly in developing countries, market mechanisms are seldom developed sufficiently for this purpose, and moreover the market may have a limited number (or no) competitive firms. Moreover, even when there is competition, potential suppliers have opportunities to collude to secure contracts with the government significantly above market rate. Again, these behaviors result in an inefficient allocation of public resources, as the products or services purchased will be of substandard quality, above market price, or both.

However, while sellers may attempt to exploit their superior information about production costs, leverage hidden relationships, or take advantage of market imperfections to secure contracts above market value, a second and perhaps more critical source of corruption in the public procurement process originates from the purchasing side. In this situation, a government official seeks to exploit their status as a representative of the monopoly purchasing

power of government to secure personal profits or kickbacks in the awarding of public contracts. This form of corruption consists of an individual or
group of individuals responsible for allocating a given contract doing so based
on private payments or bribes rather than impartial performance criteria. If
corruption is defined as the abuse of public office for private gain (Klitgaard,
1988), such behavior is perhaps the idealized case. However, while evidence is
mixed on whether this situation, commonly known as "greasing the wheels,"
has a negative impact on macro-level economic growth and development
(Dreher & Gassebner, 2013; Meon & Sekkat, 2005), it is nevertheless highly
problematic from an ethical perspective, and moreover can undermine general
trust in the government, thereby having a more diffuse impact on society.

As Kauppi and van Raaij (2014) note, however, opportunistic, self-interested behavior is not the sole factor determining a situation where the agent
does not act in the interests of the principal. Rather, this may be because
of either (honest) incompetence or a lack of information about what the
principal truly wants. As such, simply by centralizing public procurement
processes, governments can take a significant step toward improving the efficiency and effectiveness of procurement practice. An additional strategy can
be to better train procurement officials to increase the capacity of the purchasing agent.

KOREA'S PUBLIC PROCUREMENT SYSTEM

General Characteristics of Public Procurement in Korea

South Korea's central procurement agency, the Public Procurement Service
(PPS), was established first in 1961 and now operates under the Ministry of
Strategy and Finance. The agency has just fewer than 1000 full-time staff with
about 46% of these working at the PPS's headquarters in Seoul. Generally,
a centralized agency works to define procurement specifics, select suppliers,
products, and services, negotiate terms and prices, and coordinate the purchasing of subunits (Kauppi & van Raaij, 2014). Korea's PPS has several
functions and responsibilities, including the procurement of goods and services on both the domestic and international market, the management of
government-maintained stocks of various commodity goods used by Korea's
small and medium-sized enterprises (SMEs) to maintain price stability, and the
management of various government resources and properties. (Commodity
materials, which the PPS has been stockpiling since 1967, are both highly
relevant to the economy and dependent on foreign suppliers (Choi, 2010;

PPS, 2015).) Importantly, and what will be discussed in greater depth later, the PPS also oversees the operation of the country's e-procurement system, generally known by the acronym KONEPS (Korea ON-line E-Procurement System). While, like most government organizations, PPS is funded primarily through the central government budget, the agency also has a self-raised special budget funded by fees that it charges for procurement contracts it makes on behalf of other public organizations. In other words, this special budget is funded through leveraging the unique experience and expertise of the PPS on behalf of other government organizations. The special budget is used primarily to support labor and operation costs, expedited payment for goods and services, and for stockpiling the various commodities used by SMEs (OECD, 2016).

The centralization of procurement processes is known to lead to economies of scale, a streamlining of the administrative processes relevant to procurement, facilitation of concessions from sellers, better overall value for money, improved knowledge and learning, and more generally a reduction in the transaction costs associated with procurement contract formation (Celec, Nosari, & Voich, 2003; Karjalainen, 2011; Schotanus et al., 2011). In Korea, various laws govern the conditions under which it is necessary to route government procurement through the central PPS. These laws are largely financial, and different thresholds are set for different sectors. For instance, government organizations must make use of the PPS for construction projects that are valued above 2.54 million USD, or for commodities and services valued over about 85,000 USD. Laws are also different at the local level. Over the past several decades, local governments have gained greater autonomy in their procurement activities and today face few restrictions on how they procure goods, services, or larger construction works (OECD, 2016). These reforms have been part of a broader strategy to increase local autonomy in Korea. At the same time, while local governments are free to use the procurement services of their choice in most circumstances, the expertise of the PPS often makes it an attractive choice. In fact, one of the main areas of growth of buyers using PPS since 2010 has been local governments, public enterprises, as well as other governmental entities and local government enterprises, all of which have substantial autonomy in choosing which procurement service to use (OECD, 2016).

KONEPS: Korea ON-line E-Procurement System

As Korea's e-government initiative began to accelerate in the 1990s, the government also began to investigate moving existing procurement systems online. While at this time most agencies relied on traditional analog paper-based systems, a number of large purchasers began to develop and use their own online systems to streamline procurement. At this stage, however, there was little inter-agency collaboration in the planning, design, and implementation process, and consequently systems lacked compatibility and had only rudimentary information sharing capabilities. While these early attempts pointed to the future direction of procurement in Korea, more coordination was necessary before the system could produce its promised efficiencies and economies of scale (OECD, 2016).

Recognizing the need for integration, the PPS produced an e-procurement "master plan" that led, after an initial pilot period, to the government-wide rollout of the Procurement Electronic Data Interchange by 2001. This system enabled procurement-relevant information sharing across government as well as key private sector bidders, leading to efficiency gains and an overall reduction of paper-based transactions. In parallel, efforts were also expended to move bidding and payment online, and by 2001, both bidder registration and payments were available. A private contractor was hired to produce the final system, which has been available since September 2002 (OECD, 2016).

KONEPS, the Korean ON-line E-Procurement System, is an end-to-end procurement solution encompassing bidding, awarding, contracting, and payment. The comprehensiveness of this system contrasts with that of many other OECD country systems, where the role of offline operations increases as one moves through the procurement process (OECD, 2016). Security and convenience features have continuously been added to the KONEPS system, allowing the system to adapt to the emergence of mobile computing in 2008, radio frequency identification (RFID) inventory management in 2009, and the use of fingerprint identification in 2010. The system now also includes an online shopping mall made available in 2006 that standardizes a number of procurement-related processes and provides easy access to various products. These updates have been possible because KONEPS was designed as a modular system from its initiation, allowing any number of security, access, or efficiency-oriented technologies to be added as they materialize (OECD, 2016).

Some numbers suggest the scale of KONEPS (OECD, 2016). About 48,000 buyers across central and local governments use the system, with nearly 300,000 private firms registered as potential suppliers and bidders, with an additional 560,000 individual user accounts. Over 200,000 users log into the system every day, which processes a similar number of e-documents. Over 360,000 products are cataloged in the online shopping mall, in which over 11.4 billion USD was spent in 2014. Some estimates put the savings from

KONEPS at about 8 billion USD per year, with 80% of these savings accruing to private sector companies (OECD, 2016).

KONEPS was recognized early by the OECD as a "best practices" example of procurement. Based on this success, the government has been active in forming partnerships with developing countries, supporting the adoption of the KONEPS system to help achieve more efficiency in their procurement processes as well as fight corruption. Beginning in 2008, versions of the KONEPS system have been adopted in Vietnam, Costa Rica, Mongolia, Tunisia, Cameroon, and, most recently, in Jordan. The PPS has also begun cooperation with several additional countries (PPS, 2015).

Corruption Reduction and Procurement in Korea

Because of the negative economic as well as social effects of corruption in the public procurement process, reducing corrupt behaviors has become a key goal for reformers in both developed and developing countries (OECD, 2007). South Korea's economic transformation into an affluent and technologically advanced nation has often lead politicians and bureaucrats in currently developing countries to attempt to learn lessons from the Korean case that may be integrated into their own development and poverty-reduction strategies. Of course, while Korea's transformation was rapid and in some ways unprecedented, it nevertheless unfolded over several years and had to overcome many of the challenges common to developing countries today. For example, while the situation is steadily improving, Korea continues to suffer from significant levels of corruption in the public sector. During the earlier days of development, some of the causes of this corruption were structural. For instance, in the 1960s and later, few robust market mechanisms existed which government could utilize to implement a transparent and efficient allocation of national resources. As such, the government allocated resources among private companies in a largely closed-door fashion (Campbell & Cho, 2014). While it is undeniable that these practices were not entirely incompatible with economic development and moreover have, in the long run, led to the creation of some of the largest corporations in the world, nevertheless, this method of distributing national resources was highly subject to nonperformance criteria, especially funds that could be channeled into private political accounts (Kang, 2002). Moreover, precisely because these practices lead to large economic imbalances between the country's chaebol, or corporate conglomerates, and all other small and medium-sized companies, the competitive playing field as it developed became strongly biased toward a relatively small set of companies. Especially since the Asian Financial Crisis of 1997, when Korea was forced to seek a loan from the International Monetary Fund to cover short-term financial shortfalls, this economic imbalance has been a key issue for the country's democracy (Kalinowski, 2009).

Anti-corruption reforms in Korea have taken on a variety of forms (Lee & Jung, 2010). The OECD has singled out e-procurement as a key technical resource that can be used to fight corruption in the public sector (OECD, 2007). E-procurement increases transparency and standardization, which are beneficial for corruption reduction, while also improving auditing capacity by centralizing data, improving the efficacy and efficiency of monitoring, including the status of all open solicitations and ongoing contracts, and reducing the opportunity for collusion and bid rigging among bidders (Neupane et al., 2012). As such, in terms of reducing corruption in the procurement process, Korea's KONEPS system has played an important role. Because procurement in the public sector utilizes public money, there are high standards for transparency and accountability in the procurement process, and moving procurement systems online creates not only a centralized paper trail for each step in the procurement decision-making process, but also can reduce the space for individuals, either public sector purchasers or private sector providers, to act opportunistically and exploit their knowledge or position for their personal gain at the expense of the public. In this sense, rather than relying on "disciplined and ethical subjects" (Neu, Everett, & Rahanam, 2015, p. 50), e-procurement "reduces corruption-prone face-to-face contacts" between parties (OECD, 2007, p. 16), eliminating many opportunities to subvert the procurement process.

The KONEPS system is designed to create a verifiable record of all stages of the public procurement process. KONEPS allows all procurement transactions in the system to be made available to the public in real time (PPS, 2015). Making this information available to the public in perpetuity is itself a significant step toward greater transparency in the procurement process. Not only are the number of bidders, their bids, and bid winners retained and available for scrutiny, the KONEPS system tracks the procurement process through tendering to fulfillment. Given that a significant amount of corruption can take place after the bidding has finished and a tender has been awarded, this tracking and documentation of the post-bidding process provides an additional dimension upon which the efficacy of the public procurement process may be monitored and evaluated. In terms of the values that guide procurement, therefore, it can be seen that KONEPS was aimed at reconciling efficiency and transparency (Choi, 2010).

A more specific example of how the KONEPS system targets corruption in the public procurement process is its integration with the Korean Fair Trade

Commission's Bid Rigging Indicator Analysis System (BRIAS). BRIAS takes an automated, algorithmically generated approach to fraud detection in the public procurement process. Drawing on information from the KONEPS system such as bidding prices, the number of participants in a given auction, as well as the method of competition employed, BRIAS generates a bid-rigging likelihood score for individual procurement auctions. If the bid-rigging likelihood score surpasses a certain threshold, the implication is that there is a sufficiently high chance of corruption in the process. In this case, administrators are obliged to investigate further (OECD, 2016).

BRIAS generates a monthly index of bid-rigging probabilities based on daily information that it gathers from KONEPS. Over the course of a year, tens of thousands of bids are analyzed by BRIAS, which makes the system an interesting step toward the usage of big data to improve the efficiency and transparency of public sector processes. At the same time, only a small percentage of cases identified by the BRIAS system ultimately result in charges being laid. However, since the introduction of BRIAS, the voluntary reporting of potentially fraudulent actions by bidding parties has increased substantially (OECD, 2016). This suggests that, in addition to its potential to uncover collusive and dishonest behaviors in the public procurement process, BRIAS has an indirect behavioral impact on bidders, creating a pre-emptive chilling effect for individuals who may otherwise have attempted to manipulate the system for private gain.

KONEPS reduces the opportunity for corruption both on the part of government and bidders. By moving procurement functions online, publishing the details of the procurement process, and inviting public scrutiny, the implementation of KONEPS is a step toward greater transparency and integrity in the public procurement process. This is significant and represents a de-politicization of the procurement process, placing it out of reach of individuals who would otherwise attempt to exploit it for personal gain at the expense of the public interest.

Value-Based Procurement in Korea

SMEs play large and crucial role in most economies. However, despite their importance, smaller firms generally have a more difficult time competing effectively in the public procurement marketplace (Karjalainen & Kemppainen, 2008). The challenges for SMEs are numerous. Procurement processes can often be time consuming and complex, which itself can create barriers to entry for smaller firms. Moreover, on the government side, contracts can sometimes be bundled together in order to reduce administrative overhead. While this practice may lead to efficiency gains for the government, it effectively rules out SMEs that lack the scale to compete at this level. SMEs are also generally resource constrained and lack short-term human or financial capital to allocate toward learning the procurement process, even though this could result in longer-term gains. As Karjalainen and Kemppainen (2008) point out, however, public procurement processes may be designed strategically in order to alleviate these difficulties for SMEs and facilitate their greater involvement in the public procurement market.

SMEs make up nearly the entirety of businesses in Korea, with estimates as high as 99%, and account for nearly 90% of employment (Government of Korea, 2011, cited in Nicholas & Fruhmann, 2014). With a goal of achieving a more balanced future development, Korea has emphasized support for SMEs as a key value and has been one of the leaders among developed countries in the promotion of SMEs in public procurement (Jones, 2011). By 2008, at least two-thirds of total procurement has been composed of purchases from SMEs (Choi, 2010; Jones, 2011). Korea achieves SME support in its procurement process by earmarking various products that can only be purchased from SMEs, as well as by including SMEs in multiple award schedules (MAS), or stand-by contracts for product or service supply with pre-specified features and prices (Jones, 2011). Moreover, contracts are made payable prior to the delivery of the products or services, which helps to overcome short-term cash flow problems among SMEs, and additionally the PPS can also support the acquisition of loans from private institutions to facilitate contract fulfillment by SMEs. These strategies alleviate the necessities of high upfront costs that SMEs face when entering the procurement market (Choi, 2010; Jones, 2011; Nicholas & Fruhmann, 2014). Additionally, SMEs enjoy a more lenient capability evaluation for construction contracts, again facilitating their participation in public procurement (Jones, 2011). In 2014, the minimum experience required for an SME construction firm was reduced from 1 to 5 successful projects to 0.5 to 3, a change intended to attract firms with limited past performance. Additionally, unlike larger suppliers, small contractors were allowed for the first time to form consortiums to improve their bids (PPS, 2015).

Due to the importance of SMEs to employment and equity in the Korean economy, their promotion by public procurement is a significant policy. However, several specific types of SMEs receive special attention, singled out largely due to their socially relevant characteristics. First, the Korean government has introduced formal rules that favor start up and small venture capital businesses that have developed innovative, patented products.

These products can be selected under MAS contracts (Choi, 2010; Jones, 2011). Additionally, "green" products are favored in public procurement, which have been determined to have eco-friendly attributes, are energy saving, or are connected to low greenhouse gas emissions, and the government moreover fosters competition between purchasers (government entities) to make an ever-greater proportion of their overall purchases green (Jones, 2011). Public works contracts also generally have a number of green requirements (Jones, 2011). Next, regionally based businesses and women-owned businesses are targeted in procurement (Choi, 2010). Since January 2014, several public organizations had their minimum amount of direct contract for firms led by women increase from below 20 million won to below 50 million won (PPS, 2015). Contracts valued at less than 50 million won can be awarded directly to woman-owned firms, and for relatively small construction projects, only local women-owned firms can bid for contracts (PPS, 2015). Finally, since 2014, the KONEPS Shopping Mall has featured SMEs and start-ups that hire handicapped workers, encouraging government offices to purchase items offered by these organizations, which the PPS refers to as "socially vulnerable firms" (PPS, 2015, p. 19).

Finally, in addition to promoting SMEs, Korea's procurement practice has also increasingly focused on facilitating the entry of social enterprises to the procurement market. Social enterprises are privately held organizations that operate according to a so-called "double bottom line" in that they attempt to balance financial sustainability with social impact (Dart, 2004). In 2007, Korea passed the Social Enterprise Promotion Act, which was designed to promote the role of social enterprises in Korea in both employment and service delivery. The act, which also establishes a specialized agency dealing with social enterprises, stipulates that both the Ministry of Employment and Labor at the national level and each provincial and metropolitan government sub-nationally will establish a plan for the promotion of social enterprises in their respective spheres. Moreover, in addition to various other mechanisms of formal government support, the act also stipulates that the heads of public institutions shall give preferential status to goods and services produced by social enterprises. This policy has the dual purpose of increasing employment in a sector that also benefits the social welfare of society.

DISCUSSION AND CONCLUSION

The implementation of the KONEPS e-procurement system has brought with it many advantages ranging from improved efficiency in the procurement process, greater transparency and accountability, and reduced opportunities for individuals to subvert the process for private gain. Additionally, increasingly South Korea has leveraged its large public procurement purchasing program in order to attempt to favor groups with socially relevant characteristics. These changes occurred in the context of Korea's larger developmental path, which includes a stronger emphasis on anti-corruption, particularly between government and big business. While Korea's state-lead development model was exceptionally effective in reducing poverty and improving competitiveness, due to the speed of the transformation it inevitably created market distortions. As such, the transformation of the procurement system into a modern, open, and competitive endeavor represents a very significant achievement.

The challenges that Korea faced in reforming its public procurement system are not unique. Across the globe, developing countries are burdened by corruption, inefficiency, weak competition in the market, and a general inability to allocate scarce resources in an effective way. To what extent, then, can Korea's approach to public procurement be adopted by other developing countries wishing to improve the effectiveness of their public processes?

It is well-known that the government played an important role in driving economic development in South Korea (Chibber, 1999). However, in a sense public procurement policy was at the heart of its intervention in the market. Public procurement can be a key "demand-side" policy tool to facilitate innovation, both at the general and strategic, sector-specific level (Edler & Georghiou, 2007), which were relevant in Korea's developmental procurement strategy. Using what Kattel and Lember (2010, p. 389) refer to as "classical industrial policy," Korea and other East Asian countries were able to drive economic development specifically by defining the types of products and services necessary for their vision of the economy and then setting deadlines and standards to make continued progress toward the production of these. Expanding this, they write that "the successive industrial policy measures from one product to the next (from radios and light bulbs in the 1950s to computers and [computer] chips in the 1990s), East Asian industrial policy can be seen as a prolonged process of public procurement activity" (p. 370). Conceptualized in this way, procurement policy can be seen to be central to the developmental state model.

One challenge that developing countries often face is weak market competition, and over time, Korea's procurement processes strengthened competition in the market sufficiently that it could take a less active role in the economy (Kim & Campbell, 2014). While there are many determinants of the level of competitiveness, government plays a key role, either actively suppressing competition or tolerating it (Caldwell et al., 2005). Caldwell et al. (2005) argue that, under the right circumstances, public procurement can be used to both establish and maintain competitive markets, especially with regard to risk sharing, performance monitoring, and framework agreements. In more recent times, the Korean case highlights many relatively inexpensive ways that government can reduce barriers to entry for smaller firms such as by making information about procurement available as widely as possible and streamlining the procurement process. In the Korean case, the implementation of the KONEPS e-procurement system contributed substantially to this goal, and increasingly the technology to implement higher quality procurement processes is readily available to developing countries.

On the other hand, while technology transfer and innovation policy were central to Korea's procurement-based development policy, the international institutional context has significantly changed since the 1970s and 1980s. For instance, certain World Trade Organization (WTO) regulations limit the policy space for developing countries to take more aggressive actions to facilitate innovation through procurement while also strengthening domestic competition (Kattel & Lember, 2010). As Wade (2003) argues, WTO and other associated trade rules are not primarily concerned with limiting the options of private sector actors but rather limiting the options for governments to shape the behavior of these actors, both domestic and international. These agreements are also arguably more detrimental to developing countries than to developed ones (Wade, 2003). As such, while trade agreements do not eliminate the policy space in terms of procurement for developing countries entirely (Kattel & Lember, 2010), they nevertheless place nontrivial restrictions on the range of policy options available. This is a distinct challenge for contemporary developing countries that South Korea did not face with the same level of intensity.

An additional challenge faced by less developed countries in terms of utilizing procurement for development is that of bureaucratic capacity (Kattel & Lember, 2010). As Im (forthcoming, this volume) points out, in order for a bureaucracy to act as a facilitator of democratic values, it must be highly professional, sufficiently large, and have the tools necessary to secure a significant degree of independence from undue political influence. And while policy capacity has potentially been undermined worldwide due to falling support for elected officials and administrative reform (Painter & Pierre, 2005), these problems are particularly acute in developing countries. As Erridge and others have pointed out, different types of values are associated with the public procurement process; in practice, these may come into conflict with one another, creating goal ambiguity and undermining the potential of the procurement process to have a significant impact. For instance, the emphasis on short-term cost-effectiveness can come into conflict with the longer term perspective that recognizes that investment (and patience) is needed to support innovation. Balancing these needs can be expensive, time consuming, and require a level of coordination between various parts of government that is beyond the capacity of many bureaucracies. Because of this, using procurement processes to support innovation or sustainable procurement may be written off as prohibitively expensive relative to the immediate goal of short-term cost savings (Brammer & Walker, 2007; Kattel & Lember, 2010). Additionally, a high level of planning capacity is also necessary (Im forthcoming, this volume), and policy makers in the Korean context had a relatively clear idea of which kinds of products and technologies were needed in order to pursue domestic sectoral development (Kattel & Lember, 2010). Today, it is increasingly difficult to make such predictions, given that the speed of technological innovation is accelerating rather than remaining constant. As such, there is a danger for less developed countries procuring technologies that are obsolete by the time they are fully integrated into the economy.

To conclude, the case of South Korea suggests that public procurement can play an important role both in supporting economic development generally as well as facilitating market activity and autonomy among businesses deemed to have socially desirable characteristics. Moreover, Korea's e-procurement system has played a significant role in reducing corruption, which negatively affects economic competitiveness but also undermines trust in government. While the Korean case has many distinctive characteristics that make its replication challenging in alternative contexts, nevertheless, it is clear that procurement policy, in conjunction with other policy tools, can have a substantive impact on the long-term development and composition of a country's economy. As this chapter has discussed, moreover, public procurement may also be used to pursue goals that directly contribute to democratization. A robust and strategic public procurement policy should therefore be adopted by countries at all levels of development.

REFERENCES

Andrews, R., Boyne, G. A., & Walker, R. M. (2011). Dimensions of publicness and organizational performance: A review of the evidence. *Journal of Public Administration Research and Theory*, *21*(suppl. 3), i301–i319.

Brammer, S., & Walker, H. (2007). Sustainable procurement practice in the public sector: An international comparative study.

Caldwell, N., Walker, H., Harland, C., Knight, L., Zheng, J., & Wakeley, T. (2005). Promoting competitive markets: The role of public procurement. *Journal of Purchasing and Supply Management, 11*(5), 242–251.

Campbell, J. W., & Cho, W. (2014). Two faces of government-business relations during South Korea's developmental period. *Korean Journal of Comparative Government, 18*(1), 47–66.

Celec, S. E., Nosari, E. J., & Voich, Jr., D. (2003). Performance measures for evaluating the financial benefits of state term commodity contracts. *Journal of Public Procurement, 3*(1), 43.

Chibber, V. (1999). Building a developmental state: The Korean case reconsidered. *Politics & Society, 27*(3), 309–346.

Choi, J.-W. (2010). A study of the role of public procurement—Can public procurement make society better. Paper presented at the 4th International Public Procurement Conference.

Dart, R. (2004). The legitimacy of social enterprise. *Nonprofit Management and Leadership, 14*(4), 411–424.

Dreher, A., & Gassebner, M. (2013). Greasing the wheels? The impact of regulations and corruption on firm entry. *Public Choice, 155*(3), 413–432. doi:10.1007/s11127-011-9871-2

Edler, J., & Georghiou, L. (2007). Public procurement and innovation—Resurrecting the demand side. *Research Policy, 36*(7), 949–963.

Eisenhardt, K. M. (1989). Agency theory: An assessment and review. *Academy of Management Review, 14*(1), 57–74.

Erridge, A. (2005). UK public procurement policy and the delivery of public value. *Challenges in Public Procurement: An International Perspective*, 335–352.

Erridge, A. (2007). Public procurement, public value and the Northern Ireland unemployment pilot project. *Public Administration, 85*(4), 1023–1043.

Erridge, A., & McIlroy, J. (2002). Public procurement and supply management strategies. *Public Policy and Administration, 17*(1), 52–71.

Im, T., Campbell, J. W., & Cha, S. (2013). Revisiting Confucian bureaucracy: Roots of the Korean government's culture and competitiveness. *Public Administration and Development, 33*(4), 286–296.

Jensen, M. C., & Meckling, W. H. (1976). Theory of the firm: Managerial behavior, agency costs and ownership structure. *Journal of Financial Economics, 3*(4), 305–360.

Jones, D. S. (2011). Recent reforms to promote social responsibility procurement in East Asian states: A comparative analysis. *Journal of Public Procurement, 11*(1), 61.

Kalinowski, T. (2009). The politics of market reforms: Korea's path from Chaebol Republic to market democracy and back. *Contemporary Politics, 15*(3), 287–304.

Kang, D. C. (2002). Bad loans to good friends: Money politics and the developmental state in South Korea. *International Organization, 56*(01), 177–207.

Karjalainen, K. (2011). Estimating the cost effects of purchasing centralization—Empirical evidence from framework agreements in the public sector. *Journal of Purchasing and Supply Management, 17*(2), 87–97.

Karjalainen, K., & Kemppainen, K. (2008). The involvement of small-and medium-sized enterprises in public procurement: Impact of resource perceptions, electronic systems and enterprise size. *Journal of Purchasing and Supply Management, 14*(4), 230–240.

Kattel, R., & Lember, V. (2010). Public procurement as an industrial policy tool: An option for developing countries? *Journal of Public Procurement, 10*(3), 368.

Kauppi, K., & Van Raaij, E. M. (2015). Opportunism and honest incompetence—Seeking explanations for noncompliance in public procurement. *Journal of Public Administration Research and Theory, 25*(3), 953–979.

Kim, D.-H., & Campbell, J. W. (2015). Development, diversification, and legitimacy: Emergence of the committee-based administrative model in South Korea. *Public Organization Review, 15*(4), 551–564.

Kim, S. (2000). *The politics of democratization in Korea: The role of civil society.* Pittsburgh, PA: University of Pittsburgh Press.

Kim, S., & Vandenabeele, W. (2010). A strategy for building public service motivation research internationally. *Public Administration Review, 70*(5), 701–709.

Klitgaard, R. (1988). *Controlling corruption.* California: University of California Press.

Lee, M. J. (2010). An exploratory study on the mature level evaluation of E-procurement systems. *Journal of Public Procurement, 10*(3), 405.

Lee, S. Y., & Jung, K. (2010). Public service ethics and anticorruption efforts in South Korea. In E. M. Berman, M. Jae Moon, and H. Choi (Eds.), *Public administration in East Asia: Mainland China, Japan, South Korea, and Taiwan* (pp. 401–426). Boca Raton, CA: CRC Press.

Lindgreen, A., Swaen, V., Maon, F., Walker, H., & Brammer, S. (2009). Sustainable procurement in the United Kingdom public sector. *Supply Chain Management: An International Journal, 14*(2), 128–137.

Linton, J. D., Klassen, R., & Jayaraman, V. (2007). Sustainable supply chains: An introduction. *Journal of Operations Management, 25*(6), 1075–1082.

Méon, P.-G., & Sekkat, K. (2005). Does corruption grease or sand the wheels of growth? *Public Choice, 122*(1), 69–97.

Neu, D., Everett, J., & Rahaman, A. S. (2015). Preventing corruption within government procurement: Constructing the disciplined and ethical subject. *Critical Perspectives on Accounting, 28*, 49–61.

Neupane, A., Soar, J., Vaidya, K., & Yong, J. (2012). Role of public e-procurement technology to reduce corruption in government procurement. Paper presented at the Proceedings of the 5th International Public Procurement Conference.

Nicholas, C., & Fruhmann, M. (2014). Small and medium-sized enterprises policies in public procurement: Time for a rethink? *Journal of Public Procurement, 14*(3), 328.

OECD. (2007). Fighting bribery in public procurement in Asia and the Pacific. Presented at the Regional Seminar on making international anti-corruption standards operational.

OECD. (2009). OECD principles for integrity in public procurement. Retrieved from https://market.android.com/details?id=book-eArWAgAAQBAJ

OECD. (2015). Government at a Glance 2015.

OECD. (2016a). Preventing corruption in public procurement.

OECD. (2016b). The Korean Public Procurement Service: Innovating for effectiveness.

Painter, M., & Pierre, J. (2005). *Unpacking policy capacity: Issues and themes Challenges to State Policy Capacity* (pp. 1–18). New York: Springer.

PPS. (2015). *Annual report 2014: Public procurement service, the Republic of Korea.* Retrieved from https://www.pps.go.kr/bbs/selectBoard.do?boardSeqNo=21&pageIndex=1&boardId=ENG005

Rainey, H. G. (2014). *Understanding and managing public organization* (5th ed.). San Francisco: Jossey-Bass; Pfeiffer Imprints, Wiley.

Schotanus, F., Bakker, E., Walker, H., & Essig, M. (2011). Development of purchasing groups during their life cycle: From infancy to maturity. *Public Administration Review, 71*(2), 265–275.

Wade, R. H. (2003). What strategies are viable for developing countries today? The World Trade Organization and the shrinking of 'development space'. *Review of International Political Economy, 10*(4), 621–644.

Waterman, R. W., & Meier, K. J. (1998). Principal-agent models: an expansion? *Journal of Public Administration Research and Theory, 8*(2), 173–202.

CHAPTER 8

THE OLYMPICS, SOFT POWER, AND DEMOCRATIZATION: THE ROLE OF BUREAUCRACY

Kwang-Hoon Lee

ABSTRACT

Despite the privatization of its various components, the bidding process and the preparations for the Olympics are still initiated and tightly managed by central governments. Moreover, intentionally and unintentionally, governments use mega sports events such as the Olympics as a soft power medium in which to pursue their goals such as economic development and social integration and a lot of literature has already reviewed the economic and sociocultural impact of hosting the event. This chapter argues that the Olympics have been used as the medium to assist in the formation of legitimacy for a weakened authoritarian leader in the early phase of democratization in Korea. In addition, the chapter tries to explain how the bureaucracy contributed to the success of the national event and how it eventually impacted political modernization and the attitude of bureaucrats. To these ends, first, this chapter explores the influence of soft power on international competition by providing an empirical statistical analysis.

*This chapter was based on Lee & Chappelet (2012).

The Experience of Democracy and Bureaucracy in South Korea
Public Policy and Governance, 181–215
Copyright © 2017 by Emerald Publishing Limited
All rights of reproduction in any form reserved
doi:10.1108/S2053-769720170000028008

Specifically, the chapter analyzes the process by which countries compete with one another for the privilege of hosting the Olympic Games as an important field of global interaction between political actors Further, the chapter discusses which components of soft power can affect international competition. To investigate the explanatory power and concrete applicability of soft power theory, the chapter looks at the influence of democratic and government dimensions of soft power on the selection of Olympic host cities and the role of bureaucracy during that process.

Keywords: Soft power; citizen participation; government transparency, Olympism; Olympic Games bidding

INTRODUCTION

Although "hard power," wielded through either inducements or threats, is still essential for the survival of the fittest in the arena of traditional security and military order, recent social and environmental changes in global competition (such as interest in quality of life or climate change) seem to raise the importance of "soft power," a term coined two decades ago by Joseph Nye, the ability of a country to exert its influence on the actions of another through nonmilitary means such as persuasion or attraction rather than coercion (Nye, 1990). Nye's arguments about the importance and role of soft power have had an enormous impact on the theory and practice of global politics. Still, there is little agreement as to what soft power actually means, precisely how it works, and what it takes to deploy it effectively (Kroenig, McAdam, & Weber, 2010).

However, is there any realm of international competition in which a nation's democratic and transparent government as soft power affects the country's victory? Or, to follow the hard-core realism proponents' arguments, is soft power an illusion? Do all competitions between countries merely end up as zero-sum games in which the super-powerful hegemon wins all? Is there really such a thing as soft power of better democracy and bureaucracy?

To address these questions, this chapter explores soft power's presence in and impact on international competition by providing empirical evidence. Specifically, the chapter analyzes the process by which countries compete with one another for the privilege of hosting the Olympic Games as an important field of global interaction between political actors (Cottrell & Nelson, 2011).

Nye's arguments about the importance and role of soft power have had an enormous impact on the theory and practice of global politics. Still, there is little agreement as to what soft power actually means, precisely how it works, and what it takes to deploy it effectively (Kroenig, McAdam, & Weber, 2010). Further, which component of soft power can affect international competition and which have less impact? To investigate the explanatory power and concrete applicability of soft power theory, this chapter looks at the influence of democratic and governmental dimensions of soft power on the selection of Olympic host cities.

This chapter is organized as follows. In the next section, based on the theoretical background of soft power, how a bid country's citizen participation and government transparency can influence the International Olympic Committee (IOC)'s vote is explained in a review of the relevant literature and of Olympics history. The third section explains in detail the methodology used to operationalize the main hypotheses, and suggests models for analyzing the IOC's voting patterns. The fourth section presents the analysis results. In the final section, factors that had significant effect in the models are discussed and conclusions are drawn regarding the soft power of democracy and bureaucracy in Olympic bids.

THEORETICAL BACKGROUND

The Concept of Soft Power

Nye defined soft power as the ability to get others to want what you want through attraction rather than coercion or payments (Nye, 2002: 9; 2004: 10). He also explains that soft power is the ability to affect the behavior of others by influencing their preferences, and is used "to attract, and attraction often leads to acquiescence" (Nye, 2004: 5–6). Nye (2004) envisioned a country's soft power, as opposed to its hard (military and economic) power, to be a new element of international politics following the end of the Cold War. Nye (2008) pointed out that a country can wield power in three ways: threat of force (the stick), inducement with payments (the carrot), or shaping the preferences of others to get them to want the same outcomes. According to Nye, a country's soft power rests primarily on three sources: its culture (in places where it is attractive to others), its political values (when it lives up to them at home and abroad), and its foreign policies (when they are seen as legitimate and having moral authority) (Nye, 2004; 2008). As a component of soft power, culture means not only high culture like literature, art, and education, which appeals to elites, but also television, cinema, pop music, and sports, consumed in mass entertainment markets. Political values such as democracy, justice, equality, and transparency strongly affect people's preferences. A country's foreign policy also affects its soft power since it influences the attitudes, perceptions, and images that foreign citizens have of that country.

Importance of Soft Power in the Olympic System

The importance of soft power has been emphasized in the area of sports diplomacy (Cha, 2009; Chappelet, 2008; Chappelet & Kubler-Mabbott, 2008; Houlihan, Bloyce, & Smith, 2009). In this respect, Nye (2004) proposed a "three-dimensional chessboard" model, which divides world politics into three closely interdependent dimensions of influence: military at the top, economic in the middle, and soft power at the bottom. The history of Olympic bidding, in which cities and countries compete to host the largest global sporting event in the world, reveals clues about how a country's soft power is exerted.

In order to facilitate a better understanding of the underlying mechanisms how countries compete with one another to win an international sport-event bidding, an analytical framework of the 'Olympic System' proposed by Chappelet (1991), Chappelet and Kubler-Mabbott (2008), Ferrand, Chappelet, and Seguin (2012) is well worth adopting. According to a systemic approach of the Olympic Movement, which has evolved from the classical Olympic System (Chappelet, 1991) through the extended/regulated Olympic System (Chappelet & Kubler-Mabbott, 2008) to the total Olympic System (Ferrand, Chappelet, & Seguin, 2012: 17–33), the following model illustrated in Fig. 1 consists of international, national, and subnational(local/regional) stakeholders in the governmental/public sector, business/commercial sector as well as nonprofit and civil society sphere.

It can be recognized that all stakeholders in the Olympic system are extensively interdependent between the different nonprofit, commercial, and public organizations. Among them the IOC, due to its governing role of the Olympic Movement and legitimate authority based on the Olympic Charter, has considerable influence over other organizations such as IFs, NOCs, OCOGs as well as cities/countries vying for the privilege of becoming the next Olympic host city. For instance, the IOC allocates exclusive rights to host the Olympics seven years in advance in a rigorous election process that involves a series of votes by IOC members, in which the city with the fewest votes is excluded until one achieves an absolute majority.

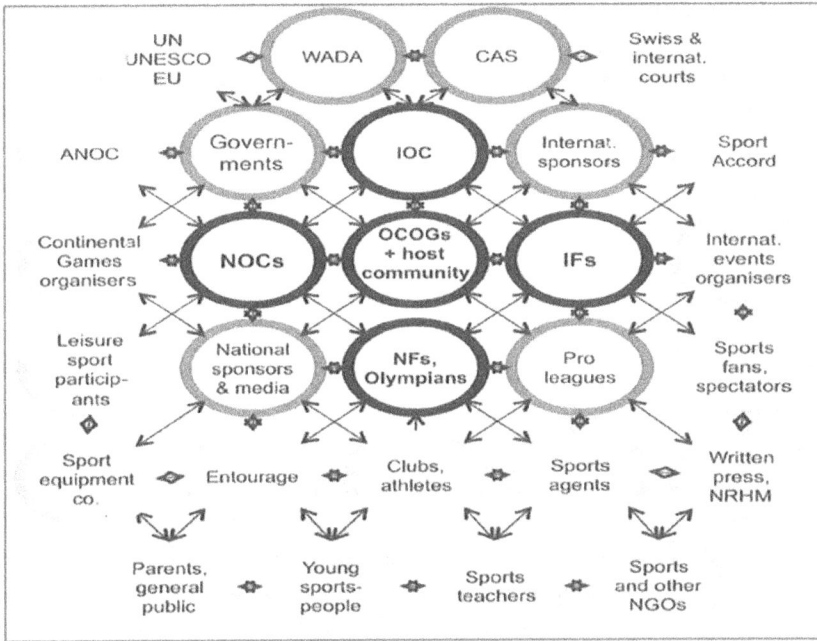

Fig. 1. Total Olympic System. *Source*: Adapted from Ferrand, Chappelet, and Seguin (2012: 31).

Several studies have argued about the political nature and dynamics of the Olympic system, calling it a microcosm of the international system, in which the IOC and other stakeholders interact with one another (Cha, 2009; Cull, 2008; Findling & Pelle, 2004; Lee & Chappelet, 2012; Poast, 2007; Toohey & Veal, 2007). In a realpolitik world (Morgenthau, 1978; Waltz, 1979), where countries fiercely compete with hard power (i.e., military strength), the Olympics has been increasingly politicized by participating countries and used as a vehicle to demonstrate the superiority of a powerful country, despite the IOC's position of maintaining neutrality on political matters. For instance, in 1936, Nazi Germany had the opportunity to host the Berlin Olympics, and attempted to use the international attention to promote a peaceful image of Nazi ideology (Findling & Pelle, 2004: 107), and several Jewish athletes chose to boycott the Games that year in response to Nazi anti-Semitism. The Cold War years, during which communist and capitalist systems sought to utilize the Olympics to promote political propaganda, inevitably consolidated the Games as a field of power politics framed as an ideological battle.

The classic examples are enumerated as the 1980 Games when the United States boycotted all participation in protest of the Soviet Union's invasion of Afghanistan, blocked voting for the Olympic hosts by Western, Eastern bloc, and Third World IOC members (Toohey & Veal, 2007). For example, the Eastern bloc tried to organize the Olympics and did so in Moscow in 1980 and Sarajevo, Yugoslavia, in 1984. It also heavily protested against the awarding of the 1988 Games to Seoul in 1981.

In contrast, in the post-Cold-War era, it is less likely that countries with strong military strength affect the event owners' decision. Rather, soft power factors such as a country's sociocultural and political characteristics can affect bid results, by way of their relationship with Olympism (Lee & Chappelet, 2012). The values of Olympism fall on the central elements of soft power, which leads this chapter to assume that the two concepts have a selective affinity. For instance, the three essential components of Olympism, i.e., excellence, respect, and friendship, are incarnated in collaborative programs such as the "'Olympism in Action" program consisting of several initiatives implemented in fields of activity such as human rights, education, democracy, and peace, which the IOC encourages and coordinates to introduce, in order to purse its aim of building a better world through sport (Ferrand, Chappelet, & Seguin, 2012: 135–136). In other words, whether a bid country is suitable for the Olympic philosophy, which portrays the Olympic movement in terms of its potential as mechanisms for achieving world peace, reconciliation, concord, and human development, can be a key criterion for host site choice.

Democratic and Governmental Dimensions of Soft Power

Impact of Democratic Participation on a Successful Olympic Bid

The essence of sport is participation itself. As Pierre de Coubertin, the founder of the IOC and reviver of the modern Olympic Games, stresses, "Winning medals wasn't the point of the Olympics. It's the participating that counts[1]." Likewise, the Olympic Movement is, in essence, linked with participation of both the Olympians and people. According to Miah and Garcia (2012), historically, the IOC has persistently advocated the idea that the Olympic movement should not engage with political issues or national governmental matters and, instead, confine itself to the business of sport, because the IOC's primary desire is to ensure that as many countries from around the world as possible put politics aside and feel ideologically able to align themselves with the Olympic values and send their athletes to the Games in order to compete in sport. As a result of this remarkable diplomatic achievement, after all, while the UN presently has 193 member states, there are 204 within the Olympic community. For example, the IOC recognized both China and Taiwan as NOCs. However, although the development of sport is admittedly the primary goal of the IOC and all sport organizations belonging to the Olympic Movement, they also consider that the values of Olympism include broader concepts related to human well-being, social responsibility, respect for universal fundamental ethical principles, and even world peace in general. As Jacques Rogge, the former IOC President stated that "as a values-based sports organization, we can't change the world on our own. But we can — and we do — help to make it a better place" (IOC, 2012: 1), the IOC's mission is to build a peaceful and better world for human development by "blending sport with culture and education" (IOC, 2011: 10). This idea of combining sport and development, with its roots in the initial vision of Pierre de Coubertin, has evolved into international cooperation for improving social and human well-being worldwide. In this respect, it could be hypothesized that if a bid country scores well on an important Olympic ideal and philosophy such as the democratic participation of citizens as well as sport athletes, the country may be recognized as an attractive host of the Games by the IOC, who wants to encourage countries to improve its people's living conditions.

Impact of Government Transparency on a Successful Olympic Bid
Governmental transparency as an ethical dimension of soft power can be defined by relying on the argument that it is exercised "when a country's culture includes universal values and its policies promote values and interests that others share" (Nye, 2004: 11). According to Nye, "Corruption is a behavior which deviates from the formal duties of a public role because of private regarding [...] pecuniary or status gains; or violates rules against the exercise of certain types of private-regarding influence." (Nye, 1967: 419) Thus, with respect to transparency and anticorruption, which are both a constituent element of soft power and elements of the Fundamental Principles of Olympism, clean sport is every Olympic family's responsibility. Keeping integrity in Olympic values extends beyond the athletes' oath of maintaining the Olympic spirit, friendship, solidarity and fair play taken at the Games (e.g., Code of Ethics, Antidoping Code which are regulated by the IOC's Ethics Commissions, World Anti-Doping Agency, Court of Arbitration for Sport and many antibetting regulations/codes/rules). Further, as the philosophy of Olympism requires ethical authority in demonstrating 'fitness' to host the Olympics, the Games has been said to involve a deep interrogation of the ethical worthiness of the hosts (Rowe, 2012: 288). The IOC's concerns for

ethical issues have been increasingly prompted and elevated by the revelation of the unethical practices of the Salt Lake City 2002 Bid Committee and the revision of more transparent bid procedures which were adopted in 1999. The old practice, in which each bid candidate enticed as many IOC members as possible to visit the attractions of its proposed Olympic sites, facilities and plans, caused side effects involving excessive giving of gifts and other enticements to IOC members and even their families, which in turn led to the "lobbying" crisis of 1998/1999 and subsequent reforms (Toohey & Veal, 2007). As a consequence, the IOC guidelines regulate contacts between candidates and IOC members, including related organizations (see IOC, 2005). The recognition of special interests and the need for transparency since the corruption scandals point to a probability that these more transparent decision-making processes are likely to lead the IOC members to favor bidding countries' transparency and ethical reputation. And the IOC could relate to widespread corruption in the bidding country to its administrative inefficiency and political instability, because members of the national Olympic organizing committee work closely in conjunction with government officials (Poast, 2007). It could thus be hypothesized that a nation's ethical image is likely to persuade the IOC to choose it as the rightful host country. That is, whether a bid country seeks to make a desirable commitment to become more transparent and/or less corrupt is likely to affect its ethical image and persuade the IOC to choose it as the rightful host country.

Hypotheses on the Impact of Democracy and Bureaucracy
in the Olympic System
Assuming that international bidding for major sports events are in a political field, i.e., the sphere of soft power at the bottom of world politics, the soft power theory (Nye, 2004) is applicable to explain the effect of country-level factors on the bidding success. Based on Nye (2004)'s argument that the effectiveness of soft power application depends on its context and recipients, a country's soft power over the event owners can be evaluated across social, cultural, political, and environmental dimensions, with a particular focus on the characteristics of the field of sport. More specifically, one can find that a bid country's levels of democratic values and government transparency as well as sporting success considering the context of sport can be assessed as main components of soft power by the IOC. In countries' biddings for Olympic sport events, the ideals of the Olympic movement, i.e., "Olympism," can influence the IOC's preferences regarding host countries, because belongings to the Olympic Movement requires compliance with the

Olympic Charter (IOC, 2011: 11). Since the early days of the Olympic system, the Charter has served as both the IOC's statutes and the procedural rules for the movement it coordinates. Accordingly, the Charter's fundamental principles governing the Olympic system include transparency, democracy, accountability, autonomy, and social responsibility (Chappelet & Kubler-Mabbott, 2008). Socially responsible activities, which date from the 1990s and are today embedded within the structures and frameworks of the IOC and its stakeholders (Ferrand, Chappelet, & Seguin, 2012: 135–136), should be pursued and reinforced by both the IOC and other Olympic organizations (Chappelet & Kubler-Mabbott, 2008: 180). Moreover, in terms of promoting the values of solidarity, peace, and human dignity which sport can channel, the philosophy and principles in Olympic sport have much in common with key components of soft power (Lee & Chappelet, 2012). Thus, in the context of soft power, a bid country's higher values of democracy and transparency in accordance with the Olympic philosophy and principles could attract and persuade the IOC to award its sporting events to the country.

Therefore, from the arguments based on the soft power theory, this study proposes the following: "If the IOC, *who seeks to obtain organizational legitimacy, chooses hosts considering the philosophy and principles of Olympism, which are related to the soft power of a bid country, then it is more likely that the Olympic Games are awarded to bid countries that have higher levels of democratic values and government transparency.*"

RESEARCH DESIGN

Models and Variables

Based on the theoretical and historical background discussed above, the main hypothesis of the study was constructed as follows: assuming that countries' hard power factors are equal, their soft power can affect the result of bidding to host the Olympic Games. In order to assess the impact of soft power on international Olympic bidding, both soft- and hard-power factors need to be included in an analytical model, so that while one factor is controlled, the influence of the other can be estimated. However, past research on hard and soft power, which used qualitative methods such as case studies, often omitted one of the two variables from the analysis, which might threaten causal inference with confounding factors or spurious effects. This chapter thus attempts to capture both hard and soft power by employing quantitative analysis.

Like two sides of a coin, the impact of a country's soft power on its Olympic bid depends on the extent to which the IOC prefers a candidate countries that have more soft power. Which countries are more likely to be preferred by the IOC as the host venue in terms of their soft or hard power? It is hard to predict how IOC members will vote, as voting is by secret ballot (Persson, 2002: 27). In addition, they are well known for voting on the basis of political and personal judgment (Chappelet & Kubler-Mabbott, 2008: 87). However, past voting results of the IOC provide clues that enable estimation of members' preferred host countries in terms of hard and soft power, assuming that not all voting members of the IOC are irrational, emotional, or corrupt. The few bribery cases in Olympic history (particularly the lobbying crisis of 1998–1999) do not prove that all IOC members engage in corrupt transactions for votes with lobbyists. It is more reasonable to assume that most members of the IOC vote based on their own beliefs or systems of preferences. In this respect, this study made several assumptions regarding the IOC's preferences and voting behaviors in order to construct estimation models. In line with revealed preference theory, which has been developed since Samuelson's (1938) seminal paper, the IOC's unobserved preferences are assumed to be revealed by their observed voting results, and their voting behaviors regarding host city choice are assumed to be rational and consistent. Fig. 2 illustrates a model of the IOC's host country selection in which members vote for candidate countries whose combinations of hard and soft power they prefer.

Regarding the dependent variable, the IOC's preferences for Olympic hosts were measured in three ways in order to ensure the robustness of the analysis. First, Host Success is a dummy variable that represents the IOC's final decision, assigning the value of 1 if a country is chosen as host and 0 if not. Second, IOC Rank represents the IOC's ranking of the bidding countries in the year t. Third, IOC Votes measures how many votes a candidate country obtained in all bidding rounds in a given year t. The IOC's preference is assumed to be reflected in the number of votes a country gets, as calculated by the ratio of individual members' votes to overall votes in a year t.

The independent variables associated with soft power are defined in political, sporting, and environmental dimensions. Based on Nye (2004)'s main constituent pillars of culture, political values, and foreign policy, a country's soft power is evaluated over the IOC across the three dimensions, with a particular focus on the characteristics of the field of sports, because soft power depends on context, as Nye stressed. First, the focal dimensions of soft power in the article include political values with respect to democratic and governmental ones as discussed above. Democratic values[2] are assessed

Soft power

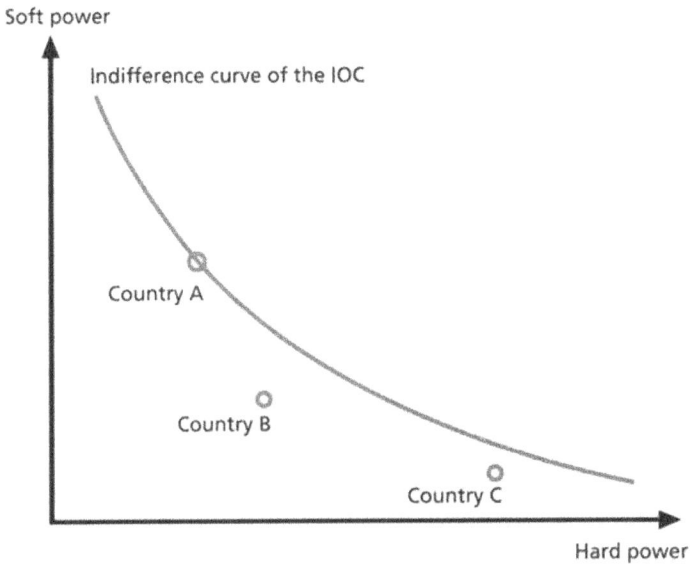

Fig. 2. A Model of the IOC's Host Country Selection. *Note*: Indifference curve is a graph showing different combinations of bid countries' hard and soft power which render indifferent or the same level of utility (satisfaction) for the IOC's choices of host countries. That is, at each point on the curve, the IOC has no preference for one country over another. *Source*: Lee and Chappelet (2012: 57).

as the level of citizen participation by two proxy valuables: A proxy variable of Citizen Participation is collected from a Voice and Accountability indicator of the Worldwide Governance Indicators, capturing perceptions of the extent to which a country's citizens are able to participate in selecting their government, as well as freedom of expression, freedom of association, and a free media; this estimate ranges from approximately −2.5 (weak citizen participation) to 2.5 (strong). Considering the specificity of the sports field, Public Opinion measures the level of public support of hosting the Olympic Games by using the IOC's public opinion poll results (%) of both bid city and country. The popularity of the Olympic bid project among local residents as well as the country's overall mood may, for example, promise to develop sports participation for all, which stimulates the IOC's recognition of better supported Olympic hosts. As the bureaucratic dimension of soft power, Government Transparency represents a country's soft power in terms of ethics. Poast (2007) and Feddersen et al. (2008) state that this can be measured by the Corruption Perceptions Index produced by Transparency International; this ranges from 0 to 10, with 0 indicating a country with an extremely and pervasively corrupt government, and 10 indicating the opposite. And another aspect of bureaucratic transparency is measured by the Rule of Law indicator of the Worldwide Governance Indicators, capturing perceptions of the extent to which agents have confidence in and abide by the rules of society, and in particular the quality of contract enforcement, property rights, the police, and the courts, as well as the likelihood of crime and violence; this estimate ranges from approximately −2.5 (weak) to 2.5 (strong).

Second, as a cultural dimension of soft power, a country's sporting success as a positive reputation in the sport field can be both appreciated for its enhancement of the Olympic movement, and seen as an effective lobbying influence in the field of international sporting diplomacy. A country's strong sporting performance, as represented by national results in the Olympic Games, is well recognized by the IOC. For example, world-popular sports stars who have won gold medals in the Olympics could influence IOC members' decision making concerning host country selection. Sporting success refers to the number of gold medals won in the previous Summer and Winter Olympic Games.

Third, a country's environmental sustainability could be regarded as a desirable value by the IOC, which seeks to host an environmentally friendly Olympics. It is critical for bid countries to comply with the IOC guideline on environmental protection and sustainable development and leave a "green legacy," including sound contributions to prevent global climate change. The more efforts a country makes to protect the environment, the more attractive it is to the IOC. The environmental sustainability of each country is measured by two environmental indexes: CO_2 emissions and particle emissions measure a country's production of air pollutants such as CO_2 (carbon dioxide) and PM10 (per cubic meter 10 or particles less than 10 microns in diameter) per GDP. These data were collected from the World Bank's World Development Indicators.

In addition, the continental diversity of the host countries, which the IOC appears to take into account (Feddersen et al., 2008; Poast, 2007), is measured by Continental Rotation as a dummy variable, assigning the value of 1 if a bidding country is located on a different continent from the host country of the next upcoming Summer and Winter Olympics, and 0 if it is on the same continent. And in order to measure hard-power factors as control variables, GDP (gross domestic product) and GDP growth were included in the models to represent a country's overall economic performance and emerging economic trends, and military expenditure was used as a proxy for military power.

Therefore, the following econometric model is proposed:

$$
\begin{aligned}
&\text{Preferences for Host (Host Success, IOC Rank, IOC Votes)}_{it} = \\
&\beta_0 + \beta_1 \text{ Citizen participation}_{it-1} + \beta_2 \text{ Public Opinion}_{it} + \beta_3 \text{ Government} \\
&\text{Transparency}_{it-1} + \beta_4 \text{ Rule of Law}_{it-1} + \beta_5 \text{ Sporting Success}_{it} + \\
&\beta_6 \text{ CO}_2 \text{ emissions}_{it-1} + \beta_7 \text{ Particle emissions}_{it-1} + \beta_8 \text{ GDP}_{it-1} + \\
&\beta_9 \text{ GDP Growth}_{it-1} + \beta_{10} \text{ Military Expenditure}_{it-1} + \\
&\beta_{11} \text{ Continental Rotation}_{it} + \varepsilon_{it}
\end{aligned}
$$

To clarify, I denotes each bidding country for t, which is the year of the IOC vote. Several soft- and hard-power-related variables receive values from the year prior to the vote $(t - 1)$, on the assumption that the IOC's decisions are based on candidate countries' status during the previous year. Table 1 summarizes all variables used in the models.

Data and Analytical Methods

The data set was constructed from all bidding countries for the Olympic Summer and Winter Games in the post-Cold-War era (between 1990, the first bidding year after the 1989 fall of the Berlin Wall, and 2015, the latest bidding year of awarding the 2022 Winter Olympics to Beijing). Thus, the estimates are based on a total of 98 bidding cities/countries, consisting of 54 Summer Games and 44 Winter Games bids.

In order to estimate the proposed econometric models, quantitative methods were employed, because large-n studies of the IOC's host city selections can identify systematic tendencies (Poast, 2007: 76) and provide statistically generalized statements concerning the relationships between a country's soft power and the choices made by the IOC. Given the panel nature of the data and characteristics of the dependent variables, the time-series cross-national aggregate level data sets were grouped by overall and summer/winter periods and regressed individually by a variety of panel data regression methods, including panel logit/probit models (against the dependent variable host success) and fixed-effects/random-effects models (against IOC vote). These panel regression methods can rule out the omitted variable bias caused by unobserved characteristics of individual countries (Baltagi, 2008; Cameron & Trivedi, 2009; Wooldridge, 2002). For instance, with the fixed-effects model, the effects of unobservable factors such as a bid country's lobbying strategies can be eliminated if these are assumed to be country specific and time invariant. In addition, a

Table 1. Variables Used in the Models.

Name	Measure	Data source
Dependent variables		
Host Success	Final decision on the host site (dummy)	International Olympic Committee
IOC Rank	Bid's ranking by the IOC	International Olympic Committee
IOC Votes	Ratio of votes that a bid country gets to overall votes	International Olympic Committee
Independent variables		
Citizen Participation	Perceptions of the extent to which a country's citizens are able to participate in selecting their government, as well as freedom of expression, freedom of association, and a free media (scale of –2.5 to 2.5)	Voice and Accountability indicator (Worldwide Governance Indicators)
Public Opinion	Level of a bid city and country's public support of hosting the Olympic Games (%)	Public opinion poll results (International Olympic Committee)
Government Transparency	Perceived government corruption in the previous year to the bid (scale of 0 to 10)	Corruption Perceptions Index (Transparency International)
Rule of Law	Perceptions of the extent to which agents have confidence in and abide by the rules of society, and in particular the quality of contract enforcement, property rights, the police, and the courts, as well as the likelihood of crime and violence (scale of –2.5 to 2.5)	Rule of Law indicator (Worldwide Governance Indicators)
Sporting Success	Number of gold medals won in the last Summer and Winter Games	International Olympic Committee
CO_2 emissions	Emitted carbon dioxide per GDP in the previous year to the bid	World Development Indicators
Particle emissions	Emitted PM10 per GDP in the previous year to the bid	World Development Indicators
GDP	Real GDP (PPP, constant 2005 \$) in the previous year to the bid	World Development Indicators
GDP Growth	Growth rate (%) of real GDP (PPP, constant 2005 \$) in the previous year to the bid	World Development Indicators
Military Expenditure	Military expenditure (PPP, constant 2005 \$) in the previous year to the bid	World Development Indicators
Continental Rotation	Different continental location from the host country of the next upcoming Summer/ Winter Olympics (dummy)	International Olympic Committee

Note: Several imputations were conducted for absent values for Citizen Participation, Government Transparency, and Rule of Law (due to being published since 1995–1996). PPP = purchasing power parity.

rank-ordered logit model (Long & Freese, 2006) was also employed against IOC rank.

To be more confident that the regression results are robust with respect to the problem of multicollinearity (Gujarati, 2003: 341–386) between independent variables (e.g., high correlation between soft power variables), reduced versions of the models that incorporate select variables to all variables at once jointly are stepwisely tested (i.e., by successively adding or removing variables, stepwise regression methods performed to check which are the best combination of variables).

RESULTS

Table 2 presents the results of the regression analyses. All soft-power-related variables were significant with signs in the expected directions. First, in all Olympic Games bids between 1990 and 2015, the significant independent variables were Citizen Participation, Public Opinion, Government Transparency, and Rule of Law, at the 5–10 percent significance level (in the model with the dependent variable of IOC Rank[3]), and Continental Rotation at the 10 percent significance level (in the Host Success model). In the IOC Votes model, Public Opinion was positively significant at the 1 percent significance level, while significant were Particle emissions and Continental Rotation, at the 10 percent significance level as well as GDP Growth, at the 5 percent significance level. Second, in the IOC Votes models for Summer Games bids from 1990 to 2013, Citizen Participation and Government Transparency were also significant between the 5–10 percent significance level, while Particle emissions was negatively significant at the 1 percent significance level. Third, in Winter Games bids from 1991 to 2015, significant variables between the 5–10 percent significance level were those associated with soft power, such as Citizen Participation, Rule of Law, Sporting Success, CO_2 emissions and Particle emissions, as well as hard-power-related GDP growth in IOC Votes models.

The results of the analysis suggest that the IOC's voting behavior is influenced by a country's soft or hard power, although several results should be interpreted cautiously due to the relatively small sample size. First of all, all soft-power-related variables had a statistically significant impact on the bid results, supporting the main hypothesis of this chapter that the host country's soft power can be a strong factor in winning an Olympic bid. In the context of soft power, a high number of Olympic medals won by world-popular athletes can also attract IOC members in favor of a country's bid. And the environmental efforts of a country may also be regarded as a desirable value by

Table 2. Estimation Results for Olympic Games Bids.

Dependent variables		All Bids, 1990–2015				
		Host success	Host success	IOC rank	IOC rank	IOC rank
Model		Panel logit	Panel probit	Rank-or-dered logit	Rank-ordered logit	Rank-or-dered logit
Independent variables		Coef. (z-stat)	Coef. (z-stat)	Coef. (z-stat)	Coef. (z-stat)	Coef. (z-stat)
Hard power	Military expenditure	−0.00 (−0.63)	−0.00 (−0.56)	−0.00 (−1.09)	−0.00 (−1.51)	0.00 (1.02)
	GDP	0.00 (1.27)	0.00 (1.13)	0.00 (0.24)	0.00 (0.63)	−0.00 (−1.25)
	GDP growth	0.04 (0.98)	0.08 (1.06)	−0.01 (−0.25)	−0.04 (−0.83)	−1.55** (−2.05)
Soft power	Citizen Participation				−0.62* (−1.92)	
	Public Opinion					−0.24** (−2.00)
	Government Transparency			−0.16* (−1.83)		
	Rule of Law					−1.72 (−1.33)
	Sporting Success	0.01 (0.68)	0.03 (0.70)	−0.02 (−0.84)	−0.02 (−0.98)	0.13 (1.25)
	CO_2 emissions	−0.04 (−0.05)	−0.03 (−0.02)	0.05 (0.08)	−0.29 (−0.44)	
	Particle emissions	−0.00 (−0.34)	−0.00 (−0.28)	−0.01 (−0.75)	−0.01 (−0.82)	
Continental Rotation		0.71* (1.87)	1.33* (1.85)	−0.34 (−1.02)	−0.47 (−1.33)	−4.43* (−1.88)
Constant		−1.94*** (−3.78)	−3.46*** (−3.53)			
N	93	93	93	93	29	29

Note: Due to missing values, regressions excluded five observations: Yugoslavia (1996), Puerto Rico (2004), Cuba (2008, 2012), and Andorra (2010). 29 values for Public Opinion are solely available for the Candidate cities/countries during 2001–2015.
* Significance at 10% level; ** 5% level; *** 1% level.

	Summer Bids, 1990–2013			Winter Bids, 1991–2015		
IOC rank	IOC votes	IOC votes	IOC votes	IOC votes	IOC votes	IOC votes
Rank-ordered logit	Random effects	Fixed effects	Fixed effects	Random effects	Random effects	Random effects
Coef. (z-stat)	Coef. (z-stat)	Coef. (t-stat)	Coef. (t-stat)	Coef. (z-stat)	Coef. (z-stat)	Coef. (z-stat)
−0.00	−0.00	0.00	0.00	0.00	0.00	0.00
(−0.72)	(−0.08)	(0.51)	(0.45)	(1.59)	(1.38)	(1.00)
0.00	0.00	−0.00	−0.00	−0.00	−0.00	−0.00
(0.74)	(0.80)	(−1.33)	(−0.84)	(−0.91)	(−0.83)	(−0.39)
−0.93**	0.04**	0.00	−0.00	0.02**	0.02**	0.02**
(−2.10)	(2.02)	(0.18)	(−0.27)	(2.13)	(2.00)	(2.34)
		0.46*	0.55**	0.07*		
		(1.89)	(2.20)	(1.65)		
−0.06	0.01***					
(−1.31)	(2.78)					
			0.10*			
			(1.74)			
−2.74*					0.06*	
(−1.65)					(1.64)	
0.00	−0.01	0.01	0.00	0.01**	0.01**	0.01**
(0.03)	(−0.98)	(0.80)	(0.57)	(2.31)	(2.34)	(2.57)
−4.36	0.03	0.03	−0.17			−0.21*
(−1.00)	(0.10)	(0.09)	(−0.56)			(−1.92)
	−0.00*	−0.01**				−0.00*
	(−1.71)	(−2.21)				(−1.72)
−1.78	0.11*	−0.06	−0.03	−0.00	0.01	−0.01
(−1.42)	(1.62)	(−0.93)	(−0.43)	(−0.00)	(0.08)	(−0.11)
	−0.30	0.32	−0.61	−0.08	−0.06	0.19*
	(−1.62)	(1.13)	(−1.23)	(−0.88)	(−0.73)	(2.08)
29	50	50	43	43	43	

IOC members, who prefer a "Green Games" ecological legacy. In addition, a good image of a country's contribution to citizen participation as well as ethical reputation for adhering to the Olympic philosophy and principles could persuade IOC members to vote in favor of a country. On the other hand, the IOC could consider widespread corruption in the bidding country as a sign of administrative inefficiency and political instability, because members of the national Olympic organizing committee interact closely with governmental officials (Poast, 2007). Thus, the ideals of the Olympic movement, i.e., Olympism can influence the IOC's choice of host city, as Pierre de Coubertin, the founder of the modern Olympics, once dreamed. Accordingly, it is critical for bid cities and countries to obtain a high level of Olympic legitimacy in the eyes of IOC members by maintaining the integrity of Olympic values.

In contrast, as components of country's hard power, military expenditure was not significant at all in any model, and GDP paradoxically had no significant effect on the success of bids. This result makes sense when we consider that the United States and China, although superpowers, have not always won their bids. However, the IOC has also preferred, in the past, countries with better economic performance in terms of GDP growth rate. The economic considerations of the IOC include a candidate's financial ability to stage the games, and monetary profitability from the potential host market. For example, when countries with emerging markets—such as China (for the 2008 Summer Olympics) and Brazil (for 2016)—have been chosen by the IOC, China's bid campaign linked economic development to Olympism (Haugen, 2005), and Brazil used media strategies that frame the bid with Olympic-related developments (Carey et al., 2011). These imply that hard power alone (GDP, GDP growth rate, and military expenditure) is not sufficient to win an Olympic bid. In this regard, Nye (2008) went one step further and argued for the need to deploy "smart power," which is the ability to combine hard and soft power effectively.

Next, the continental rotation factor (which represents the goal of not hosting the Olympics on the same continent twice in a row) also contributed substantially to host success. This means that the IOC tends not to choose countries from the same continent for two Games in a row. It can be thus concluded that IOC members have taken the principle of continental rotation into account in their decision making, despite the fact that it is not an official rule but an informal consensus. Based on Nye's (2004) argument that even nonstate actors such as international organizations frequently wield soft power, it could be argued that the IOC enhances its legitimacy by following the continental rotation rule, thus increasing its soft-power influence. Therefore, countries need to time their bids appropriately to appeal to the

IOC's continental rotation rule, or to the spirit of Olympism and the legitimacy of spreading the Olympic movement and the games throughout as many regions of the world as possible.

DISCUSSION AND CONCLUSION

Sports and Government

Before the birth of the modern nation, the sport was not the domain of government intervention. Sports were considered as the free activities of the participants and functioned as mode of entertainment and spiritual abundance. The sport was considered to be simply implied in participation and spiritual upheaval. Therefore, the sport did not have to artificially intervene in the country, spread the fostering policy, or regulate it. Avery Brundage, who served as chair of the IOC in the 1950s and 1960s, also expressed negative views about the involvement of central and local governments in sports. In the idealistic thought that sports activities are separated from the selfish and computational world and provide pure and human experience and space, the government should not restrict sports activities, and should not even support them (Seong, 2002).

Prior to the modernization of the nation, sport was mostly in the private realm. However, after the industrialization, institutional sports such as the Olympics appeared, and sports professional leagues were born and administrative intervention in sports started. With the development of society, sport has become a target of national intervention, the degree of intervention is getting stronger, and the range of intervention is also expanded. The policy intervention of a government in any area means that the sector has a great meaning for the nation and the people. Government started to see sports as the soft power medium of pursuing their goals as following.

Sports as a Means of Economic Growth
In the eighteenth and nineteenth centuries, industrialization has increased the power of the masses to emerge sports as a professional league. In addition, international sports events such as the Olympics appeared in the international scene, and the scale of the sports appeared. Industrialization and globalization have transferred sport from the area of leisure to the domain of industry and market. Sports have been evaluated as promoting not only intangible

benefits such as health promotion and mental elevation, but also reborn as an industrial field that generates tangible and economic benefits from industrialization and internationalization. The sports industry is an economic activity that generates added value by producing and distributing goods and services related to spectator sports and participatory sports (National Sports Promotion Corporation, 1999). The characteristics of the sports industry can be implied in several ways.

First, sports industry is a type of economic activity that not only has a direct impact on the national economy, but also indirectly contributes to the national economy. The improvement of the people's physical fitness and the quality of life caused by the sports activities can strengthen the productivity of the industrial manpower. In addition, the experience of raising sportsmanship, cooperation, and competition is a way to raise the level of human capital in the country. Furthermore, since sport is a community activity, it is an opportunity to secure social capital such as social trust and contribute to economic development.

Second, the sports industry is highly connected with other industries. The sports industry includes a number of subindustries such as sports facilities construction, sporting goods manufacturing, sports betting, sports marketing, sports media, and sports education. In modern times, sports-related markets have been formed and economic transactions have been increased in many fields such as manufacturing, operating, construction, marketing, and lottery.

Lastly, the sports industry has a great effect on job creation. The players, supervisors, and referees who participate in sports are all people. In sports games, mechanization and automation are limited, so the replacement of manpower with capital is relatively low. In addition, since sports tend to be enjoyed by cultural products and tourism products, and indirect employment inducement effects are also very high.

Sports as a Catalyst for Social Integration
Sport is a very effective means of integrating society. There are many ways in which sports contribute to social integration. Nixon and Frey (1972, 2002) approached the role of sport in national development from a functionalist point of view and emphasized five main functions of sports for national development.

The first is the role of domestic political stability and national identity. Sport plays an important role in achieving social stability in times of turmoil. If winning an international match or attracting a sporting event can induce national unity within the country, it will be an indicator that internationally demonstrates its supremacy externally. Cuban Fidel Castro attempted to institutionalize the athletic program in order to restore the confused political and social order after the 1959 revolution to receive public support (Arbena, 1993; Nixon & Frey, 2002). When the subject of interest is transferred from society to sporting events, it is found that the stabilization of the domestic situation can be achieved. A similar example is the sports policy of the 5th Republic of Korea. The 5th Republic of Korea created slogan of "3S (Sports, Screen, Sex)" for promoting healthy physical education, but the truth behind the sports promotion was the unity of nation. It can be seen that sports can be a useful tool to transform to the understanding of the government.

Second, sports play a role as a channel for communication for changes in social institutions. In particular, large-scale sports facilities provide a space for the public to inform the public about the economic and social changes of the nation. African leaders have used the sports arena to communicate changes in agriculture, health and maternity policy to the people (Nixon & Frey, 2002; Uwechue, 1978) and the Cold War Soviet Union played a major role in the socialist construction process (Riordan, 1980; recited in Nixon & Frey, 2002).

Third, sports play a role in coordinating social organizations. In other words, the sport promotes the institutionalization of the cooperation between the related organizations, because the central government and the local government must cooperate and coordinate activities on the planning and execution of sports policies or events. When coordination and cooperation are institutionalized into a single network, it is possible to reduce the waste caused by conflicts in jointly implementing sensitive policies between central and local governments.

Fourth, sports play a role in developing human resources. Leaders of sports organizations can improve their ability to communicate and plan, and citizens will develop ways to act in accordance with standard rules. In other words, sports will cultivate the capacity of sports personnel and citizens to build human infrastructure and contribute to social development.

Finally, sports help modernize values and culture. Today, many countries around the world enjoy modern forms of sports. It is a result of actively accepting modern sports as a means to reduce the primacy of the culture of the country. In addition, the hosting of sports events may be regarded as a stepping stone to raise public awareness. For example, in preparation for the 88 Seoul Olympic Games, Korea promoted to participate in volunteer activities such as urban environment preservation, order keeping, and kindness campaigns (Do, 1988).

1988 Olympic Host City, Seoul

The 1988 Summer Olympics were an international mega-sport event held from September 17 to October 2, 1988 in Seoul, South Korea. These sixteen days of events were considered as a significant event in Korean history since the Olympic was opportunity to demonstrate how Korea overcame Korean War and progressed economic development through the media to all over the world. Prior to the event, the image of Korea was still depicted as one of the poorest countries with full of homeless, vagrants, and orphans by international media and press due to the colonial period and war (Jung, 2001). Therefore, being host for the Olympic Games was more than just hosting mega-sport-event that the ultimate goal was to break the prejudice about the obsolete image of Korea.

According to PWC (Price Waterhouse Coopers) report, the Games of Seoul 1988 showed that Seoul significantly improved its infrastructure by hosting an Olympic. The city upgraded its transport and telecommunication infrastructure as well as constructing new urban centers with housing, retail, and other community facilities that have been fully integrated into their metropolitan areas. Economic impacts of Games were beyond the financial viability of the event itself, but approximately, affected to increase 1.4% of GDP, about 1,846 billion won of economic impact and created 336,000 jobs. In order to host mega event, such as Olympics, needs enormous amount of political, financial, and social support especially government support is critical before, during and even after the event. In the late 1980s, countries of hosting Olympic cities used the Olympic Games to social and economic development.

Since Korea's industrialization commenced in 1962, the economy reached its peak during the fifth economic planning period (1982–1986) with the strong government support. Nevertheless, at the same time, political instability continued due to the assassination of President Park in October 1979. The government behind the Seoul Olympic in 1988 was the Chun Republic which was in some ways a continuation from the previous Park military regime. However, the power of the military government was weakened, which affected the political, economic, and social spheres.

The economic environment that the Chun administration faced was different from that which Park managed. The economy became increasingly sophisticated and complicated. Especially, chronic inflation rates and a heavy defence burden were critical issues. An oil-shock and political instability after the assassination of Park caused a negative economic growth rate in 1980 which was the first economic decline since the 1960s. In this situation, the

Chun Republic readjusted its development strategy fundamentally by adopting two major shifts of policy. The first was its emphasis on the development of soft infrastructure. The Five-Year Economic Plan, which was initiated by Park, was officially renamed the Fifth Five-year Plan of Economic and Social Development (1982–1986). Second, the fundamental development strategy shifted from rapid growth with inflation to continuous, stable growth with price stabilization. Government intervention and a closed economy strategy was readjusted to a more liberal economy open to foreigners. In that sense, changes in the economic direction were aligned with the reasons to host the Olympic games. When Seoul was awarded the 1988 Olympic Games on September 30, 1981 at Baden-Baden during the 84th IOC Session, the main official objective of the Seoul Olympic was to display national strength, upgrade Korean sports to an international level, consolidate ties of friendship with countries all over the world, create the proper atmosphere for establishing diplomatic relations, and solidify national unity.

In reality, the Korean government used the Seoul Olympics to pursue its political legitimacy in diplomatic, security, social, and economic development through the Seoul Olympic's official coordination process with international organizations. Unintentionally, this led to a democratization process in Korea such that the preparation simultaneously became a political development process toward democracy because the political situation in Korea was watched by the world, and everyone watched with curiosity, tension, and expectation.

Olympic Preparation Process as Stimulus of Democratization in Korea

On a national level, the Seoul Olympics had a substantial impact on citizens' awareness of democracy. The hosting of the Seoul Olympic Games allowed a reduction in the gap between bureaucrats and citizens. In order to earn citizen support, bureaucrats had to engage more with citizens. Bureaucrats, in particular, felt that they were contributing to the development of politics and public administration, and more broadly to globalization. The Olympics, rather than having a direct effect on political and administrative development, worked to enhance the public's awareness of democracy as well as to foster an international outlook and greater self-confidence. Bureaucrats felt that the Seoul Olympics played a critical role in stimulating a more open, independent, and democratic administration with a greater emphasis on service functions. Most feel, however, that there was a greater impact on increased service functions than on the independence of the administration.

Including the 1,435 employees of the Seoul Olympic Organizing Committee
and the 18,608 employees dispatched from national organizations and corporations, over 20,000 operations personnel received training in international
administrative structure, administrative skills, modern administration management theories, and top-quality administrative service. Furthermore, they
had a chance to accumulate on-the-job training. Such training and experiences helped them in their future work, and there are great expectations that
they will function as adaptable reserve forces for administrative development.

The Olympic bid itself was made to announce the start of sports diplomacy in Korea. In the previous regime, meetings with the IOC were planned,
but they were not actually invited. However, after the Olympic bid was confirmed, the Korean government had various opportunities to have agreements with other countries. Sports are actually used as a diplomatic means in
the field of international politics. Until the Seoul Olympic Games, there was
almost no international invitation, but sports exchanges expanded dramatically on the occasion of the Seoul Olympics. Since sport entered the national
agenda, the government established the Ministry of Sport in March 1982.
The Ministry of Sport was comprised of a planning and management office
and three divisions. Fig. 3 shows the structure of the Ministry of Sport.

Since the Olympic bid was decided in March 1983, a sports exchange
agreement was first signed with the Dominican Republic, followed by Iraq

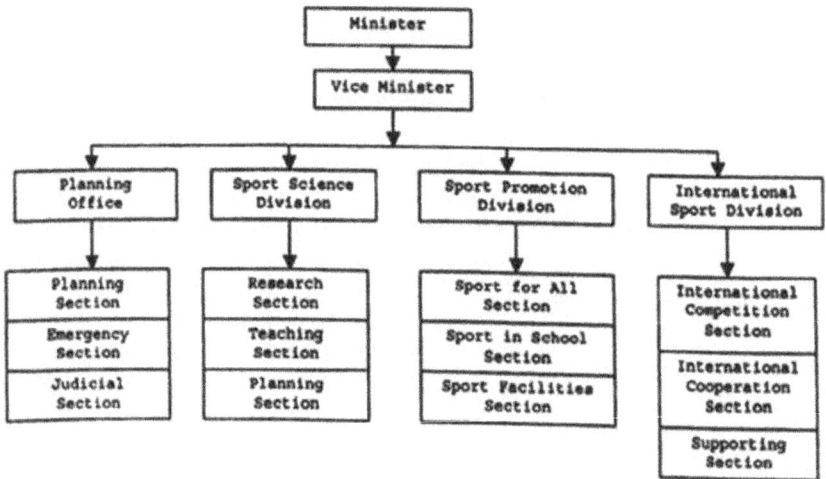

Fig. 3.   Structure of the Ministry of Sport in 1982. *Source*: Adapted from
Kim (1999: 205).

in 1984. And the 1988 Olympic Games boosted respective sports agreements various countries in Asia, Europe and Africa (Kim, 1999:195).

For the specific task of making the Seoul Olympics a success, the Seoul Olympic Organizing Committee was prepared before the actual official work. First of all, the urgent task was to collect information about new fields that the country had no experience with at the time. The committee gathered and analyzed official reports from past host countries of the Olympic Games, various sports information materials, recorded movies, and invited experts to ask for advice. The committee used the benchmarking technique that is often used in administration. The committee dispatched an investigation team to the host city of the previous tournament and collected information and materials extensively. They also worked closely with national Olympic committee officials, IFA executives, prominent athletes and journalists in various countries, and participated in the athletic diplomacy function for the successful hosting of the Seoul Olympic Games.

The Seoul Olympic Organizing Committee pursued efficiency as its main objective. Historically, the Olympic Games, which had been organized and held in urban centers until the 1930s, were held under the leadership of the central government in 1936 during the Berlin Games. In the case of the Tokyo Convention, the Japanese government appointed the Olympic substitute and provided intensive government support, thus making the economic leap forward. The Olympics were not a private form of organization like today, but more of a government-centered organization.

Korea also decided to use the Olympics as a tool for national development. In this context, the organizing committee of the Seoul Olympic Games aimed at more than simply playing athletic events to secure the success of the Olympic Games on a smaller budget. In other words, 'The Reform of the National Consciousness' was selected as the ultimate goal. Specifically, the Seoul Olympic Games strived to focus on the nation's capabilities by declaring that it would become a "gesture that recognizes the wisdom of all peoples and showcases the kindness and fairness of the people, and shows the world that is Korea a first-class cultural nation."

The preparation process of the Olympic Games in Seoul created a political atmosphere and the basis of a democratic environment in Korea. The Olympic Games stimulated the development of democracy due to the following reasons:

- Increased level of awareness of morality and legitimacy in bureaucracy
- Fostering a stronger democratic attitude for both citizens and bureaucrats
- Coordinating with other international organizations

- Increasing the public spirit of participation
- Increasing the freedom of the media and awareness of globalization

After 1988 Seoul towards 2018 PyeongChang Olympics

There are criticisms that the Olympic Games in Seoul used sports as political tool, destroyed the natural environment, and neglected the human rights of the people. However, it is also true that in terms of results, it has produced many positive effects. For example, government built various athletic facilities for the Olympic Games. The Jamsil Olympic Stadium began construction in 1977, but construction was delayed due to a lack of funds. However, with the bid to host the Olympic Games, the company made big progress in construction and was able to complete it in 1984. Various stadiums including tennis, weightlifting, fencing, gymnastics, and cycling were also built. The Olympic Games presented the opportunity to supply physical facilities that were lacking in quantity and diversity at the time. In addition, Olympic athletes and journalists made housing for residents in Jamsil, and after the Olympics, they were converted into apartments.

The rotation principle is best illustrated by the successful bid of PyeongChang in Korea, which had been defeated in two consecutive Olympic Winter Games bids by Vancouver in 2010 and Sochi in 2014. In its 2011 bid for the 2018 Winter Games, the Korean bid committee used the slogan New Horizons to acquire Olympic legitimacy in the eyes of the IOC, and emphasized its Drive the Dream Projects, in which the Korean government supported winter sports in developing/emerging countries (Merkel & Kim, 2012). This strategy appealed to the IOC by suggesting that the 2018 Winter Games should be hosted in Asia, not in Europe (two key competitors were France and Germany).

The promotion of internationally recognized Olympic champions or athletic celebrities, who are regarded legitimate contributors to world sport, thereby being attractive to IOC members, has been a widely used strategy by Olympic bidders. World-popular sports stars who have won gold medals in the Olympics can persuade IOC members' concerning host country selection. The persuasion strategy was enhanced when Yu-Na Kim, the 2010 Winter Olympic gold medalist in figure skating, participated in the final phase of the bid process and told the IOC that staging the Winter Olympics in Korea would be her personal dream come true and would inspire young athletes in Korea and the Asian region, where winter sports are not as developed as in Europe and North America (Lee, 2011). Another contender, Munich, Germany, also had a figure skater, double Olympic champion Katarina Witt, as the chairperson of its organizing committee, again suggesting the important lobbying role of popular sports stars. Korea's win over Germany sheds light on the interaction of the continental rotation rule with a country's sporting success[4]—wielding soft power via a "message" coupled with "messenger" (Nye, 2004), because a receiver's behavior can be changed when both the content of the message and the sender are tailored to appeal to the receiver (Sohn, 2011: 80).

In addition, Fig. 4 illustrates the impact of South Korea's soft power on the results of PyeongChang bids to host the 2010, 2014, and 2018 Winter Games. Here, the country's soft power factors during 2010–2014 were not sufficient to win the bids, whereas South Korea benefited from a higher level of citizen participation, public support, government transparency, and rule of law as well as other soft power factors (except CO_2 emissions) in the bidding for 2018.

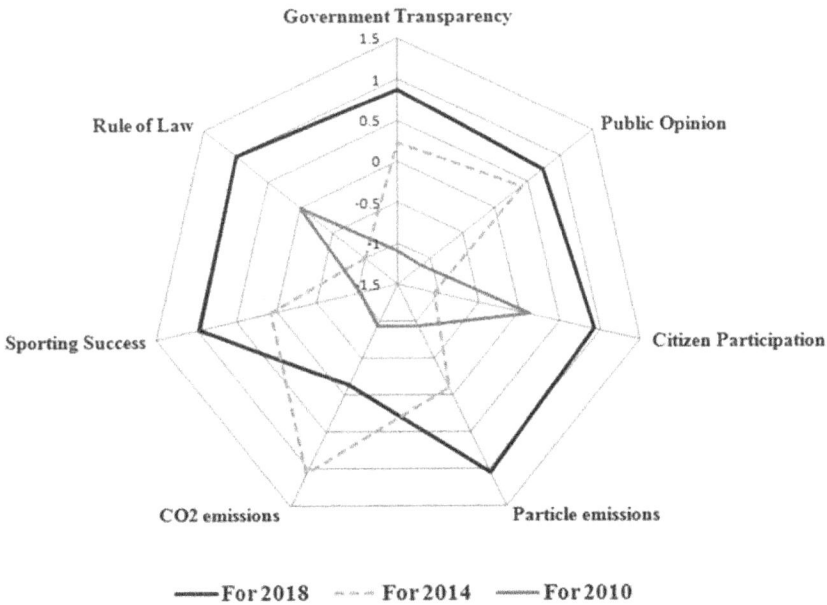

Fig. 4. Change of South Korea's Soft Power for the PyeongChang Bids (2010, 2014, and 2018). *Note*: Values for each variable were standardized as z-scores and displayed on each axis. In order to be directionally consistent with the other indicators, the reciprocal values of CO_2 and particle (PM10) emissions were used. *Source*: Author's own elaboration.

In fact, the key success factors of PyeongChang's 2018 bid include the full support from the national government as well as other public institutions at the regional and local levels. The Minister of Culture, Sports and Tourism, for instance, announced that a total of 500 million dollars would have been invested for the development of winter sports by the year 2018. Furthermore, while the previous two Olympic Bid Committees in charge of the application functioned as an organization that reported to the regional government of Kangwon province, the official PyeongChang Olympic Bid Committee in charge of the 2018 candidature operated as a legal entity within the remit of the Ministry, which changed the bid from merely locally driven effort to a national effort as a government-led project primarily managed and coordinated by the national government in partnership with local authorities and sports organizations (Merkel & Kim, 2012: 2376).

Most notably South Korea's government has pledged to help PyeongChang's bid by speeding up the improvement of infrastructure, which is a good sign to the IOC. That is, this reliable commitment of the Korean government was appreciated by the event owner of the mega-event as a signal to successfully organize the Olympic Games given the time and resources available[5]. Moreover, the 2018 bid's more centralized yet inclusive approach resulted in widespread public support, leading 91.4% of the South Korean public and 93% of the Kangwon province populations to overwhelmingly back the bid (Merkel & Kim, 2012: 2376).

In conclusion, the Olympic Games in Seoul acted as an opportunity to shake the world of the Republic of Korea. Korea achieved miraculous economic growth in the wake of the war and a lot of literature only focused on the success of the economy. However, this chapter suggests that the soft power of democracy and bureaucracy is effective in international cooperative systems such as the Olympics. In general, soft-power factors including citizen participation and government transparency were more important than hard-power factors: among the latter, the only significant factor was GDP growth rate, whereas all soft-power related variables had significant impacts on bid success between 1990 and 2015. The continental rotation rule also affected IOC decision making, by both constraining a "hard power takes all" approach and facilitating bidding countries' soft-power persuasion strategies.

Therefore, the IOC, which is a full-fledged member of the Olympic movement in accordance with the Olympic Charter, will choose a bid country following the philosophy of Olympism, which is in turn related to soft power, as the host of the Olympic Games. In this light, countries that have a higher level of democratic values, government transparency as well as sporting success and environmental responsibility may use these sociocultural, political, and environmental images and reputations as a means of marketing strategies for bids in order to showcase themselves as ideally fitting the Olympic values.

NOTES

1. "The important thing in the Olympic Games is not to win, but to take part; the important thing in life is not triumph, but the struggle; the essential thing is not to have conquered but to have fought well." (Quotes from Pierre de Coubertin, 1966: 19–20).

2. As this "political" pillar of soft power is inherently biased toward Western ideals of government and democracy, nondemocratic countries may face an immediate disadvantage in any assessment of relative soft power (McClory, 2011:19). Thus, this article mainly focuses on an assessment of citizen participation at the actor-level, instead of the systemic level such as democratic or authoritarian regimes.

3. In regards to the interpretation of the results of rank-ordered logistic model, it needs to be pointed out that the directions of all independent variables' signs are opposite to other models. For instance, the negative sign of Government Transparency in the model can be interpreted, in a reverse way, that the higher a bidding country's level of transparency is, the higher its probability of winning the bids is (i.e., the smaller numerical value of the ranking it gets).

4. South Korea had made in fostering winter sports in its nation before the 2018 bid. As a result, South Korea emerged as an athletic powerhouse in the winter sports arena. The 2010 Vancouver Olympics saw a significant turning point with the total of 14 medals (six gold, six silver, and two bronze) in South Korea's Winter Olympic medal performance (Merkel & Kim, 2011: 2370). The country, which in the past had heavily relied on the outstanding performance of short track athletes, also won three gold and two silver medals in speed skating. Moreover, the well-known and iconic figure skater Kim Yu-na won the gold medal in the Ladies' Singles.

5. To assess each Applicant City and its country's current conditions and the potential to organize successful Olympic Winter Games in 2018, the IOC commissioned a number of studies, appointed a number of experts, including experts from the International Federations (IFs), National Olympic Committees (NOCs) and the IOC Athletes' Commission, and established an IOC Candidature Acceptance Working Group (hereafter the "Working Group"). The IOC Working Group based its analysis on the information provided by the Applicant Cities in their Application Files and during the video conferences organized during the Working Group meeting in Lausanne from 21 to 23 April 2010, as well as the reports provided by external experts and their own expertise (IOC, 2010: 5). The technical criteria concerning government support, legal issues, and public opinion (including compliance with the Olympic Charter and the World Anti-Doping Code) was assessed based on a grade (a scale of 0 to 10) comprising a minimum and maximum number. As the following table lists the grades attributed to each Applicant City, Pyeongchang's government support, legal issues, and public opinion was highly evaluated by the Working Group (IOC, 2010: 15).

REFERENCES

Baltagi, B. (2008). *Econometric analysis of panel data.* New York: John Wiley.
Cameron, A. C., & Trivedi, P. K. (2009). *Microeconometrics using stata* (Vol. 5). College Station, TX: Stata Press.
Carey, M., Mason, D. S., & Misener, L. (2011). Social responsibility and the competitive bid process for major sporting events. *Journal of Sport and Social Issues, 35*(3), 246–263.
Cha, V. D. (2009). A theory of sport and politics. *The International Journal of the History of Sport, 26*(11), 1581–1610.
Chappelet, J.-L. (2008). Olympic environmental concerns as a legacy of the Winter Games. *The International Journal of the History of Sport, 25*(14), 1884–1902.
Chappelet, J.-L. (2008). *The International Olympic Committee and the Olympic system. The governance of world sport.* UK: Routledge.
Cottrell, M. P., & Nelson, T. (2011). Not just the Games? Power, protest and politics at the Olympics. *European Journal of International Relations, 17*(4), 729–753.
Coubertin. P. (1966). *The Olympic idea, discourses and essays* (Transl. J. C. Dixon, C. C. Diem), pp. 19–20. Institut an der Deutschen Sporthochschule.
Cull, N. J. (2008). The public diplomacy of the modern Olympic Games and China's soft power strategy. In *Owning the Olympics: Narratives of new China by price.* Ann Arbor, MI: M. E. University of Michigan Press.
Feddersen, A., Maennig, W., & Zimmermann, P. (2008). The empirics of key factors in the success of bids for Olympic Games. *Revue d'économie politique, 118*(2), 171–187.
Ferrand, A., Chappelet, J.-L., & Séguin, B. (2012). Chapitre 1. Le système olympique. *Management & Sport, 37*–53.
Ferrand, A., Chappelet, J.-L., & Séguin, B. (2012). *Olympic marketing.* UK: Routledge.
Findling, J. E., & Pelle, K. D. (1996). *Historical dictionary of the modern Olympic.* Westport, CT: Greenwood Press.
Gujarati, D. N., & Porter, D. C. (2003). *Basic econometrics* (4th ed.). New York: McGraw-Hill.
Haugen, H. Ø. (2005). Time and space in Beijing's Olympic bid. *Norsk Geografisk Tidsskrift-Norwegian Journal of Geography, 59*(3), 217–227.
Hong, E. (2011). Elite sport and nation-building in South Korea: South Korea as the dark horse in global elite sport. *International Journal of the History of Sport, 28*(7), 977–989.
Houlihan, B., Bloyce, D., & Smith, A. (2009). *Developing the research agenda in sport policy.* UK: Taylor & Francis.
Im, T., Yang, I., Kwon, H.-K., & Han. B.-H. (2016). Organizations in Olympic governance: A comparison between Olympic organizing committees for Seoul Olympics and Pyeongchang Olympics. *The Korean Journal of Organizations, 13*(3), 149–182.
I.O.C. (2005). *Rules of conduct applicable to all cities wishing to organise the Olympic Games.* Lausanne: Switzerland.
I.O.C. (2010). *2018 working group report/XXIII Olympic winter games.* Lausanne: Switzerland.
I.O.C. (2011). *Olympic charter.* Lausanne: Switzerland.
I.O.C. (2012, June 4), *Factsheet: Development through sport.*
Kang, Y.-S., & Perdue, R. (1994). Long-term impact of a mega-event on international tourism to the host country: A conceptual model and the case of the 1988 Seoul Olympics. *Journal of International Consumer Marketing, 6*(3–4), 205–225.

Kim, C.-G. (1989). *Impact of the Seoul Olympic Games on national development*. Korea Development Inst.

Kim, S.-J. (1999). *Sports and politics in the Republic of Korea*. British Library Document Supply Centre.

Kroenig, M., McAdam, M., & Weber, S. (2010). Taking soft power seriously. *Comparative Strategy, 29*(5), 412–431.

Lee, K.-H., & Chappelet, J.-L. (2012). Faster, higher, softly stronger: The impact of soft power on the choice of Olympic host cities. *The Korean Journal of Policy Studies, 27*(3), 47–71.

Lee, S.-Y. (2011, July 8). Kim Yu-na charms IOC members. Korea Herald. Retrieved from http://news.asiaone.com/News/Latest+News/Sports/Story/A1Story20110708-288091.html

Long, J. S., & Freese, J. (2006). *Regression models for categorical dependent variables using Stata*. Stata Press.

McClory, J. (2011). The new Persuaders II: A 2011 global ranking of soft power. *Institute for Government, 1*, 24.

Merkel, U., & Kim, M. (2011). Third time lucky!? PyeongChang's bid to host the 2018 Winter Olympics–politics, policy and practice. *The International Journal of the History of Sport, 28*(16), 2365–2383.

Miah, A., & Garcia, B. (2012). *The Olympics: The basics*. UK: Routledge.

Morgenthau, H. J. (1978). *Politics among nations: The struggle for power and peace* (5th ed.). New York: Library of Congress.

Nye, J. S. (1967). Corruption and political development: A cost-benefit analysis. *American Political Science Review, 61*(02), 417–427.

Nye, J. S. (1990). *Bound to lead: The changing nature of American power*. New York: Basic Books.

Nye, J. S. (2003). *The paradox of American power: Why the world's only superpower can't go it alone*. UK: Oxford University Press.

Nye, J. S. (2004). *Soft power: The means to success in world politics*. Public Affairs.

Nye, Jr, J. S. (2008). Public diplomacy and soft power. *The Annals of the American Academy of Political and Social Science, 616*(1), 94–109.

Persson, C. (2002). The Olympic Games site decision. *Tourism Management, 23*(1), 27–36.

Poast, P. D. (2007). Winning the bid: Analyzing the International Olympic Committee's host city selections. *International Interactions, 33*(1), 75–95.

Rowe, D. (2012). The bid, the lead-up, the event and the legacy: Global cultural politics and hosting the Olympics. *The British Journal of Sociology, 63*(2), 285–305.

Samuelson, P. A. (1938). A note on the pure theory of consumer's behaviour. *Economica, 5*(17), 61–71.

Sohn, Y. (2011). Attracting neighbors: Soft power competition in East Asia. *The Korean Journal of Policy Studies, 26*(1), 77–96.

Toohey, K., & Veal, A. J. (2007). *The Olympic Games*. A social science perspective: CABI.

Waltz, K. (1979). *Theory of international politics*. Addison-Wesley series in political science. New York: McGraw-Hill.

Wooldridge, J. M. (2010). *Econometric analysis of cross section and panel data*. Harvard, MA: MIT Press.

APPENDIX: INTERNATIONAL OLYMPIC COMMITTEE VOTES

Year of Vote	Winning Bid	Bid Countries	Voting Results					IOC Rank	IOC Votes
			1st	2nd	3rd	4th	5th		
2015	2022 Winter Beijing, China	China	44					1	0.523809524
		Kazakhstan	40					2	0.476190476
		Norway						6	0
		Poland						6	0
		Ukraine						6	0
		Sweden						6	0
2013	2020 Summer Tokyo, Japan	Japan	42	49	60			1	0.536842105
		Turkey	26	45	36			2	0.326315789
		Spain	26	—				3	0.136842105
		Azerbaijan						6	0
		Italy						6	0
		Qatar						6	0
2011	2018 Winter PyeongChang, Korea	Korea	63					1	0.663157895
		Germany	25					2	0.263157895
		France	7					3	0.073684211
2009	2016 Summer Rio de Janeiro, Brazil	Brazil	26	46	66			1	0.480836237
		Spain	28	29	32			2	0.31010453
		Japan	22	20	—			3	0.146341463
		United States	18	—				4	0.06271777
		Azerbaijan						7	0
		Qatar						7	0
		Czech Republic						7	0

Year	Event	Country					Rank	
2007	2014 Winter Sochi, Russia	Russia	34	51		54	1	0.440414508
		Korea	36	47		50	2	0.430051813
		Austria	25	–		–	3	0.129533679
		Kazakhstan					7	0
		Georgia					7	0
		Spain					7	0
		Bulgaria					7	0
2005	2012 Summer London, United Kingdom	United Kingdom	22	27	39	54	1	0.351485149
		France	21	25	33	50	2	0.319306931
		Spain	20	32	31	–	3	0.205445545
		United States	19	16	–	–	4	0.086633663
		Russia	15	–	–	–	5	0.037128713
		Germany					9	0
		Brazil					9	0
		Turkey					9	0
		Cuba					9	0
2003	2010 Winter Vancouver, Canada	Canada	40	56			1	0.444444444
		Korea	51	53			2	0.481481481
		Austria	16	–			3	0.074074074
		Andorra					8	0
		Switzerland					8	0
		China					8	0
		Spain					8	0
		Bosnia-Herzegovina					8	0

(Continued)

Year of Vote	Winning Bid	Bid Countries	Voting Results					IOC Rank	IOC Votes
			1st	2nd	3rd	4th	5th		
2001	2008 Summer Beijing, China	China	44	56				1	0.483091787
		Canada	20	22				2	0.202898551
		France	15	18				3	0.15942029
		Turkey	17	9				4	0.125603865
		Japan	6	–				5	0.028985507
		Thailand						10	0
		Egypt						10	0
		Cuba						10	0
		Malaysia						10	0
		Spain						10	0
1999	2006 Winter Turin, Italy	Italy	53					1	0.595505618
		Switzerland	36					2	0.404494382
		Finland	–					6	0
		Austria	–					6	0
		Slovakia	–					6	0
		Poland	–					6	0
1997	2004 Summer Athens, Greece	Greece	32	62	38	52	66	1	0.439252336
		Italy	23	44	28	35	41	2	0.296728972
		South Africa	16		22	20	–	3	0.135514019
		Sweden	20		19	–	–	4	0.091121495
		Argentina	16		–			5	0.037383178
		Turkey						11	0
		France						11	0
		Brazil						11	0
		Russia						11	0
		Puerto Rico						11	0
		Spain						11	0

Year	Games	Country						Rank	Share
1995	2002 Winter Salt Lake City, USA	United States	54					1	0.606741573
		Sweden	14					2	0.157303371
		Switzerland	14					3	0.157303371
		Canada	7					4	0.078651685
		Austria						9	0
		Spain						9	0
		Slovakia						9	0
		Russia						9	0
		Italy						9	0
1993	2000 Summer Sydney, Australia	Australia	30	30	37	45		1	0.401129944
		China	32	37	40	43		2	0.429378531
		United Kingdom	11	13	11	–		3	0.098870056
		Germany	9	9	–	–		4	0.050847458
		Turkey	7	–	–	–		5	0.019774011
1991	1998 Winter Nagano, Japan	Japan	21	30	36	46		1	0.378917379
		United States	15	27	29	42		2	0.321937322
		Sweden	18	25	23	–		3	0.188034188
		Spain	19	5	–	–		4	0.068376068
		Italy	15	–	–	–		5	0.042735043
1990	1996 Summer Atlanta, USA	United States	19	20	26	34	51	1	0.348837209
		Greece	23	23	26	30	35	2	0.318604651
		Canada	14	17	18	22	–	3	0.165116279
		Australia	12	21	16	–	–	4	0.113953488
		United Kingdom	11	5	–	–	–	5	0.037209302
		Yugoslavia	7	–	–	–	–	6	0.01627907

Source: Adapted from Lee and Chappelet (2012:70–71).
Note: – stands for the bid was eliminated in the ballot.

CHAPTER 9

THE CEILING STRATEGY AS POLICY: LIMITING BUREAUCRATIC EXPANSION AND DEMOCRATIZATION[*]

Hyemin Choi and Jisu Jeong

ABSTRACT

It is commonly recognized that the transition to democracy in Korea was associated with economic progress. However, not many scholars have given attention to the role of bureaucracy during the process of democratization, due to the fact that bureaucracy is usually thought of as belonging to politics, not democracy. As a refutation of this general view, first, this chapter argues that bureaucracy has been an important contributor to political modernization. Since the post-1945 period, the 'ceiling' strategy, which limits the total number of civil servants, was introduced into the personnel management method and system of checks and balances to limit undue political influence over staffing and to control bureaucratic expansion. Second, through this strategy as policy, the bureaucracy legitimately tried to avoid undemocratic political power by standardized process and

[*]This chapter was previously published as The Ceiling Strategy as Policy: Limiting Bureaucratic Expansion and Democratization, in *The Korean Journal of Policy Studies*, Vol. 32, No. 1 (2017), pp. 175–198.

The Experience of Democracy and Bureaucracy in South Korea
Public Policy and Governance, 217–240

doi:10.1108/S2053-769720170000028009

*allow coordination. The ceiling policy is originally the product of histori-
cal context during colonial and authoritarian period, but the bureaucracy
utilizes it as the instrument to reduce corruption. The contribution of this
chapter is provoking the new insights about democratization from bureaucrat's perspective which is rarely highlighted.*

Keywords: Ceiling law; bureaucratic expansion; democratization;
personnel management

WHY DOES THE NUMBER MATTER IN DEVELOPING COUNTRIES?

The total number of national civil servants is expected to hit a record of more
than 1 million this year in Korea.[1] The number is surprisingly more than double if the calculation includes quasi-public sector employees who are partially
paid through government subsidy. These numbers are almost 6.5% of the
nation's total working population. Every year, the central and local governments hire about 40,000 new employees, which is almost same as the combined number of top four chaebol companies recruited. Government is an
active employer and recruiter that is as significant as the private sector in the
job market. Public sector jobs are often preferred due to the job security, social
security provisions and welfare. Despite the low payment, there is a prevalent
perception that a career in civil service provides a good quality job with stable
working conditions because of the continuous demand for civil services.

Strong government implies not only the driver of economic development,
but also the group of elite bureaucracy. Nevertheless, when GDP increases,
government is praised, but ironically, when the number of bureaucrats increase,
government is blamed. We have stereotyped perception that the economic
development is positive and the bureaucracy is negative impact to our society.
In fact, a negative perception of the bureaucracy is inevitable because civil servants are working in a political environment. The bureaucratic system is always
politically vulnerable unless all civil servants have clear and unbiased political
neutrality. Also, higher ranking civil servants and ministers frequently intervene in the recruitment and appointment of personnel to expand their power
and create unnecessary positions. This is usually the root cause of the bureaucratic expansion that is common in both developed and developing countries.
Parkinson (1957) summarized this phenomenon as Parkinson's Law, which
states that bureaucratic expansion is not due to an increased amount of work
but rather the result of creating unnecessary positions.

Therefore, the absolute number of public servants is easily manipulated as evidence of a dysfunctional bureaucracy. Since this number is a common way to measure efficiency, sometimes a large number suggests the wrong assumption. A large number does not necessarily create a good image of the bureaucracy and the impression is that bureaucratic expansion will be inefficient, consume more taxes and generate more red tape. Furthermore, since the work of bureaucracy is mainly office work, the increased size of bureaucracy symbolizes increased personnel and budget. Therefore, the power of bureaucracy is all about the number game.

Common Bureaucratic Expansion Phenomena in Developing Countries?

Increased unnecessary positions within the bureaucracy have been a common dilemma that many developing countries are facing. Furthermore, these positions are easily used as the channel of corruption. In Ecuador, entry into the Civil Service is based on merit and competitive examinations. However, there is also occasional and temporary direct recruitment through civil contracts when a person is engaged by a public entity to provide a temporary service that cannot be covered by one of its permanent employees. They are not career staff but still have the same duties as public servants. Although they have a fixed-term contract, usually their term is renewed several times, which results in the reduction of career staff (OAS report). In Mongolia, the size of the bureaucracy fluctuated extensively after the parliamentary elections of 1996 and 2000, when the party in power changed. Almost 60% of all government staff, including civil service employees, were terminated and replaced. Turnover after the 2004 Parliamentary elections, when the same party remained in control, is estimated between 30% and 40% of the staff. They are then replaced by staff chosen based on political patronage, including those who worked or contributed to the campaigns, regardless of whether or not they possess the capabilities or skills required by the jobs to which they are assigned. The bureaucracy is also used to provide jobs to members of Parliament who have lost an election (USAID report, 2005). In Algeria, there was a remarkable expansion of the bureaucracy since the arrival to power of Bouteflika in 1999. As a result of an unmanaged bureaucracy, the government has announced a hiring freeze in most parts of the public sector, which already accounts for 60% of employment (Ford, 2016).

This chapter views that the limiting of bureaucratic expansion can function as a system of controlling undemocratic power in an authoritarian context. Despite Korean bureaucracy evolved in the context of colonial and authoritarian era for long time, bureaucracy implemented their own strategy to democratize the administrative organization. In this chapter, we conceptualize the democratization as the standardization of process by the rule of law. The law limits arbitrarily operated discretions. From that perspective, the process of developing a bureaucratic procedure to limit the size can be viewed as democratization in a developmental state. Through the examination of a Korean policy, 'The Ceiling Law²', which was initiated top down approach by bureaucracy, this chapter argues that the bureaucracy in developing countries can take an active role to help democratization.

BUREAUCRACY AND DEVELOPING COUNTRIES

The Role of Bureaucracy in the Developmental State

Why does bureaucracy expand beyond a desirable size, especially in developing countries? In the case of Korea, the main reason behind bureaucratic expansion was economic development. The number of personnel in the bureaucracy has continuously increased due to the characteristics of the developmental state. Especially during the stage of 'condensed industrialization', the role of government was broad and aggressive to catch up to industrialized countries. For example, from the mid-1960s to late 1980s, the Korean government set goals in five-year economic development plans, and the bureaucracy took on the role of a bank or enterprise and enjoyed the 'late benefits' of industrialized countries in late industrialization (Gerschenkron, 1962). Elite civil servants continued to increase their power and capacity as the state actively maintained the state-led administrative structure until the 1997 economic crisis. Many studies agree that the government played an important role in the growth process of the Korean economy.

The developmental state is often conceptually positioned between a liberal open economy model and a centrally planned model. However, the theory of the developmental state is not about a dichotomous choice between capitalist and socialist systems. The developmental state is based on combinations of positive advantages of private business and the positive role of government (Bolesta, 2007). Often, the positive role of government was interpreted as the power of state intervention from an economic perspective to govern the market.

In that sense, Lariaux argued that 'the developmental state is an embodiment of a normative or moral ambition to use the interventionist power of the state to guide investment in a way that promotes a certain solidaristic vision of national economy' (Lariaux in: Woo-Cumings, 1999). Wade (1990) moved one step further and viewed the role of government in developmental state as entry-exit decision maker from an organizational perspective: 'A pilot agency or economic general staff is one of the core features. The pilot agency decides which industries ought to exist and which industries are no longer needed in order to promote the industrial structure which enhances the nation's international competitiveness'. Chang (1999) explained the role of government as not only regulating the economy, but also in relation with politics in a developmental state. However, the economic environment was continuously at the center of the developmental state discussion in a lot of literature, but there seems to be very little debate about the political environment necessary for a developmental state.

During the developmental stage, the Korean government was acting as both planner and implementer of the national economy. In this process, the role of bureaucrats was that of a mediator who scales down an ambiguous [ambitious?] vision to transform it into practice. The transferring method was through the characteristics of Weberian bureaucracy: the chain of command, procedure, hierarchical organization, expert, rule of law and documentation. These characteristics were based on scientific management and administrative principles in the combination of the government and the market. As Weber mentioned, bureaucracy is an inevitable consequence and result of modernity.

Korea between the 1960s and the 1980s probably provides the most 'extreme' case of the developmental state in organizational terms (Chang, 1990). This period was a turbulent developmental stage with strong government-driven economic development planning by the Park government. In a relation to that, the goals were not limited to economic growth, but also to the development of human resources, national land reforms and a self-reliant national defense. The ambitious plans for policy reforms and socioeconomic development increased the workload of bureaucrats, and more government employees had to be hired as a result (Bello & Rosenfeld, 1990, Boyer & Ahn, 1991). However, unfortunately, additional public servants were hired who were not trained enough to achieve this goal [?]. In trying to upgrade the human resources of the bureaucracy, an alternative strategy was to create a new organization with fresh people. Powerful pilot agencies, such as the Economic Planning Board, the Ministry of Finance and the State-owned bank, were established during this economically turbulent stage. These types of government agencies required completely different skills and knowledge from public servants. Especially, the Economic Planning Board, which not only managed the (indicative) planning exercise but also controlled the budget and the foreign fund, needed diversified experts from across the spectrum including economics, law, international affairs, language and financing. Also, since the EPB coordinated the activities of the Ministry of Commerce and Industry, the banks and other state-owned enterprises, highly educated individuals were desired from various disciplines. Young PhD scholars who had studied abroad with Fulbright grants or academic professors were also [a high priority to be hired] in great demand.

Since the State Council Secretariat was abolished and reorganized as the Ministry of Government Administration in 1963, personnel administrative functions were still managed in the Personnel Management Bureau in the Ministry of Government Administration. However, due to the rapidly increasing number of public servants, MGA's personnel administrative workload increased drastically. Not only preparing and supporting cabinet meetings and promulgating new and revised legislation, ordinance and law, the ministry was in charge of public servant personnel management, managing all government organizational structure and quotas, improvement of general administrative work, managing public servants' insurance and retirement, merit system evaluations, training programs and managing government building facilities. The change in the political culture of citizen participation also increased the demand for public servants. After the democratization of the late 1980s, citizens believed that they were now in a genuine democracy and a democratic political culture emerged. They started asking actively about what they wanted from the government. Not only the quantity of demands, but also the specific and detailed nature of the demands was problematic. To satisfy their requests, government needed more human resources. Partly in response to this, the retirement age of street-level bureaucrats was extended from 58 to 61.

Causes of Bureaucratic Expansion in Developing Countries

Underdeveloped Private Job Market

One simple answer for the reasons of bureaucratic expansion in developing countries is that becoming a civil servant is a decent job due to the underdeveloped private job market. Since the private market is not fully structured and developed, most businesses are rather small-scale productions or family oriented businesses. Even though periods of economic growth have the largest impact on reduction in the exit rates, the market size is still small and small firms' survival rate is also low. Therefore, the private sector cannot guarantee job security, particularly during periods of political uncertainty (Klapper et al., 2009). Often the available private sector jobs are blue-collar work in the industrial sector, especially manufacturing. In this context, working in government as a career civil servant is a privileged job in developing countries and considered white-collar work.

For example, to become a civil servant in Korea, there are two ways: entering by passing the strict qualifying exam or entering through a temporary position and surviving to become a career civil servant. The law of open competition for public servants in the recruitment system (Articles 28, 1963) allows any talented individual to enter the bureaucracy. This merit-based system of recruitment carried out through open competition was not a new idea in Korea. Traditionally, Korea's public service system is rooted in its Confucian heritage such that public servants were typically either appointed by the royal court or recruited through highly competitive national exams. Regardless of social class, anyone who passed the national civil service exam, Gwageo, could become a public servant during the Joseon Dynasty Period (1392–1910).

Korea's economic and political situation was similar to that of many other developing countries, especially in the late 1970s to 1980s. Although the career civil servant system had been continuously elaborated through law, it was not followed because of the under developed job market. During the 1960s and 1970s, large private companies expanded in parallel to the country's economic success. However, the number of large private companies was very small and available jobs were mostly in the manufacturing sector, which does not require a university degree. Furthermore, since the economy was still developing, the survival rate of companies was low, and job security in the private sector was low as well.

Undemocratic Political Power
Another problem was inherited culture of familialism. Scholars have characterized Korean administrative culture as hierarchical, authoritative, paternal, emotional, irrational and familial (Cho, 1994; Paik, 1982). Also, especially in the context of Confucian familialism, hiring people through personal networks is still frequently considered a cultural norm in an agriculture-dominated society. Mainly, the root cause of the bureaucratic expansion was due to these appointed temporary workers recruited through the familial network.

The merit-based recruitment system was officially considered as the only way to become a career civil servant by law. In reality, however, only 20% of all civil servants were hired through the merit-based open competition system (Cho, 1968). Behind the scenes, career civil servants who entered as appointed temporary workers made up the majority of the bureaucracy. The familial network can be easily manipulated to offer bribes for jobs and corruption. Career civil servants who entered as appointed temporary workers usually had a low quality of manpower and their concern was survival rather than performance, which degraded the quality of the overall bureaucracy. In this context, undemocratic political power means unequally treated and distributed opportunity using abuse of discretion.

The implication of this phenomenon is that the bureaucracy is a hindrance for democratization, rather than facilitator. However, even in Western countries, networking is a critical method for job recruitment, and hiring people through the network is encouraged. Therefore, the matter is not about the characteristics of temporary positions via the familial network, but the uncontrollable increase in the number of positions through undemocratic political power.

CASE STUDY: THE CEILING POLICY[3]

In order to control the expansion of temporal public servants and prevent the size fluctuation caused by undemocratic political power, Korean bureaucracy implemented their own policy called 'The ceiling law'. The Law of General Rules on organization and the ceiling of administrative agencies was enacted under The Government Organization Act in 1977. The purpose of the law is to set a rational standard of personnel ceiling management in order to manage administrative organization efficiently. The ultimate common goal of the ceiling was controlling and prediction for a stable bureaucracy.

The Ceiling as Number Strategy: Table of Organization

Korean bureaucracy has been managed based on headcounts from the beginning. The ceiling strategy originated from the concept of TO which stands for Table of Organization. This is a table listing the number and duties of personnel and the major items of equipment authorized for a military unit. Originally, a table of organization and equipment (TOE or TO&E) is a document published by the U.S. Department of Defense which prescribes the organization, staffing and equipment of units. TOE provides information on the mission and capabilities of a military unit as well as the unit's current status.

The history of the TO-based personnel and organizational management system in Korea begins in the era of Korean War. After the Japanese colonial period ended, the American Military Government created a new administrative structure in South Korea on the basis of a democratic system that affected the process of the formation of the Korean bureaucracy from 1945 until the establishment of the Republic of Korea on 15 August 1948. During the United States occupation period, the Military Governor General Hodge was ordered by the U.S. government to impose an American Military Government on the framework of the Choseon Governor General and the first urgent task was to form some kind of administrative structure. In order to meet the day-by-day problems of governing more than 17 million people, the Military Governor needed a great number of competent civil officials trained for the purpose. For General Hodge, personnel management was driven by the U.S. army system. By the end of 1945, the total personnel in groups and companies was only 541 officers and 1918 enlisted men whereas the number required by the TO for these organizations called for 638 officers and 2882 enlisted men (Lee).

An Office of the Military Governor document states that *there were approximately 175,000 positions to be filled both in government and public corporations*, which shows that government officials are calculated as 'positions' and something needed to be 'filled' based on the structure of the 'table of organization'. The inherited ceiling concept during this period still endures in the system of bureaucracy. The position is still considered a unit of individual personnel. Furthermore, the 'seat' is the metaphor of the position which represents 'rank', 'task', 'seat' and 'job'.

Within Central Government Organizations: System of Checks and Balances

Since bureaucratic expansion in central government and local government occurs in different contexts, they share the same goal of a ceiling law, but their strategies are developed differently. Within the central government, the ceiling strategy was to create a strict administrative procedure in order to limit the increase of each ministry's total number of personnel. The Ministry of Government Administration was the control tower of this whole process. MGA (1948–1998) was first established with The Ministry of Interior Administration right after the official Republic of Korea Government was founded in 1948. Since then, the MGA has dealt with overall government administration, organizational management, personnel management, document system administration, office administration and government general affairs as overhead functions. In addition to that, the MGA also functioned as the central personnel administration for long time.

The MGA has been a crucial ministry within the central government. Although the MGA covered overall government administration with a broad spectrum of work, since it was considered as general administrative work, the ministry was constantly exposed to decomposition or abolition. However in 1963, the MGA was re-established with a new mission to create a stable working environment for civil servants, led by then MGA Minister Lee.

Since Minister Lee had a military background and a close relationship with President Park, he could exercise strong leadership for administration reform without political intervention. Major achievements were the revision of the existing public service law with more detailed requirements and more specifically described procedures. As a result, laws in relation to the recruitment system, remuneration policy, the incentive system, and welfare and pension were restructured. The revision included centralizing recruitment and selection, improving examinations, installing a performance rating system, adapting a new training system, improving pay administration and installing a position classification system (Cheng, Haggard, & Kang, 1998).

In particular, MGA tried to restructure the foundation of the personnel system including the law of open-competition for the public servant recruitment system (Articles 28, 1963) and the career civil servant system. Although the career civil service system had been continuously reformed through the law to protect it from undemocratic political power, the minister's centralized personnel decision power was still used to hire individuals to unofficial positions. Therefore, the frequent replacement of ministers eventually resulted in the frequent replacement of bureaucrats. Consequently, every time a new minister was appointed, the size of the bureaucracy expanded.

Due to the merit-based recruitment system, central government regularly filled with competent personnel. Therefore, within the central government bureaucracy, the more problem was not about total personnel, but balanced allocation of personnel among ministries. If one ministry has more personnel than other ministries, that may cause an unbalanced power distribution. Also, since each ministry has overlapping functions, a redundant work force can emerge. Therefore, the ceiling strategy for the central government was created based on a strict schedule of checks and balances.

The law precisely describes the procedures that each ministry has to follow in order to revise their staff ceiling number every year. This strict procedure forces each ministry to prepare the following year's specific projects and to plan in advance. Planning is not only for filling the gap of the currently needed workforce, but also for preparing needed workforce in the future. In order to estimate the needed seats, each ministry has to consider both the internal situation and the external environment. Internally, they need to decide where work should be focused and which projects will be outsourced. Project planning and scheduling is strongly related to personnel and not only full-time but also fixed-term public servants and the temporary workforce should be considered. To assign the right number of people, with the right attitude and skills, in the right place at the right time, defining a clear goal and mission is a necessity.

As shown in Fig. 1, every year, each ministry applies a revision of organizational structure and a new ceiling number for approval. At this stage, each ministry has to submit a long-term strategy plan for their ministry that includes the reason for requesting a new ceiling number. Additional supporting documents can be requested by the MGA. Once the MGA accepts the application from each ministry, the managerial level first prescreens the applications and checks the requirements. Once each MGA manager confirms the requests, an official organizational evaluation is initiated. During this process, the organizational review and the ceiling number review are processed separately. The main purpose of the organizational review is to evaluate the function of the ministry. The ceiling number review is to evaluate the requested number of personnel based on the proposed organizational structure and long-term strategy. Once both reviews are completed, the next step is a budget review by the Ministry of Finance and Economy and a legislative law review by the Ministry of Government Legislation. Both are steps in the checks and balances system.

Central-Local Government: Rational Scientific Model

A large number of bureaucrats in central government belonged to an elite who had been selected through the merit-based system. On the other hand, in the 1970s, bureaucrats in local governments were less competitive and highly influential through undemocratic political power, so that the central government had to limit local governments' bureaucratic expansion. Local government had strong bond with community and local interest group. Their power was uncontrollable and inhibits the equal opportunity. In order to limit undemocratic discretions in local government, the central government used the ceiling strategy to provide a legitimate total number of public servants. Those tasks were managed by the Ministry of Interior Administration (MIA, 1948–1998).

MIA was established in 1948 with the MGA. Compared to the MGA, which was managing the central government, the MIA was founded to manage home affairs including mainly administrative management for

```
┌─────────────────────────────────────────────┐
│      Ministry of Government Administration    │
│      announces the guidelines of Government   │
│          Organizational Management            │
└─────────────────────────────────────────────┘

┌─────────────────────────────────────────────┐
│      Each ministry submits application for the│
│         approval of revised organizational    │
│      structure and new ceiling number based   │
│              on the guideline                 │
└─────────────────────────────────────────────┘

┌─────────────────────────────────────────────┐
│        Prescreened (MGA) Data Collection      │
└─────────────────────────────────────────────┘

┌─────────────────────────────────────────────┐
│        Organizational Evaluation (MGA)        │
└─────────────────────────────────────────────┘

┌──────────────────────┐  ┌──────────────────────┐
│    Budget Review     │  │  Legislation and Law │
│ Ministry of Finance  │  │        Review        │
│    and Economy       │  │ Ministry of Government│
│                      │  │     Legislation      │
└──────────────────────┘  └──────────────────────┘

┌─────────────────────────────────────────────┐
│         Vice minister's meeting               │
│         Cabinet Council Meeting               │
└─────────────────────────────────────────────┘

┌─────────────────────────────────────────────┐
│            President's consent                │
└─────────────────────────────────────────────┘

┌─────────────────────────────────────────────┐
│      Approved - Officially Announced          │
└─────────────────────────────────────────────┘
```

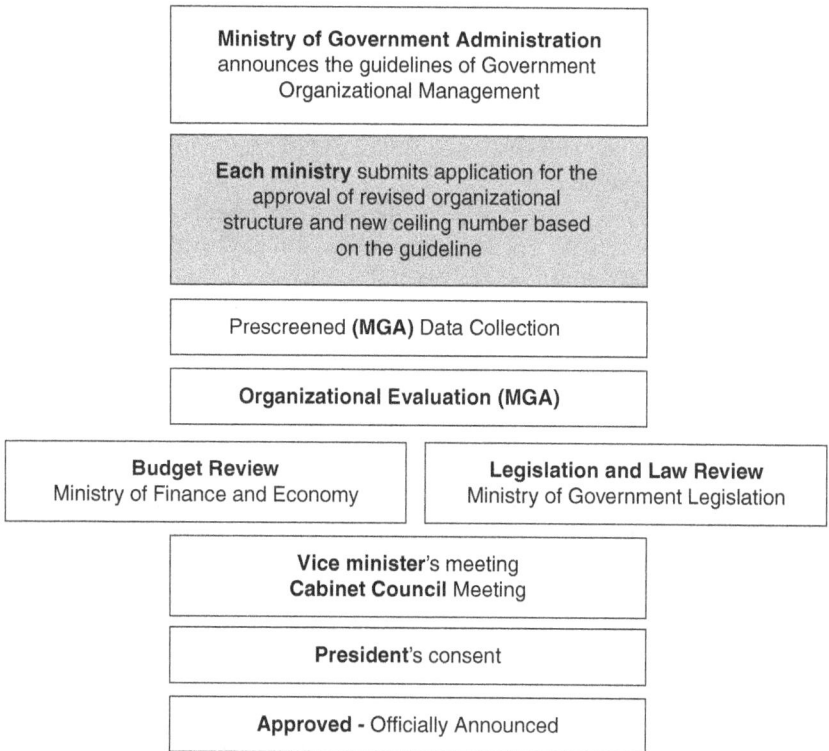

Fig. 1. Central Government Organizations: Annual Ceiling Number Approval Process. *Source*: Ministry of the Interior Website.

local and public security such as civil defense training, disaster management and fire services. The enacted local autonomy law (1949) aimed to strengthen local government, but it took 20 years to initiate the local elections of the mayors of Seoul and Pusan, provincial governors and local councils. Even that attempt was placed on hold under the system of military rule during 1961–1970. During this period, major cities were under the direct control of the central government in that provincial administrations and mayors directly reported to the Ministry of Interior Administration. Even most personnel were appointed by the political power. The mayor of Seoul was appointed by the president and usually was regarded as his close confidant. Heads of other administrative divisions were recommended by the minister of Interior Administration for presidential approval. Mayors of ordinary cities and managerial levels of local career civil servants were recommended by the provincial governor for appointment by the president. Therefore, until 1988, personnel management was based on the individual approval system.

The MIA adopted the ceiling system, which was characterized by a slightly different approach from the MGA's ceiling strategy. MIA's ceiling strategy was not a procedure, but rather a rational scientific model with the aim to set the number. This ceiling number was driven by a simple regression to predict needed personnel for the future. Not only that, the ceiling number was a reasonable source of defense when local governments asked to hire more personnel. In terms of the local government, there was no ceiling for the local government until 1988 due to the inactive local autonomy system. Until then, the central government fully controlled local government, and every request had to be approved by the MIA.

Independent Variables for the Ceiling Number

In academia, efforts have been made to study the demand and the capacity of civil servants in Korean context starting with the article of Cho Suk-Choon (1976) Predictive Model of Public Personnel and Manpower in 1982. The focus was prediction rather than reduction. Therefore, the concept of personnel is framed more as the capital of budget. In order to develop a regression model, the following variables had to be considered (Table 1).

Table 1. The Enacted History of Ceiling Law.

	Ministry of Government Administration (MGA)	Ministry of Interior Administration (MIA)
Purpose	Managing civil servants in central government	Managing civil servants in local government
		Coordination of central-local government
	Coordination between ministries	
Method	System of checks and balances	Rational scientific model
Enacted law	The approval procedure (1977)	Individual approval system (~1988)
		The standard ceiling system (1988–1994)
		The total ceiling management (1994–1996)
		The new standard ceiling system (1997–1998)
	Emerged as **Ministry of Security and Public Administration (1998)**	
Enacted law	The new standard ceiling system (2003–2006), The fixed budget (2007–)	

Choi and Jeong (2017)

Population Variable

The population can be simply defined as a group of people. However, the population age structure, which is the summary of the number of individuals of each age, depicts the actual characteristics of the population. It is useful in understanding and predicting future population growth, because each age group needs different services and administrative goals. For example, normally, older adults have different health care needs than younger age groups, and this will affect the demands placed on the health care system in the future. Therefore, the administrative demand can fluctuate based on the age structure. The central government and the local government must plan ahead to allocate human resources in order to supply rudimentary services for the survival and well-being of the people. The politically relevant strata of the population multiplies the demands for government services, and thus stimulates an increase in governmental capabilities, a broadening of the elite, increased political participation and shifts in attention from the local level to the national level.

Social System Variable

The characteristics of economic and social systems can affect civil servants' workload. Esping-Andersen (1999) argues that the 'East Asian Confucian states' such as China, Japan, Korea, Taiwan, Singapore and Hong Kong have an exceptionally low number of civil servants in comparison with Scandinavian countries such as Norway, Sweden, and Finland. The size of the public service sector relative to the population in Scandinavian countries is exceptionally large compared to other OECD countries. From the standpoint of the welfare system, the expansion of the role of the state for social welfare has been caused by the demand side triggering the expansion of the national service, the political aspect aiming at redistribution and the institutional aspect of the government organization seeking expansion of the budget (Boix, 2000). These factors affect the expansion of government.

Size of Economy Variable

From an economic point of view, depending on whether the nation is market-oriented or government-centered, the required function and capacity of the bureaucracy varies. In the market economy, it is important to pursue minimum regulation and market autonomy. In this case, the role of public servants is to support legitimate competition with minimum manpower, and to maintain stable international relations through diplomatic security. On the other hand, in the case of the government-centered economy, the government acts as the regulatory entity such that an increase of regulation means the expansion of the public service. Regardless of the economic regime, as the economy grows, the number of taxpayers increases. Therefore, more local tax offices are needed, including the personnel in the finance department.

Territorial Context (Area) Variable
The size of countries is very diverse. China, one of the largest countries in the world, has 9,597,000 km² of land; Tuvalu, the smallest country with a seat in the UN has an area of 26 km². European countries have relatively small land areas, but a typical European citizen is governed by a series of up to six levels of governments, from a city council to the European Union. The spatial process of change which includes the level of urbanization across regions and countries also affects administrative territories and the size of the bureaucracy.

Workload (Administrative Demand) Variable
Workload means the total amount of administrative work that the government should carry out. Conceptually, this is deducted [normalized?] as workload per worker. As such, administrative demand is the most direct determinant of public service demand, and even if it is difficult to quantify, the work-load should be analyzed in any model. Administrative demand may change based on the following questions: Will the function of government expand? Can some administrative demand be outsourced to the private sector? Will there be additional investment? How will policy priorities will change? Will the population of beneficiaries increase? Therefore, in predicting civil serv-ant demand, clear assumptions and quantitative plans or estimates of these problems must be made in advance. However, this is in fact a matter for the jurisdiction of high-ranking decision makers. Therefore, it is hard to expect realistic long-term plans.

Mode of Administration Variable
Mode of administration means the manpower dependency in administrative processes. It has the same meaning as the combined ratio of manpower and capital as the production factor (production mode). Even if the demand for public administration remains constant, if the dependency on manpower in the administrative process is high, the demand for civil servants will increase accordingly. The mode of administration should be reformed by the sim-plification of decision-making processes and administrative procedures for

performance improvement. Eventually, it will require a smaller number of civil servants. Therefore, to predict the optimum workload in the future, administrative reform should be made in advance. However, a change of administrative style takes a relatively long time to implement. Administrative reform (improvement) should be considered separately because it is a task to be pursued continuously. Rather, the problem of mechanization or computerization of administration should be examined as a competitive alternative to the problem of increasing or decreasing manpower.

Quality of Manpower
The higher the qualifications of civil servants, the lower the quantitative demand for civil servants. In other words, quantity and quality of manpower are mutually substitutable attributes. To estimate the required number of civil servants, their qualitative level should be anticipated in advance. The quality of civil servants is closely related to the incentive system, training and education, which need investment. Manpower supply includes both quality and quantity, and the estimates of manpower should be classified based on the level of education and technical skills.

Budget and Revenue (Finances) Variable
In reality, the size increase of the civil service is implemented under a specific policy system, and the biggest constraint is often a financial reason to increase or decrease labor costs. Therefore, if the workload determines the aggregated total demand of civil servants, the decision type is determined by the financial conditions of the government.

Analytical Method for Estimating Ceiling Number for Local Government

In 1980s, based on consideration of independent variables, the standard ceiling was driven by a simple regression to predict the number needed in the future. This first ceiling strategy applied to local government in the late 1980s under the Local Government Act. The first model (1) of the standard ceiling only used the basic variable of population, land size of local area, number of local public organizations and local revenue were considered as statistically significant variables.

$$Ceiling\ Number = [1,086,245 + (0.0015 \times Local\ Population)] \times 1.05 \quad (1)$$

The regression model was periodically revised and the independent variables such as number of administrative districts, administrative workload (added in 1990), number of administration districts (added in 1991) were included for better prediction. However, criticisms were received that the independent variables in the simple regression model (1) treat each local government homogeneously. Therefore, in order to consider unique local characteristics, a more complex regression model was developed and introduced.

$$EMP_{ij} = \beta_0 + \beta_1 X_{1ij} + \beta_2 X_{2ij} + \beta_3 X_{3ij} + \beta_4 X_{4ij} + C_{ij} + T_{ij} \qquad (2)$$

Compared to the first model (1), the complex model (2) considered local factors and included various dummy variables to strengthen the model. X_1 is local population in each administrative area. X_2 represents number of public organizations in that area and X_3 is the land size of each administrative area. X_4 means settled revenue of general account. In the second revised model, dummy variables which considered local context are also reflected. The purpose of these models was not to provide the true number of public servants. Rather, it allowed both central and local governments to control themselves before hiring. Additionally, it provided legitimacy for the central government to control local government.

Post-Ceiling Strategy

Fixing the total personnel number in advance with a rigorous procedure stabilized the size of the bureaucracy, but there was also a dominant view that the government was limiting the ministry's autonomy and the resiliency of the organization too much. From a top-down perspective, planning fixed total personnel number in advance was efficient only at the ministry level. However, from a bottom-up perspective, projects were always exposed to unexpected challenges in the environment and faced the risk that a team would need more personnel or less personnel depending on the situation (Table 2).

Because of these contingencies, the government introduced the Fixed Budget for Personnel Policy which allocates the total budget for personnel instead of imposing government-wide ceilings on staffing numbers. This aligned with the change from rank classification-based recruitment to job classification-based recruitment so that recruiting experts were allowed in each ministry to select and hire what they actually need. In the past, the personnel number was only planned by rank and even though organizations sometimes needed more entry-level public servants, they had to hire middle level officials according to this plan. This mismatching problem could

Table 2. Variables for Analytical Model.

Year	Model	Dependent Variable	Independent Variable	Calculation
1989	Simple linear regression OLS	Ceiling number	• Population • Area • Number of public organizations • Revenue	$[1{,}086{,}245 + (0.0015 \times Local\ Population)] \times 1.05$
1995	Least squares dummy variable (LSDV)	Ceiling number	• Population • Area • Number of public organizations • Revenue • Dummy variables*	*differentiate geographical and time context
1999	Standardized index (SI)	Ceiling number	• Population • Area • Number of public organizations • Revenue • Number of public servants • Park area, recipient of livelihood program	$[2067.8 + (0.00022240 \times Local\ Population) + (0.00060543 \times Revenue)] + (\text{Fixed dummy variables})$

* This model considers geographical and time context for variables

be resolved. Of course, a close monitoring of the procedure by the central personnel administration in the Ministry of Government Administration and Ministry of Finance still continues, but ministries could recruit, control and coordinate their personnel autonomously within their allocated budget.

In a broader sense, the *Total Fluid-Personnel Policy (1997)* was also introduced as the improved version of the Fixed Budget for Total Personnel so that the personnel can be directly transferred or rearranged between ministries. However, there was a tendency that powerful ministries that receive a large amount of budget from the government would ask for more personnel from less powerful ministries. Personnel only flowed from the less powerful ministries to more powerful ministries so that it was difficult to maintain balance among them. The power relationship worsened because the powerful ministries became larger and acquired more human resources while the less powerful ministries became smaller (Im, 2003). In order to address these problems, the *Fixed Total Occupations Policy (2013)* was implemented. Since the Korean government's central model of controlling the total number was generally done at the ministry level, similar characteristics of teams or departments were created in each ministry. In order to avoid this redundancy, the government decided to manage not only a fixed number of public servants by ministry, but also the number of seats by position. The government asked each ministry to select 5% of their total positions as redundant positions, and they had to remove them by 1% every year. The main purpose was to reduce each ministry's size by managing redundant positions and reutilize them elsewhere. However, which positions to eliminate is still an unsolved question.

THE CEILING LAW AND DEMOCRATIZATION

Developing Procedure to Eliminate Undemocratic Power

A further problem of undemocratic political power is unpredictability. For example, when the bureaucracy expands in the spoils system, an organization cannot predict what kind of positions will be filled and generated. Since the expenditure for existing positions in the bureaucracy is drawn from taxes, the wrong estimation eventually leads to a waste of public money.

Since the law operates within a predictable, consistent and limited framework, the value of the rule of law is to reduce arbitrary power and to ensure an orderly society ruled by a responsible and principled government (Raz, 1994). Democratic power means the rule of law and legitimized procedure. Weber also emphasized that the ideal type of bureaucracy is driven by principles such as 'division of labour' and 'rule of law'. Weber argues that these principles are typical of modern bureaucracy such that it is the obligation of the bureaucrats to follow the procedures of carrying out their duties by law, and it is the duty of all to obey the orders of the public officers justified by them.

In that sense, the 'ceiling' policy was an instrument to control undemocratic power within the bureaucracy and external political influence. The term 'ceiling' symbolizes the maximum number. In personnel management, the ceiling implies a limit of the number of personnel assigned to an institution or department by law. The purpose of the law was to set the rational standard of personnel management through a scientific model and to forecast the needed total number of personnel every year.

An organization is a combination of functions and personnel that are organically inter-related to each other. However, the concept of the personnel ceiling states the optimum size of manpower that can achieve the organization's goals efficiently. Since the concept of manpower itself refers to human resources in terms of economy, the estimation of manpower demand is generally calculated as a specific output, that is, the quantitative scale of the labor force to achieve the production amount. Therefore, the optimum number of the personnel ceiling policy refers to the process of finding a reasonable number of personnel in accordance with the organization's workload and nature of work (Kim, 1980).

The Role of Bureaucracy and Democratization

Bureaucracy and democracy are typically considered antithetical (Etzioni-Halevey, 1983). Usually, the terms bureaucracy and democracy are thought of as the contradiction between control and autonomy. Even though the logic for institutionalizing the bureaucratic form of organization was to ensure efficiency, equal treatment, good record keeping and justification for every decision, the bureaucracy is often stereotyped as hierarchical, legalistic and even authoritarian (Du Gay, 2000; Goodsell, 2004; Peters, 2010). Contrarily, democracy is conceptualized as an effective and reflective system that supports collective decisions by participants who express their preferences. The construction of democratic legitimacy is based on voting, interest aggregation, constitutional rights or even self-government, but as Dryzek (2000) argues, the essence of democracy itself is now widely taken to be deliberation. Also, he argues that the level of democracy is dependent on the capacity for autonomy.

In that sense, democracy is closely related to the concept of participation. However, this chapter defines democracy as a procedure which is driven by the rule of law. The law operates within a predictable, consistent and limited framework. Therefore, the value of the rule of law is to reduce arbitrary power (Raz, 1994). From that perspective, controlling the size of the bureaucracy is strongly related to democracy because it is about the process of removing undemocratic political influence and avoiding centralized power among a small number of civil servants. This also can be applied to Weber's ideal type of bureaucracy which is driven by principles such as 'division of labour and 'rule of law'. These principles are typical of modern bureaucracy and oblige bureaucrats to follow the procedures and carry out their duties consistent with law, and it is the duty of all to obey the orders of the public officers justified by them. In that sense, the ceiling policy, as a form of coercive law, was instrumental in controlling undemocratic phenomena in the bureaucracy during Korea's developmental stage.

CONCLUSION

Huntington (1965) argues that four sets of categories recur continuously in the definitions of political development. These are rationalization, nation building, democratization and participation. Among them, the democratization approach focuses on pluralism, competitiveness and equalization of power. In that sense, the ceiling policy as law, political development in the bureaucracy is that of movement towards democracy. The ceiling policy was a procedure that allowed other ministries to participate in the ministry's future organizational structure, long-term vision and personnel number. Also, the ceiling policy controlled bureaucratic expansion and enhanced the competitiveness of the bureaucracy, which was an essential aspect of political modernity (Coleman et al., 1960). Furthermore, the ceiling policy helped to distribute centralized power.

The ceiling management strategy reflects bureaucrat's will to avoid undemocratic political influence. The ceiling policy acted as a regulatory-type instrument. Within the authoritarian context, the hide-and-seek process was a constant process between political powers, which try to expand their power in the bureaucracy, and the rule of law, which focuses on the prevention of intervention. The ceiling policy was gradually elaborated through the law by bureaucrats themselves to strengthen the stability and predictability of the bureaucracy. The ceiling system has fostered democracy insofar as it has worked to control undemocratic phenomena in the bureaucracy.

Since the ceiling strategy has innate characteristics of top-down approach and evolved through authoritarian government, there is limit to link democratization. However, democracy needs to be constantly reinterpreted in various perspectives. In this sense, the contribution of this chapter is to recognize the new debate on democratization in the Asian context especially in developing countries in relation to the bureaucracy.

NOTES

1. Korean government and OECD have different standard of calculating public servants. In Korea, Ministry of Security and Public Administration annually announces official number of national civil servants. In 2016, official total number of national civil servants is 1,027,561. This number includes public servants in central government (61%, not only general administrators but also teachers, police officers, and post officers), local government (36%), National Assembly, The Supreme Court and Constitutional Court. https://org.moi.go.kr/org/external/dept/deptReportIntro.jsp

2. Japan and United States also have similar law. In Japan, personnel were managed by *the fixed total number law* (1967). In United States, *Federal Workforce Recruiting Act of 1994* has similar function. However, both of laws are different from Korean Ceiling Strategy because of two reasons. First, Japan and United States use ceiling as the size reduction in order to achieve "small government." Second, Japan uses fixed

total number law as reduction, pooling, and redistribution of personnel. United States use ceiling strategy in order to induce retirement. Both countries are using ceiling strategy as the perspective of reduction. On the other hand, the uniqueness about Korean Ceiling Strategy is oriented from the idea of prediction.

3. The ceiling policy only applies to administrative employees whom are working in central and local governments. The ceiling policy is also called as *Government manpower ceiling*, *Total personnel system*, and *Personnel quota system*. They convey similar meaning but translated differently by scholars.

ACKNOWLEDGMENTS

This research is supported by National Research Foundation of Korea (NRF-2014S1A3A2044898). We thank *Tobin Im* for valuable insights and comments.

REFERENCES

Alesina, A. (2003). The size of countries: does it matter?. *Journal of the European Economic Association, 1*(2–3), 301–316.

Bello, W., & Rosenfeld, S. (1990). *Dragons in distress: Asia's miracle economies in crisis*. Institute for Food and Development Policy.

Boix, C. (2000). Partisan governments, the international economy, and macroeconomic policies in advanced nations, 1960–93. *World Politics, 53*(1), 38–73.

Bolesta, A. (2012). China as a post-socialist developmental state: Explaining Chinese development trajectory. Doctoral dissertation, The London School of Economics and Political Science.

Boyer, W. W. (1991). *Rural development in South Korea: A sociopolitical analysis*. Newark: University of Delaware Press; London: Associated University Press.

Breton, A., & Wintrobe, R. (1975). The equilibrium size of a budget-maximizing bureau: A note on Niskanen's theory of bureaucracy. *Journal of Political Economy, 83*(1), 195–207.

Cho, S. C. (1976). Public sector manpower forecasting model and the size of manpower in 1982. *Korean Journal of Public Administration, 14*(1), 1001.

Cho, S. C. and Im, T. (2010). (2nd ed.), Paju, Kyuggi. BupMunPress

Choi, B. S. (1988). Political and economic democratization and its impact on the government-business relationship in Korea. *Korean Journal of Policy Studies, 3*(1988), 30.

Choi, S. Y. (2012). Comparison of civil service reform in the United States and Korea: Central personnel agencies and senior civil service systems. *Korean Journal of Policy Studies, 27*(3), 101–123.

Chung, J. Y., & Kirkby, R. J. (2005). *The political economy of development and environment in Korea* (Vol. 73). UK: Routledge.

Dryzek, J. S. (2002). *Deliberative democracy and beyond: Liberals, critics, contestations*. Oxford: Oxford University Press.

Du Gay, P. (2000). *In praise of bureaucracy: Weber, organization, ethics*. London: Sage.

Entwistle, T., Guarneros-Meza, V., Martin, S., & Downe, J. (2016). Reframing governance: Competition, fatalism and autonomy in central-local relations. *Public Administration, 94*(4), 897–914. doi:10.1111/padm.12210

Esping-Andersen, G. (1999). *Social foundations of postindustrial economies.* UK: Oxford University Press.

Etzioni-Halevy, E. (1985). *Bureaucracy and democracy: A political dilemma.* New York: Taylor & Francis.

Evans, P., & Rauch, J. E. (1999). Bureaucracy and growth: A cross-national analysis of the effects of Weberian state structures on economic growth. *American Sociological Review, 64*(5), 748–765.

Fiorina, M. P. (1977). The case of the vanishing marginals: The bureaucracy did it. *American Political Science Review, 71*(1), 177–181.

Foweraker, J., & Krznaric, R. (2002). The uneven performance of third wave democracies: Electoral politics and the imperfect rule of law in Latin America. *Latin American Politics and Society, 44*(3), 29–60.

Gerschenkron, A. (1965). *Economic backwardness in historical perspective: A book of.* Cambridge, MA: Harvard University Press

Goodsell, C. T. (2004). *The case for bureaucracy: A public administration polemic* (4th ed.). Washington, DC: CQ Press.

Grinyer, P., & Yasai-Ardekani, M. (1981). Strategy, structure, size and bureaucracy. *Academy of Management Journal, 24*(3), 471.

Holton, R. J. (1989). *Max Weber on economy and society.* London: Routledge.

Huntington, S. P. (1965). Political development and political decay. *World Politics, 17*(3), 386–430.

Im. T. (2003). Bureaucratic power and the NPM reforms in Korea. *International Review of Public Administration,* 89–102.

Im, T. (2014). Bureaucracy in three different worlds: The assumptions of failed public sector reforms in Korea. *Public Organization Review, 14*(4), 577–596.

Im, T. (2017). *Public organizations in Asia* (1 ed.): New York: Routledge.

Jeong, M. & Lee, J. (2016). Determining factors of employment size in local governments. *Journal of Korean Association for Local Government Studies, 28*(4), 73–101.

Johnson, R. N. (1994). *The Federal civil service system and the problem of bureaucracy: The economics and politics of institutional change.* Chicago: University of Chicago Press.

Kang, H. & Shin, W. (2004). Study on local government ceiling management. *The Journal of Korean Policy Studies, 4*(1), 37–55.

Kang, I. (2008). Comparative study of local government personnel in OECD countries. *Korean Public Administration Review, 42*(2), 169–190.

Kim, S. (1980). Projection of the aggregate number of civil servants and techniques for estimating the numbers by organization. *Korean Journal of Public Administration, 18*(1), 1112.

Kim, T. (2000). Comparisons of public sector implement between Korea and other OECD countries. *Korean Public Administration Review, 34*(1), 117–135.

Lee, E. (1995). A comparative study of public sector's manpower growth in Korea, Japan and USA. *Korean Policy Studies Review, 4*(1), 146.

Lee, H. (1997). Local autonomy and the interior department's personnel size control. *Korean Public Administration Review, 31*(3), 89–105.

Lee, W. (1976). The embryo of Korean bureaucracy in 1945. *Korean Quarterly, 7,* 32–49.

Lerner, D. (1960). The politics of the developing areas. Gabriel Almond, James S. Coleman. *American Journal of Sociology, 66*(1), 96–97. doi:10.1086/222829

Maravall, J. M. A. (2003). *Democracy and the Rule of Law* [electronic resource]. In A. Przeworski (Ed.), *Cambridge studies in the theory of democracy*. Cambridge: Cambridge University Press.

Meier, K. J. (2006). *Bureaucracy in a democratic state: A governance perspective*. Baltimore, MD: Johns Hopkins University Press.

O'Donnell, G. (2004). Why the rule of law matters. *Journal of Democracy, 15*(4), 32–46.

Park, J., & Ham, J. (1995). A study on flexible personnel management: Focusing on the system of total government workforce. *KIPA Research, 13*, 59–91

Parkinson, C. N. (1957). *Pakinson's law and other studies in administration*. Boston, MA: Houghton Mifflin.

Peters, B. (2010). Bureaucracy and democracy. *Public Organization Review, 10*(3), 209–222.

Przeworski, A., & Maravall, J. M. (2003). *Democracy and the rule of law*. In J. M. Maravall, A. Przeworski (Eds.). Cambridge, UK: Cambridge University Press.

Raz, J. (1994). *Ethics in the public domain: Essays in the morality of law and politics*. Oxford: Clarendon Press.

Sen, A. K. (1999). Democracy as a universal value. *Journal of Democracy, 10*(3), 3–17.

Shin, W., & Jeon, B. (2010). The optimum size model for local government. *Journal of Governmental Studies, 16*(3), 143–183.

Ulrich, D., & Barney, J. B. (1984). Perspectives in organizations: Resource dependence, efficiency, and population. *The Academy of Management Review, 9*(3), 471–481.

Yong Duck, J., Yoon Ho, L., & Deok Soo, K. (2011). Institutional change and continuity in Korea's central agencies, 1948–2011. *Korean Journal of Policy Studies, 26*(1), 21.

Wade, R. (1990). *Governing the market: Economic theory and the role of government in East Asian industrialization*. Princeton, NJ: Princeton University Press.

INDEX

www.ingramcontent.com/pod-product-compliance
Lightning Source LLC
Chambersburg PA
CBHW050338270326
41926CB00016B/3511